GRACIAS PERÚ

A MISSIONARY'S MEMOIR

by

TOM SHEA, CSC

βίος Books
New York

βίος Books
An imprint of Woodwrit, Inc. Editions

ISBN-13: 978-0692080153
ISBN-10: 0692080155

DEDICATED TO

JORGE MALLEA, C.S.C.

SINCERE, STEADFAST

COMPANION IN HOLY CROSS

With grateful acknowledgement
to Ted DuBois for his help.

CONTENTS

GRACIAS PERÚ

1. MY CALL TO PERU

For several years I have considered writing about my life in Peru. Friends have encouraged me to do so, but I hesitated to begin. I already have written several papers on the history of Peru between the years 1963-2009 for the Holy Cross History Association, so I questioned whether I should write more about my life there. However, after returning recently from a five-week visit to that beloved country, I decided to undertake the project, in order to share my life experience there with you, my family and friends. I also want to put down on paper the names of the many people I have known in Peru, to thank them personally for being an important part of my life's journey there. I want, as well, to record the many people in other places who have been important to me.

I recognize a guiding hand in my life, especially in getting me to Peru in the first place, and in sustaining me while I was there. I call that guiding hand GOD. I hope that my personal journey might help readers to see the presence of a guiding hand in their own journey, especially in light of the many changes that have occurred in our world and in the Catholic Church since the 1960's.

MY BACKGROUND

I was born in Albany, New York, on June 9, 1941 to Frank X. Shea and Anne M. Riedy who were married in 1931. My family with my brother Francis Robert ("Bud") born in 1933, had just moved from the Irish ghetto of North Albany to the new Pine Hills neighborhood they thought quite ritzy. A recent book I read about Albany neighborhoods points out, however, that the section of Hamilton Street and Hudson Avenue where we lived was not at all upscale. My mom would turn over in her grave if she realized that; she was so proud to be living there! Hudson Avenue was a street with people of various ethnic backgrounds and diverse religions. Quite "ecumenical." Those of us who were kids back then still gather together today when I am in Albany to celebrate our long lives of close friendship. When I left home in September 1959, the world and the Church were about to change more than any of us would ever have imagined.

1959 was the year of the Cuban revolution. The Cold War between the Soviet Block and the West was still at its height. John F. Kennedy was about to be elected the first Catholic president of the United States. The thin, austere Pope Pius XII had died, and kind, warmhearted, chubby Pope John XXIII was the new pope, shaking things up in the Catholic Church after centuries of stagnation. He wanted to open the windows! He summoned an ecumenical council, a worldwide gathering of bishops, to update and renew the Catholic Church, which had not had such a council since the nineteenth century. The world and the Catholic Church were about to change. So also was the life of a skinny and shy boy, Tom Shea! I was about to begin a journey that I never would have thought possible for myself.

I probably was an ordinary Irish Catholic for that time. I went to Sunday Mass and weekly confession. I attended daily Mass during Lent and prayed the rosary every day. Even though I had thought about becoming a Catholic priest since an early age, I never had been an altar boy like my brother Bud, and I was not overly devout. In that way, I was more like my dad than my mom who tended to say a lot of novenas and other prayers each day. Occasionally as a child I enjoyed playing at celebrating Mass against the wall of our living room and singing the Gloria in Latin. What was about to happen to me was nowhere in a plan I had in mind for myself at that time. So, I will be sharing with you the story of my growth and call to new life and change during these evolving times in the Church and in the world.

I also want to enjoy walking through my life again giving thanks to God, my guiding light, for both the joyful and the sorrowful parts of it. For the journey has brought me much joy, but it also has brought some conflict into my life, just as evolving situations in the world and in the Church have brought into the lives of people I will be writing about. We all have different personalities and viewpoints developed in our families and in our theological preparation and life experiences. These have brought each player in this story to make decisions affecting the direction of his own life and the lives of others. Like me, most of us started out in a world and the pre-Vatican II Church that were quickly disappearing. Both I and others would mature in a changing world where the Catholic Church and with it our Religious congregation were called to renewal. It was a call to synchronize with the modern world after centuries of complacency.

This will be the story of my life in Peru as I moved into the new Latin American Church and the new social order emerging in most of Latin America at that time. I am sure that it will be like the stories of many other people my age who have had to grow and stretch themselves into a new era, some with more success than others, but all carrying the wounds of change and the conflicts that change brings in its wake. I hope the account of my life in Peru will help you to consider your own life's journey to be a gift from God, one that you try to carry forward through joys and struggles as best you can.

I left home in September 1959 at the age of eighteen to travel to Stonehill College in Easton, Massachusetts, to join the Congregation of Holy Cross. A Religious community of priests and Brothers founded in Le Mans, France, in 1835 to respond to the educational and pastoral needs of post-revolutionary France, Holy Cross is now represented on every continent, serving those needs across the entire Catholic Church.

Peru was never in my personal vocational plans when I joined Holy Cross. I wanted to be a high school teacher in the United States. I always was impressed with the ministry of the Holy Cross Brothers who taught at my hometown parish high school, Vincentian Institute, in

Albany, New York. I wanted to be a teacher like the Brothers. I wanted to be like Brother Renatus Foldernaur especially, one of my vocation pillars and my spiritual mentor. Renatus was director of the school's symphonic and marching band, and the school band was my life when I was in high school.

During my novitiate year in Holy Cross 1960-1961, when we prepared ourselves with study and prayer to join the Congregation, culminating with our pronouncing the three temporary vows of poverty, chastity and obedience, we also were encouraged to take what was called the fourth vow. A person took this vow if he was interested in ministering in a culture outside his own. I never wanted to be a missionary! I had not even been a boy scout! So, I never took nor intended to take this fourth vow. My plan was to be a teacher like Brother Renatus! My thanks to you, Brother Renatus. Yet God had other plans for me.

In 1964 I finished my B.A. degree in philosophy at Stonehill College, which at the time was still a new, small, liberal arts college founded by the Congregation of Holy Cross in 1948 for the children of the Portuguese immigrants in southeastern Massachusetts. In August, after a summer as I had spent the previous two, counseling at our camp for boys at Lake Sebago, Maine, I pronounced my final, perpetual vows in Holy Cross. In September I was sent by my Holy Cross Congregation to study theology at the Jesuit-run Gregorian University in Rome, Italy, and to live at our international house of studies there.

The Council of Vatican II, the worldwide meeting of the bishops of the Catholic Church that Pope John XXIII opened in October 1962, was about to begin its third session. John XXIII had died in June 1963, and now newly-elected Pope Paul VI was in charge. He was continuing the Council, trying to follow in the footsteps of his predecessor, but of course in his own way.

The Council already had approved radical changes in the Catholic liturgy by permitting Mass facing the people and the use of the vernacular, the common language of a place, rather than Latin. One of the basic documents of the Council about the Church itself, called "Light of the World," also already had been approved. It emphasized that the Church is composed of all the people of God, all the baptized, who all are the priesthood of the faithful. The hierarchy (deacons, priests and bishops) are those who have been called to serve the people of God with the Scriptures and the sacraments. This was a totally new way of seeing the Catholic Church at that time.

Later documents of this Council would remind Catholics of the importance of reading and studying the Holy Scriptures. This practice previously had often been considered something mainly Protestants do. So, Bible studies became important for Catholics, too.

Another major document, named "The Church in the Modern World," would call upon the Church to be involved in current world problems involving economics, the arms race, scientific and technological advances, and such matters. It encouraged the Church to step out from a ghetto mentality to become a sign, a sacrament, of Jesus' love for all humanity amid the suffering in our world, to be a sign of hope that we can build a better world together.

A document that was important for me concerned the renewal of Religious life, that of priests, Brothers, and Sisters bound together by vow, which invited Religious congregations to return to their roots, the original reason that they had been started by their founders. It called them to renew their lives by putting their original gift to the Church into practice in our present modern times.

The Council also invited the laity to become more involved in ministries of service inside the Church, and most importantly to be the light of Christ in the secular world, taking up their baptismal commitment to be Jesus alive amid world affairs, in their families, as well as in their places of work and study. It encouraged them to become involved in politics, science, and economics to contribute to building the kingdom of God, the kingdom of justice, love and peace, here among us.

During those years of the Council in Rome, I had many opportunities to attend conferences given by the great theologians of that time, many of whom formerly had been silenced because of their ideas, considered radical, like Karl Rahner, Hans Kung, John Courtney Murray, Henri de Lubac, Edward Schillebeeckx, and others. I had landed feet first in a whole new world of Church thought.

I also had discovered on my shipboard journey to Rome that most of the world was not like Albany! I had never before seen so much poverty as I did in the Madeira Islands and Casablanca in Morocco and other ports where the boat docked.

I began to find theological studies at the Gregorian University very academic and dry, especially the juridical, moral, canon law theology of a professor like Zalba and the speculative approach to doctrine of many of the teachers. I was enlivened more by the new moral theology of Fuchs who taught us that not every little act like missing Mass on Sunday was a mortal sin as we had been taught in our growing-up years. In fact, he taught that it is very hard to commit a mortal sin. One had to turn ones' life completely away from God. I spent a lot of time during my years in Rome reading the books of these theologians.

I also had the opportunity to make a "Better World Retreat" (*Movimento per un Mondo Migliore*) during my second year in Rome, just after an Easter visit by my parents. I was becoming discouraged with the studies at that time and beginning to question my vocation. This retreat opened me to new ways of connecting the Bible to the real world. It made the Bible come alive and become more meaningful for me.

THE CALL

It was shortly after this *Mondo Migliore* retreat that I suddenly felt that I was being called to go to my province's recently-opened mission in Peru. Bob Nogosek, the superior of Collegio di Santa Croce, Holy Cross' international theology house on Via Aurelia Antica in Rome, was the one who without knowing it set off the idea in my head. One evening while we were having dinner outside as we often did on Sundays in good weather, Bob, who was shy and conversationally awkward and with whom I usually felt uncomfortable, chose to sit next to me. He suddenly turned to me and said, "Shea, why don't you go to Peru?" I am sure he meant well, but in his awkwardness I took it as if he was saying, "Shea, why don't you get lost!" I went upstairs angry, when suddenly I felt I *heard* an inner voice that seemed to say to me, "Why not, Tom?" I asked myself if that was God talking to me. And from that time on I began to plan to go to Peru.

In 2009 I met Bob Nogosek again at a national conference of the Small Christian Communities Movement held at Nativity parish in Brandon, Florida, where I was ministering to the Hispanic community. It was an opportunity to share this story with him and to thank him personally for being the one who got me to start thinking about Peru. I often have told young people who are trying to discern God's will for themselves that sometimes the voice of God comes through people who are not always our best friends. Thank you again, Bob, for conveying God's voice to me!

The following summer I began to study Spanish, even though I was still struggling with mastering Italian and French. We used French as well as English in our international house, and of course we needed Italian for living in Rome. Sad to say our classes were taught in Latin rather than in Italian. I went to Spain for two summers, first to a course in Madrid and the next year to another in Santander in northern Spain. I did not learn much Spanish either time, because most of the students were English speakers, and we mostly spoke English.

Gonzalo Martin who was from Spain, and who had met Holy Cross priest Jerry Lawyer while Jerry was working there with the Family Rosary Crusade, was considering joining Holy Cross and so was studying with us in our house in Rome. He was helpful, tutoring me in Spanish a couple of times a week, and I learned more from him. He will reappear later in this story. Thank you, Gonzalo!

During my last year in Rome I wrote to the provincial superior Richard Sullivan asking him if I could go to our new mission in Peru after ordination. When I did not hear back from him I wrote a second letter suggesting a second option. At that time, Holy Cross had a high school in Bridgeport, Connecticut, to which I did not want to be assigned because I had heard rumors of tensions within that Holy Cross community. I asked instead to be assigned to one of the Holy Cross Brothers' high schools if Peru was not now possible. The provincial misunderstood the motive behind my second letter, thinking that it was my way of saying I no longer wanted to go to Peru, so he assigned me to teach religion and be chaplain at the Brothers' high school in West Haven, Connecticut. Fortunately, I had a chance to talk with him personally before I left Rome in June 1968 to clear up the misunderstanding. Dysfunctional communication will be a constant theme in my life journey!

I was asked to go to Peru in July 1968 while I was on vacation with my family after celebrating my first Mass in my home parish of St. Vincent de Paul in Albany, New York. The assistant provincial, Jerry Lawyer, came up to Albany to talk to me about it. He told me that one of the men already in Peru, Don Abbott, a good friend of mine who had been a year ahead of me in studies in Rome, was having some personal problems and wanted to return to the United States, so the mission in Peru needed another priest. I knew that my mother was hoping to have me around after my being away for four years in Rome, but my dad was very supportive, telling me to follow my heart. So I said "Yes," and off I went, after spending a month helping in my childhood parish of St. Vincent De Paul in Albany and visiting for a month with family, friends and Holy Cross community houses in the northeast.

I sailed for Peru with Jim Chichetto in mid-October 1968. Jim had entered Holy Cross with me back in 1959 and had studied theology at the Holy Cross Mission house in Washington, D.C., in preparation to go to the missions in what was then East Pakistan (now Bangladesh), since unlike me he had taken the mission vow after novitiate. When he was unable to obtain a visa to go there, he decided to join us in Peru. My mom was in the hospital sick with bronchial asthma the day I was to sail, so my dad and brother Bud took me to the boat in New York. It was the Magdalena owned by the W.R. Grace Company. I recall that my aunt Bess, my first cousin Betty Christenson and her daughter Pat were there to see me off.

The trip down to Peru was a great adventure for me. Three elderly women who had been traveling together on vacation for more than fifteen years adopted Jim and me and another young laywoman on her way to do missionary work in Ecuador. We had a great social life on the boat playing bingo and participating in activities. I remember I had to be initiated by King Neptune and his court when I crossed the equator. As a punishment for winning at bingo too often on the ship I was showered with grease and other liquids before being pushed into the swimming pool. We visited the various ports where the boat docked, Port Au Prince in Haiti, Curacao, Cartagena in Venezuela, Panama, Buenaventura in Colombia, and Guayaquil in Ecuador, where once again I witnessed the poverty in our world. I stayed in touch with these three women until each died. One of them, the youngest, Josephine, was a computer expert. I visited her several times in New York City when I returned from Peru on family visits.

Jim Chichetto has written a short novel about our trip down to Peru and our first years there which is a great read. I do not believe it has been published, but I encourage you, Jim, to do so.

2. CARTAVIO 1968 - 1973

We arrived in Peru on October 25, 1968. Both George DePrizio, who had been provincial superior at the time of the opening of the Holy Cross mission in Cartavio in 1963, and Larry Olszewski, who was a few years ahead of me in formation and who after finishing his theology studies in Montreal had been assigned to Peru in 1966, met us at our boat in the port of Callao near Lima. What anticipation I felt for this new life of mine that was about to begin! I knew little or nothing about Peru at that time, but I was very excited because, without knowing why, I felt in my heart that I was being called to live and work in this land. We spent a few days in Lima, visiting the city, doing paperwork on our visas and getting Jim settled into language school there. I remember that Larry took us on a city tour. We even went to a bullfight and a concert. I had seen bullfights before in Spain when I was studying Spanish there during summers from Rome. Jim and I also began the long bureaucratic process of getting residence papers for Peru.

Jim was to stay a few months in Lima to study at the St. James language school in Barranco, a district of Lima. The St. James Society with headquarters in Boston was founded around 1960 for diocesan priests who wanted to do missionary work in Latin America. They opened a language school in Lima for Church people coming to

Latin America after Pope John XXIII in 1960 asked Religious communities and dioceses to send ten percent of their personnel to Latin America to help the local Church there during that time when Communism was growing on the continent. Many Latin Americans were dissatisfied with the promises of capitalism in their countries and had seen the success of the revolution in Cuba. They saw Communism as a viable alternative to how they were living then under capitalism.

George DePrizio had recently moved from Cartavio to Lima where he was living and serving as chaplain with the Immaculate Heart of Mary Sisters from Philadelphia who had a school for wealthy girls on Avenida Arequipa in a nice sector of Lima called Miraflores. During the following years, Jim and I would stay there with George when we came down from Cartavio to visit Lima.

After those first days Larry and I began the ten-hour trip by car on the Pan-American Highway up the Peruvian coast toward Cartavio, our destination about a forty-five-minute drive north of the city of Trujillo on Peru's northern coast. On the way, I remember that one of my first surprises was that there is no jungle on the Peruvian coast. From my very limited studies of Latin America in grade school, I had had the impression that Peru was all jungle. I discovered that the coast is desert except for fertile valleys where the rivers run down from the mountains to end in the small coastal towns and cities. At first I thought I was in the Sahara in Africa! I never had seen desert before, but I began to appreciate its beauty. The fact is that Peru's jungle is on the other side of the Andes mountains. I really knew so little about the country I was about to live in. I also discovered that Peru, although located halfway down the western side of South America, is in the Eastern time zone, directly under New York City. I always had had the impression that the South American continent was located vertically below North America. There were so many new things to learn.

CARTAVIO

I remember our arrival in Cartavio in the early evening after the long drive from Lima. Cartavio was a large sugar plantation (*hacienda*) owned and operated by the W.R. Grace Company of New York. There was a sugar factory there surrounded by the workers' homes much as in old American company towns. Fields filled with sugar cane spread out for miles as we left the Pan-American Highway just past the large city of Trujillo and drove onto the hacienda's bumpy roads bruised by the huge tractor trailers that carted sugar cane from the fields to factory.

Cartavio was still a hacienda then, but in June 1969 it would be declared a cooperative by the new revolutionary military government of Juan Velasco Alvarado, a military general with a vision of a Peru free of exploitation by the local Peruvian oligarchy and foreign investors. The new government had just expropriated at the beginning of October 1968 the oil refineries in the north of Peru from the Standard Oil Company. It was a time of political change throughout Latin America including Peru. And there was a fear by some of the threat of Communism.

The town of Cartavio had about thirty thousand people who mostly lived in long, narrow company houses along narrow, dusty streets. The leftover molasses from the sugar cane was used on the streets to keep the dust down. I remember that it stuck to my shoes when it was fresh off the truck. For this reason, too, there was a sweet smell in the air of the town that slowly would grow on me.

The night I arrived in Cartavio was the evening of the final procession of Our Lord of the Miracles on the streets of Cartavio. For the people in Peru, this fiesta in the month of October takes the place of the Church's traditional season of Lent. The Church's liturgical calendar is based on the seasons in the northern hemisphere, so, in the southern hemisphere where Peru is located, the liturgical Lent falls inconveniently during the summer. The feast of Our Lord of the Miracles dates from the sixteenth century in Lima when there was an earthquake. The image which had been painted on the wall of a church for African slaves outside Lima was the only wall that survived the earthquake. It was considered miraculous by the poor slaves, who then started this devotion which over the years spread throughout Lima and to many other parts of Peru.

During the month of October the people dressed in purple, the penitential color. Every night in Cartavio that month the image moved in procession from neighborhood to neighborhood as crowds followed it with songs and prayers. In October Mass was celebrated among the people in their neighborhoods rather than in the main church building. It was a great way for the priests like me to get closer to the people, especially those who did not come often to Mass in the parish church. I will always remember a band playing the special song dedicated to Our Lord of the Miracles that I heard on the first night I arrived in Cartavio.

When I entered our large house at Calle Real #6 on the main street near the church, Don Abbott whom I was sent to replace was standing at the door with his bags packed. He immediately announced to Larry and me that he would be leaving the next day to return to the United States! I knew Don was experiencing a lot of personal problems, but he was supposed to stay for at least six months until I mastered Spanish a bit more! At that moment in time, I could barely speak or understand the language. I had studied only two brief summer courses in Spain, but the provincial superior Richard Sullivan was convinced that I had sufficient formal studies and would pick up the language quickly with the help of tutoring.

The next day I was told by Larry, who was acting pastor, that I would have to teach Don's religion classes at the state high school in town beginning the following week and, in addition, that I also would be the pastor of the parish beginning in mid-November while he was away on a three-month vacation in the United States. It would be his opportunity to visit his family after not having seen them for three years. The actual pastor in Cartavio was Holy Cross Steve Lambour who had come to Peru with George DePrizio years before. He was at that moment in the United States on vacation until January. So, I would be left alone in Cartavio except for Gonzalo Martin, who as a seminarian had tutored me in Spanish in Rome and who had come to work in Peru in 1967 after his ordination to the priesthood.

Gonzalo still had not formally entered the Congregation of Holy Cross, which requires a year in the novitiate and pronouncing the three vows of chastity, poverty and obedience. Thus, he still was considered a postulant (a person who is considering joining the Congregation). For that reason, Gonzalo could not be assigned as pastor in Cartavio. Talk about baptism by fire for me!

THE LANGUAGE

In the meantime our neighbor Wilda Cardenas, a former grade-school teacher and principal, became my Spanish tutor. She was a well-educated Peruvian woman who lived with her husband and five children right next door to us. She spoke no English, so we had to speak together in Spanish. In fact, no one in the town spoke English! That was a plus for me, because it forced me to use the language. Each weekday morning I went to her house for two hours of class. I had the Spanish books that were used at the language school in Lima where Jim was studying, and we worked our way slowly through these texts. She was a skilled teacher and very patient with me. She also would correct my Sunday homilies, which I preferred to try to ad lib without writing them out beforehand. Thank you, Wilda, and everyone who helped me to learn Spanish! After Jim arrived in December 1968, he, Larry, and I decided to speak only Spanish among ourselves to facilitate our learning the language. It was a great idea, and we all improved our Spanish language skills that way.

One comical incident as I was learning Spanish occurred at one of my first Masses when I was experimenting with preaching the homily without first writing it out. I wanted to say that I was embarrassed by my poor Spanish, but I employed the Spanish word *embarazado*, thinking it meant "embarrassed," but in Spanish it means "pregnant." So, the people got a good laugh at my expense.

THE HIGH SCHOOL

I began teaching in the public high school a few days later by writing out my classes. Enrique Urquiaga, a young Peruvian sacristan at the parish church and a student at the school, helped me to understand the questions students asked me. Enrique would sit in the front row and repeat their questions very slowly for me. I tried to answer in my broken Spanish. The students in general were very kind to me and helped me to learn the language quickly. I sometimes wondered how the experience of a Spanish-speaking teacher who did not speak much English would compare in a school in the United States at the time.

Some of the students often came to the house in the evening and invited me to go out with them to walk around the nearby main square. Then they would quiz me on vocabulary and force me to try to converse in Spanish with them. All of us enjoyed many good laughs at my many mistakes! I loved teaching at the state high school all those years. The students were very kind and friendly to me. I especially remember my good friend Antero Ruiz who was one of the first students I knew. He is still a faithful friend even today when he is nearing his 65th birthday. Thank you, dear Antero!

With some students from school I formed a parish youth group we named "Cultural Roots" (*Raíces Culturales*). I remember planning an activity with them to go to a movie in the neighboring city of Trujillo, where we saw "Who's afraid of Virginia Woolf?" There was so much dialogue in the lengthy movie and so little action, I think they all were bored silly! Another night we went together with other parish members to Trujillo for the first music event of their Spring Festival. Raul Vasquez, a young and at that time unknown artist-composer won, becoming famous for his song "The Funeral Wailer" (*La Plañidera*). Now I have a CD recording of that festival, and I often listen to it both in my room or while driving a car to remind me of those wonderful days.

I remember that shortly after I arrived, the Peruvian government began an educational reform calling for group work instead of just memorization and repetition of what a teacher dictated. I was enthused with this methodology and used it in all my classes. I would invite the students to use books at the library located in the parish hall to prepare a class in groups. That gave me contact with them at the parish center in the afternoons as well, so I got to know them better. I think they enjoyed this method. I know that I did. I continued to use it all my years in Peru.

During my first years teaching at the school, classes often were canceled Friday afternoons for various reasons, such as a teachers' meeting or marching practice for a parade, or a sports event. On the other hand, the students had religion class only once a week, and three of my classes were scheduled for only Friday afternoon; so sometimes I didn't get to see those students during the entire semester. When it came time to grade them, I told the principal that I could not in conscience give them a grade since I had never had class with them! He was quite shocked by my attitude. The following years I insisted on not having classes on Friday afternoons. Such was life often in the Peruvian state schools. I had a lot to learn about Peruvian ways. At first difficult for a *gringo* like me, over time I became quite used to dealing with these annoyances.

One day the director of the night section of the high school, Lorenzo Santillán, a friend who often visited us at our house, suggested that the three of us who each taught a few of the religion classes put all the class hours in the name of one of us. Since I was the only one really interested in teaching full-time, it was decided that the other two would continue to teach a few classes but under my name. That is how I got a permanent teaching position with the Peruvian government which is called a *nombramiento* in Spanish. I would keep this *nombramiento* and move it around with me during almost all my years in Peru until I retired with thirty years of service in 2001. Thank you, Lorenzo Santillán!

It was a highlight of my time at the Cartavio school when in 1973 the senior class elected me to be one of their class advisers. We planned a two-week bus excursion to Cuzco and during the year organized activities to raise money for it. The trip was a wonderful experience. Fifty-five of us went, including four adults (three teachers and a parent). We traveled down to Lima and then up from Lima to Huancayo, down through Ayacucho to Cuzco, then down to Juliaca and Arequipa and back up the coast to Cartavio. It was the first time I traveled around Peru.

I was disappointed in Ayacucho which is known for its many Spanish churches. No priests or Sisters in the churches or religious schools there would allow us a space to sleep on the floor when we asked for it. They did not want to dirty their schoolrooms they said, even though we told them that we would clean up well. What they did want to do was show us the jewels in their churches! We had all been sleeping on the bus for several nights until then, and we really needed to stretch out somewhere to have a good night's sleep. A university student who over-heard us speaking about our difficulties in the Ayacucho main square offered his small room to us! I felt like Joseph looking for a room for Mary and child! To me the only Christian I met was this poor university student! That's what I told the students, too!

Cartavio was a great place to begin ministry in Peru. The people were the poor from the northern mountain villages and towns of Peru where their first language often was Quechua. They had been brought down to the coast to work in the sugar cane fields and in the sugar factory. There were several other haciendas besides Cartavio in the fertile Chicama valley around Trujillo owned by wealthy Peruvian families like the Larcos and Gildermeisters. The mountain people were promised a better life on the coast, but often became indebted to the company town and were not able to move elsewhere until they paid off the bill. A modern-day form of slavery? These people were very kind and very hospitable to *gringos* like me who did not speak their language well or understand their culture, customs or religiosity. I learned so much of Peruvian culture and spirituality from them. Thank you, people of Cartavio!

HOLY CROSS IN CARTAVIO

At the beginning of my years in Cartavio, we were five Holy Cross priests there, Steve Lambour the pastor, Larry Olszewski, Gonzalo Martin, Jim Chichetto and I. Steve had replaced George DePrizio, the founding provincial of our Peru mission who in early 1968 recently had moved to Lima, the capital city, to minister in the new Catholic charismatic movement he established there with an American Dominican priest. It was a movement like the Protestant Evangelical one of praising the Lord with songs and shouts of joy.

We hoped to have more young priests from the U.S. Eastern Province join us, but they never appeared. Two of them fell in love during language school in Mexico. In June 1969 Steve Lambour, the pastor, returned to the United States for personal reasons, and Gonzalo went to our formation house at Notre Dame, Indiana, for his novitiate year to enter the Congregation of Holy Cross. He returned as a professed member of Holy Cross in late 1970, and was assigned to the new mission in Chimbote of which I will speak in the next chapter.

So, in June 1969, Larry, Jim and I were alone in Cartavio, where we three lived an enjoyable community life. We had our meals together. We went on outings together to the mountain city of Cajamarca, about a five-hour drive from Cartavio, or to the town of Cascas, some two hours by car in the mountains near Cartavio. We often went to Trujillo for dinner and movies. Every three months each of us spent a few days in Lima to relax. We usually traveled by *colectivo* (a car carrying four or five passengers). Lima was a ten-hour trip from Trujillo by car in those days, a 350-mile ride on the two-lane, narrow, very heavily traveled Pan-American Highway. We seldom made the trip by plane, because it was quite expensive. In the beginning, we stayed with George and the Sisters whose chaplain he was in Lima. Thank you, George! May you rest in peace! You were a most gracious and hospitable host, as were the Immaculate Heart of Mary Sisters.

Every day in Cartavio we picked up our meals in a lunch bucket and brought them to our house from a little restaurant owned by Rebecca, a great cook, who kept us well-fed and healthy. It took me with my Irish roots about a week to get used to having rice rather than potatoes as a part of the main course. At home in Albany rice was always a dessert with raisins in it. Now of course I love rice and miss it here in the United States.

When Holy Cross accepted to work in the mission in Cartavio, the Grace company who owned the hacienda offered at that time to pay our salaries and take care of our needs. The issue would become a problem for all of us later, because we appeared to be and were workers for the

Grace company! We employed two young men who were brothers, Victor and Juan, to help with domestic work in the house. Thank you Juan, Victor, Rebecca for all that service to us! The hacienda also furnished us a chauffeur named Roman and a truck for our transportation needs. We lived well thanks to the sugar company's paying for all these workers! I remember that once I went with Roman, Victor, Juan and others who helped us out at home or in the parish on a three-day car trip up to Peru's border with Ecuador in the north. It was a great outing together to thank them for all they did for us. We also took an annual day trip to the beach with them each year.

When we arrived in Cartavio, Jim and I did not have Peruvian driver's licenses. So, one day we went to Trujillo to obtain them. Since both of us still had difficulty with Spanish, we were accompanied by one of the hacienda's supervisors. Nice service, no? When Jim did not pass the written exam (since he was just beginning to learn Spanish) and I did not pass the eye exam (I have one bad eye), the plantation official offered the examiner fifty pounds of sugar for each of us to ensure that we would receive the driver's licenses, since we needed them to travel to the outlying villages around Cartavio. I could not believe my eyes and ears! It was my introduction to Peruvian ways that were so generally accepted by all the people in Peru. One more cultural custom I would need to get used to!

Another cultural difference I had to learn was the unimportance of time. I remember arriving for an exchange of rings ceremony (a pre-marriage custom in Peru) in a home at the exact time stated on the invitation.

However, the ceremony did not begin for another three hours. In fact, when I arrived the family members were still cleaning the floor of the living room where the party was to take place, and so I sat there as they cleaned around me for three hours! After that experience I knew that 7:00 pm meant 9:00 or 10:00 pm, and so I adapted.

Yet another cultural lesson for me was that people usually gave you the answer they thought you expected rather than their honest one. They did this to not offend you. For example, I would ask the young people if they wanted to go to the beach, and all would answer yes, but then no one would show up. So, I learned to be flexible.

A typical day in Cartavio started with Mass at the Sisters' chapel at 6:00 am followed by the 8:00 am Mass in the church, and then sometimes a 9:30 Mass in one of the villages. After each Mass, we were invited for coffee and black olive or butter sandwiches in the house of the person who had asked for the Mass intention. During the day we often had religion classes at the high school from 8:00 am to noon, and from 2:00 to 5:00 pm. We also visited the sick in their homes and in the town hospital, and then went to the homes for baptism preparations. Each day at 5:00 pm we had Benediction at the Sisters' chapel and a 7:00 pm Mass at the church, followed by a meeting with one of the parish groups. Sometimes we also had classes from 7:00 to 11:00 pm in the night section of the same public school where we taught during the day. That section existed for young adults who had not been able to finish high school in the daytime because they had to work to help their families. So ours was usually a full day. It required at least two priests to be able to do it all. Thank God most of us were young and full of energy!

On Sundays, we had several Masses. The 6:00 am at the convent with the Sisters was open to the public. The 7:00 am was celebrated in the sector called Santa Rosa, where the pigs and other animals belonging to the families who worked in Cartavio were kept. Family relatives who did not work in the hacienda lived there in very poor conditions, because the workers' houses were usually tiny and overcrowded with their own immediate family members, with little room for these relatives to live with them. There followed an 8:00 am Mass in the church, and then a 9:00 am in the town of Santiago de Cao, about a half-hour drive from Cartavio. For a short while there also was an 11:00 am Mass for the upper-class hacienda workers, but that was discontinued. In the afternoon, there were religion classes taught by the Sisters and some lay men and women from the parish, sometimes with a Mass in one or more of the four outlying villages, each located about a twenty-minute drive from Cartavio. In the evening we had a 6:00 pm and a 7:00 pm Mass in the parish church, as well as a 7:00 pm Mass in a chapel in the Ingenio sector of Cartavio, and an 8:00 pm in the neighboring hacienda of Chiquitoy, a sugar plantation owned by a Polish count and his family, absentee landlords. Sunday was a long day!

Besides Masses in the main church in Cartavio, and visits to the sick at the Cartavio hospital and in their homes, we had duty days in the parish office once or twice a week when we had to remain available for people who might stop in with some need. Each priest also was given a duty day in one of the churches in the outlying villages. I was assigned to the old 16th-century town of Santiago de Cao. I remember my first day there. During the week, Santiago was like a ghost town. I would stand outside the church and not see a soul. I would walk around town and not see a soul! So, I decided to spend my time rearranging the many, many statues on the side altars of the church. Did I ever learn a lesson! You don't move the statues! The next Sunday when I arrived for Mass, all the statues were back in their original places! Sunday Mass there was well attended, however.

I also was assigned to Nepen, one of the four very small outlying villages that were about a twenty-minute drive from Cartavio. I enjoyed my time in Nepen more than Santiago even though it, too, was like a ghost town during the week. I got to know some of the people there little by little during my visits, and they were interested in gathering at night once a week in one of their homes to read and reflect upon and pray with the Bible. So, we started what is called a "small Christian community," a Church gathering where the people read and reflect on the Bible in the context of their life problems and hopes.

The "small Christian community" was an innovation that originated from Church pastoral experiences in Brazil in areas where there were few Religious or priests, and it became a national movement. It was hoped that these gatherings would keep the faith alive in those areas. This was the beginning of my interest in working with "small Christian communities." Once again, we were involved with the growth of lay leadership in the Church! It was a great experience for me to see the faith of these very simple and poor people come alive. They knew so little about the Bible, and they were very happy to learn more about it and to see how it could be applied to their daily lives. This became one of my main ministries in Peru all my years there.

Besides all the sacramental activities in the parish like baptismal visits in the homes and marriage preparations, we also had marriages and funeral Masses. As I slowly grew accustomed to life in Cartavio I remember especially enjoying the visits for baptism preparation that we did in the people's homes. It was a great way to get to know them on their own turf where they were more at ease, but also a way to see the poverty in which most of them lived. Believe me, that was an education for me! And I will never forget their hospitality. They would receive us into their small, poor, adobe houses, sit us down on perhaps their only chair, and offer us something to drink or eat. I remember that they seemed much more comfortable with us there in their homes than when they were visiting us in the parish office. This reminds me of today when Pope Francis is encouraging us priests to go out to where the people are!

In the parish there also were several social action groups representing national and international Church movements, such as the Legion of Mary Movement, the Christian Workers Movement (MTC), the Christian Family Movement (CFM), the Young Christian Workers Movement (JOC), and the Cursillo Movements. All of these were great for helping people to grow in their faith and to do ministry in the parish and in society without being overly dependent on the parish team. The Legion of Mary was founded in England in the early twentieth century. The group gathered for prayer each week that centered on devotion to Mary and the rosary. The Christian Family Movement gathered each week to discuss their family and married life with reflection from the Bible. The Cursillo Movement had an intense three-day retreat to promote personal Christian renewal, and then weekly gatherings to keep the new commitments alive.

The other social action groups which dated back to the beginning of the twentieth century in Europe were the Young Christian Students (JEC), the Young Christian Workers (JOC) and the Christian Workers (MTC). These movements were founded originally in Europe to respond to the Church's desire to work again among the working classes and poor. In their weekly meetings, they discussed their labor problems or youth problems using the method of See, Judge and Act. You look at your lived reality (*see* it); *judge* or illuminate it with the Scriptures; and then *act* to better or change it. This methodology would be important to me during all my years in Peru, and continues to be today.

We Holy Cross Religious priests in Cartavio were the spiritual guides to these movements. I personally enjoyed working with the Young Christian Workers groups (JOC), one of men and another of women, and with one of the three Christian family (CFM) groups. As you can see, there was not a dull moment. However, we were young at the time (not one of us over thirty years of age!)

and energetic, and very enthused about the changes in the Church brought about by Vatican II and by the Latin American bishops' documents at Medellin calling for the Church to have a preferential option for the poor.

In late May 1970, there was an earthquake in northern Peru. Larry was away in the United States for the provincial chapter. Jim and Gonzalo and I were in Cartavio. I remember that I was taking a nap when it occurred. My bedroom was on the front of the house on Calle Real, and the tractor trailers that carried the sugar cane passed by often. Hearing the rumbling, I thought it was one of those trucks. Then my bed began to rock, and the front windows were vibrating. I got up and ran outside and grabbed onto our truck which was parked on the street. The ground was heaving up and down and the trees and lampposts were rocking back and forth, as was our church building on the corner. What a terrifying experience! And the shaking continued all night long. We were unable to communicate with the outside world for over a week. Of course, our families and our community in the United States were concerned.

I remember how the parish youth group came to us and wanted to take up a collection of food and clothing to bring to Chimbote, about three hours away by car, which was very close to the earthquake's epicenter near Casma and Huaraz. I thought that we would be able to do the collecting quickly, because most of the people in Cartavio were poor; but it took us three days! When we went through the poorer sections of Cartavio, we filled the back of the pick-up truck every half block! Then we brought what was collected back to the parish hall where other volunteers separated the food and clothing. When we went to the wealthier part of town, many people did not even come out of their homes, so we passed through quickly. What a lesson that was for me! Those who are needy themselves are often the most generous in times of the suffering of others! The next week Sister Dolores, some of the older youth and I drove to Chimbote and then up to the town of Jimbe where we distributed the donated goods. That was a learning experience, too, since we witnessed how the corrupt leaders in the town tried to favor their own families with the donations by using a list overloaded with the names of their friends and relatives. The people protested this list of names, so we used the system of each person getting in line.

One of the parish youth groups, the Young Christian Workers (JOC), did a survey on the treatment of the women and men who worked in domestic service in the houses of the wealthier people in Cartavio. Domestic men and women worked long hours for low pay, with no benefits and very little free time and no days off. We published the results of the survey in the Sunday parish bulletin, and of course there were outcries from these wealthy families and from the Sisters who thought we were Communists doing political work. We responded by saying that we were just following the Peruvian bishops recent document on Justice in the World. The same youth group also produced plays with the theme of social justice, particularly regarding the domestic workers' problems, to try to raise consciousness about the injustice of their situation in Peru and the lack of legal recourse for them. That event received a lot of criticism, too, especially since two of the youth group, Toni Villalobos and Gabi Vega, were children of the wealthier families. They both have continued to stand with the poor even in their lives today. Thank you, Toni and Gabi, for your courage even way back then!

All those years I engaged in what some called "Tom's beach ministry." I often went to the ocean with groups of students and members of the parish youth groups to play soccer there. It was a great way for me to get to know the young people and to talk with them more informally. To this day many of those young persons are still close friends and meet up with me when I visit Cartavio and Trujillo where some of them live now. One is my *compadre* (father of my godchild Isaac) Felipe Calderon who presently lives in the city of Callao near Lima. A godfather at baptism in Peru becomes a member of the child's family and becomes a co-father in the extended family. Being a godfather has considerable cultural significance and creates obligations on both sides to help and care for one another.

Another of my beach ministry friends is Antero Ruiz whom I mentioned before as one of my students who helped me to learn Spanish. I made many other friends, like Ricardo Avila, Willie Quezada, Felipe Jorge Monzon, Douglas Vergara, Nelson Gonzales, Santos Guanilo, and Gonzalo "Archie" Gutierrez and Manuel Morgado, as well as Toni Villalobos, Gabi Vega, Iris Vega, Marlene Vega, Tomasa Julca, Julio Julca, Segundo Mendoza, Carlos and Jesus Bacilio and many others who were members of the parish youth and social action groups and participants in my beach ministry. Thank you one and all for this wonderful learning experience with all of you in Cartavio and for your constant deep friendship throughout the years!

I also remember with fondness Patan, Larry's bulldog who lived with us in the house on Calle Real. Patan often accompanied the youth and me to the beach to play soccer with us. He was so funny running and using his nose to push the ball! They were wonderful years of happiness for me, and I cherish their memory in my heart always.

A TIME OF CHANGE

When I arrived in October 1968, Peru was at the beginning of a social revolution. In June 1969 the military government of President Juan Velasco Alvarado expropriated all the large haciendas in Peru, including the Cartavio hacienda owned by W.R. Grace Company of New York, and was preparing to transform these large haciendas into cooperatives owned by the workers themselves. For years, the rich oligarchy, the aristocratic class, had dominated Peru politically and economically.

The Peruvian Church, too, was in the process of implementing the Vatican II documents. Recently, in 1968, a Latin American conference of bishops had been held in Medellin, Colombia, where they formulated revolutionary guidelines encouraging the formation of a Church with a preferential option for the poor. They spoke about social sin, the unjust structures that in most of Latin America enslave and oppress the population. They invited priests and Religious to live simply and to move into the poor areas of their cities and the countryside. For years, the Church had stood politically and economically on the side of the upper classes, for the most part. Now there was a desire to insert Church people more into the poor areas of Peru to serve and to stand with the poor in their struggles for justice in a corrupt, unjust society.

I arrived during those social, political, economic and ecclesiastical upheavals and changes. Of course, many people in Church and society, especially among the upper classes, were not happy with the documents of Vatican II or of Medellin. These documents strongly affected my spirituality and pastoral ministry during my first years in Peru. They gave it new life beyond the dry neo-Scholastic, classical, philosophical theology that I had received so recently at the Gregorian University in Rome.

It also was the time of a new Biblical renewal. I learned how to read the Bible with one eye on the reality these people were living and with one eye on the Biblical text. It was not sufficient just to know, read and study the Bible as a book, without understanding both the context in which the text was written and the present context of people's lives. For me it was a whole new ball game. And one that I grasped eagerly and enthusiastically.

Before I arrived in Peru, some priests there organized themselves into a movement called the National Office of Social Information (ONIS). Well-known Peruvian diocesan priests like Gustavo Gutierrez, considered the founder of Liberation Theology, and Jorge Alvarez Calderon, who worked tirelessly for years with social action lay groups, were, together with many others, the founders of ONIS.

This group, becoming a movement, tried to unite priests in their efforts to put the Vatican II and Medellin documents into practice in a new Peruvian social, political and ecclesial reality by furnishing them with the information they needed for their pastoral work.

The ONIS group in the northern part of Peru was composed of priests and Sisters working in the dioceses of Chimbote, Trujillo and Chiclayo. We Holy Cross men in Peru were all members of ONIS. Often Religious Sisters also joined with us in our meetings. We met at our house in Cartavio because it was a natural mid-point between the northern dioceses involved. It was the beginning for me of years of collaboration on pastoral planning between many different Religious congregations and diocesan clergy. We were not involved in just a Holy Cross work but in a much wider and broader experience of being Church.

Those of us priests and Sisters working in 1969 on the sugar plantations (*haciendas*) that were being transformed into cooperatives by the new military Peruvian government formed a special sector of ONIS in the north to deal with the specific reality that was ours at that moment of time. I remember especially the Canadian diocesan priests from London, Ontario, who ministered on the sugar plantation in Cayalti near the city of Chiclayo, about a three-hour car ride north of Cartavio, and the Sisters of Charity from Halifax, especially my good friends Sisters Zelma LeBlanc and Kay Conroy, who visited us often in Cartavio and who also worked in the Chiclayo diocese. We visited them, as well, at their home among the poor on the outskirts of Chiclayo. We have remained friends all these years, often working together in other areas of Peru or gathering for summer theological courses in Lima. Sister Zelma died a few years ago. May she rest in peace.

To help with the transition from the plantation system to the cooperative system, we also spoke often in our homilies and classes on the benefits of the latter which we all thought would help the people in Cartavio. We encouraged the people to participate more fully in the change-over process from the hacienda to the cooperative system.

We also belonged to the Trujillo group of ONIS priests which included other priests from the Archdiocese of Trujillo in which the parish of Cartavio was located. Practically all the members were native-born Peruvians except for us, and that was a great learning experience for me. I especially enjoyed the years in Cartavio because the Church in Trujillo did not have so many foreign-born clergy as other dioceses did at that time. These Peruvian priests were wonderful men, so dedicated to their people, especially to the poor in the city of Trujillo, which was about an hour's ride from Cartavio. They usually held other jobs like teacher or lawyer during the day to support themselves.

We had many regional and national assemblies of ONIS, too, that were always an educational opportunity for me, both for the Peruvian socio-political reality and the history and present reality of the Peruvian Church. These meetings helped me to see the role of Church as humble servant at the service of those in need of liberation, which is so different from the clerical, sacramental Church I had experienced up to then.

I especially enjoyed the talks by Peruvian diocesan priest and theologian, founder of Liberation Theology, Gustavo Gutierrez. I had to relearn and further learn so much about the Bible. In my studies at the Gregorian University in Rome, the emphasis had been on dogma courses. The Bible was used essentially to defend dogma. Gustavo made the Bible come alive for me in a way that I had not experienced it before. He especially helped me to comprehend the Book of Exodus in the light of people coming out of slavery, called by their God to a new life of freedom to live in a new fraternity of equality. He helped me to see that the Creator God's love for all humankind is also the Liberator God's preferential option for those who are poor or enslaved or oppressed by others. For me this is much like a parent who might take care of his most needy child while still loving all his other children too. All that opened my eyes to discover Jesus in the Gospels calling us to do the same—to follow Him amid so much suffering to new life now in His Spirit. I saw this in the context of Cartavio where the owners and those who worked in the fields and factory lived quite separately and lived very different lifestyles.

All these conferences helped me to make the connection between the real life problems of the poor and the Scriptures. This is something I have never forgotten and continue today to try to connect in my homilies and Bible classes. It makes faith seem more an essential part of life rather than just intellectual doctrine or beliefs. This new way of reading the Bible influenced my whole life in Peru and still does even now here in the United States. Thank you, Gustavo and team!

In early 1969 Gonzalo and some of the ONIS priests in the Trujillo archdiocese participated in an organized protest of the new, luxurious golf course in Trujillo. The city had used public money to build a golf course for the rich, rather than for giving safe water and electricity to the poor sectors of the city. Archbishop Jurgens of Trujillo, who was a good friend of the city officials, was angry with the priests who had participated in the protest. He removed from his archdiocese three Spanish priests who worked at the regional seminary and dismissed several others, including Gonzalo. There was a general protest in opposition to the archbishop's actions in many parishes throughout the archdiocese. In Cartavio we participated in that protest by canceling all the Sunday Masses except for one during which we explained to the people what we were doing and why. The archbishop finally relented.

Shortly afterwards the priest group ONIS expanded into a lay branch called *Iglesia Solidaria* (Church in Solidarity with the Poor). This name was later changed to *Fe y Acción Solidaria* (Faith and Action in Solidarity with the Poor) because some bishops interpreted the first name to mean we were founding a new church! Most of the lay people who participated actively in the parish became members of this movement, which organized many assemblies among the participating parishes in Trujillo.

It was a time in the Church when priests, Religious Sisters and Brothers and lay folk worked together on pastoral plans combining themes of faith and social justice. The new orientation given by the Latin American bishops at Medellin and by the Peruvian bishops in their recent wonderful document on Justice in the World in 1970 and another document on Evangelization in 1971 called for the Church to unite the work of faith with justice for all people, especially those excluded and marginalized in Peruvian society. Many like Archbishop Jurgens and some of the Franciscan Sisters in Cartavio and other Church people considered all this to be only political work since it defended the poor. It did not fit into their pre-Vatican II mentality or point of view.

In February 1973, for example, I needed to obtain from Archbishop Jurgens his Church approval to teach. When he had visited Cartavio in 1970, he told us that our parish was a model for his archdiocese; but since then he had become more upset with the Vatican II changes in the Church. He told me that he did not want me to teach because Larry had returned to the United States at the end of 1972 and so I was acting pastor that year. I gave him examples of other pastors who were full-time teachers in their schools and who also were alone in their parishes. I at least had the help of Fred Serraino (who had arrived in 1971) in the parish in Cartavio. Suddenly, he slapped me in the face. I was so surprised and angry and furious that I marched out of his office. His secretary came running after me and pleaded with me to return, where I found the archbishop sobbing. He apologized to me, telling me he was under a lot of pressure these days. Our Holy Cross founder, Basil Moreau, had problems with his bishop, too. I often wonder if it is part of our Holy Cross charisma.

During those years, we also had some difficulties with the Franciscan Missionaries of Mary Sisters who had a large convent of about twenty Sisters in Cartavio. The active Sisters staffed the hospital, taught in schools and ran a kindergarten. Many others were elderly and retired. They were accustomed to the pre-Vatican II Church and wanted a lot of Church services in their own convent chapel. We asked them to come to the parish church which was only a block away from their convent, which Vatican II had recommended Religious do. But they insisted on having Mass at their own convent chapel which also served as a special church for the wealthier folk in Cartavio who did not like to rub shoulders with the field and factory workers. Finally, though, after some dialogue with us they accepted to come to the parish Masses.

The few Sisters who worked with the parish team were impressive, but they often were mistreated in their own convent. Some of the Sisters did not like our social justice orientation in the parish. Their thinking was more in line with the archbishop's. One year their provincial superior suddenly ordered Sister Maria Dolores who was on our parish team to go to Lima for a new assignment. I was away at the time in the mountain town of Cachicadan visiting with the Calderon family whose two young sons, Pablo and Felipe, lived with us in our house on Calle Real. Some of the women in the parish went to the convent and refused to leave until they could speak with the provincial superior, to explain to her why Sister Dolores was so important at that moment on the parish team. They finally got to talk with her late at night. The provincial told them that she was not aware of all that Sister Dolores was doing in the parish, and she allowed her to stay and finish out the year.

Another example of these differing Church mentalities occurred the year I needed to obtain permission to teach from the Sister in charge of the Diocesan Office for Religious Education (ODEC). Each diocese in Peru has an office in charge of assigning the religion teachers in the state schools. She was treating all the lay teachers very rudely. As usual I was not dressed in clerical garb. So, when I arrived at her desk she behaved towards me the same way as she did towards the others, until I told her I was a priest. Did she change her manners quickly! I told her then that I thought she might try to treat everyone in a respectful way and not just those of us who are priests! That was a common occurrence in Peru in those days when there was still a very clerical Church. Sad to say, such still is the clerical attitude in our Church sometimes even today!

We tried to follow the new Church orientation flowing from the Vatican II documents that view the Church as the people of God and holiness as the practice of justice and love of neighbor. This tension in the Church would exist all my years in Peru, and it persists today here in the United States, as well. Many want a purely sacramental Church which does not get involved in social problems. But at that time the pope was Paul VI who continued to support the changes recommended by Vatican II, and most Latin American bishops also were in favor of the changes. We studied the Church documents in groups together and tried to follow their direction.

TENSIONS IN HOLY CROSS

As I described, the people in Cartavio were mostly from the mountain towns and villages near Trujillo. They were beautiful, simple people whom I learned to love. They were very hospitable to me and others despite our linguistic and cultural differences. I felt very much at home there. Cartavio was a very good place to start out in Peru. However, from the very onset of Holy Cross' plans to work in Cartavio, there was contention in Holy Cross over our presence there.

From the beginning in 1963 there was a concern in the Congregation of Holy Cross, voiced especially by our superior general in Rome, Father Germain Lalande, about having American-born Religious working on an American-owned sugar plantation (*hacienda*) in Peru. Even some in Holy Cross' U.S. Eastern Province, of which I am a member and which oversaw the mission in Peru, wanted us to move out of Cartavio. I was saddened that this difficult situation had not been explained to me before sending me to work there.

The expropriation of Cartavio by the military government in June 1969 changed all that. How could we leave now with this new development? It would look like we were working all this time for the Grace Company! So, after many letters back and forth between the provincial superior in the United States, Richard Sullivan, and those of us in Peru, the provincial decided that we would stay a while longer in Cartavio and then we would open a new mission elsewhere. Larry and I went looking at several places on the northern coast between Trujillo and Lima. We settled on the possibility of the commercial city of Barranca about halfway between Cartavio and Lima as a new possible mission for Holy Cross.

Previous attempts had been made to expand outside Cartavio into Trujillo and Huanchaco by the second pastor and former provincial George DePrizio, but it had never panned out due to personnel problems in the Holy Cross community during the first five years. Most of the initial Holy Cross men who arrived in Peru between the first group on September 10, 1963 until my arrival in October 1968 returned to the United States after a few years or even months in Peru. It was a time of many personal vocational difficulties perhaps exacerbated by Vatican II and the sudden changes in the Church. There also were at times personality conflicts among the small group of Religious which did not make community life in Peru easy. Some just could not adapt to the Peruvian culture, language or poor living conditions. Others were dealing with their own vocational problems. Despite all that, between 1963 and 1968 the mission continued forward.

The people in Cartavio made life there so pleasant for me that any other difficulties that I personally might have experienced disappeared easily and quickly. There was a lot to do in this exciting time in Cartavio. We remained for at least a few more years, keeping Holy Cross community contact with George DePrizio who was residing in Lima and with Dave Farrell who was in Chimbote.

Dave who will appear frequently in this story, especially in the latter part, had been with me for two years during our formation at Stonehill College. Then I was sent to Rome. He was sent to study theology in Chile from 1964 to 1968. While he was there he came each summer for a few months to do pastoral work in Cartavio. On returning to Peru after his ordination to the priesthood, celebrated in the United States in October 1968, he was assigned at first to Cartavio. However, due to difficulties with Archbishop Carlos Jurgens of Trujillo, our provincial superior Richard Sullivan decided that Dave should go to work in the Prelature of Chimbote where Dominican North American Bishop James Burke was friendlier to the ONIS priests. So in early 1969, Dave went to help a Peruvian diocesan priest, Bertino Otarola, in the parish of our Lord of the Miracles in the center of the city of Chimbote. Larry, Jim and I occasionally drove the three hours to Chimbote to visit Dave, and he also came to visit us in Cartavio, especially on holidays like Christmas.

Dave was the one who from the beginning encouraged us to participate in ONIS meetings. He was very interested in the Peruvian political situation. He also was someone with whom Jim, Larry and I disagreed frequently, due mainly to his very strong opinions and personality.

One of those early disagreements occurred in early 1969 when we were debating whether to stay or to move out of Cartavio. The provincial Richard Sullivan and the assistant provincial Jerry Lawyer, both of whom admired Dave highly and respected his political views, had a lot of what we called "secret communication" with him about the future of Cartavio that did not include Larry, Jim and me who were living and working in Cartavio. At a community meeting in Cartavio during the provincial visit in April 1969, all that "secret communication" came out. Of course, Jim, Larry and I expressed our displeasure that it had been carried on without our participating in the conversation. At the end of that meeting the provincial assured us that in the future we all would share in the discussion.

In 1971 Larry took a year of personal renewal, called a sabbatical year, in Spain. Jim Chichetto also decided to return to the United States for personal and health reasons at the end of 1971. Fred Serraino, a good friend of mine from formation days, arrived to work in Cartavio that same year after finishing Spanish studies at the language school in Lima. Bob Baker who also will appear frequently in this story also came to Cartavio for six months during that year. Both Fred and Bob had studied theology in our theology house in Washington, DC.

When I visited Notre Dame High School in Bridgeport, Connecticut, where Bob was teaching in 1970 when I was on family visit leave, Bob told me of his desire to work in the Hispanic ministry in the United States. I suggested that he might think about coming to Cartavio for a few months during 1971 to help us out while Larry was away. He could study Spanish with Wilda Cardenas our neighbor and practice with us in the house where by that time we all spoke Spanish together. Bob had been a class-mate of Dave Farrell, and he had studied with Dave and me for two years at Stonehill College. So, we all knew one another from our early days of formation.

Before Larry left on his sabbatical in 1971 we formed a parish council with leaders of the social action move-ments, namely, the Legion of Mary, the Christian Family Movement, and a few others who held leadership posi-tions in the neighborhoods of the parish. Larry's idea was that they advise the pastor and us priests. Little by little while Larry was away, Fred Serraino and I decided to give the council more decision-making powers. All members would vote, one vote each on major decisions concerning the parish. We also decided to put the Mass collection money into a joint account requiring two signatures, one of the pastor and one of the parish council president. When Larry returned from his sabbatical year, he found these changes difficult to accept. He believed the pastor should make the important decisions after listening to other opinions and should be in control of the money in the parish.

In 1971 during a community gathering Fred and I, together with Dave and Gonzalo who were now both in Chimbote, began to speak about the need for Religious like us to give witness to a simpler lifestyle by moving into a smaller house in the working-class section of Cartavio. Dave and Gonzalo had already done this in Chimbote. We waited until Larry came back to make the final deci-sion. After considerable discussion, the three of us decided to move to a house at Calle Grau #19 which was located near the parish church and office but in a poorer working-class neighborhood. The house was a bit larger than the other poorer houses in Cartavio. This community decision, like the one about the parish council, created some tension within our small Holy Cross community in Cartavio, due to different visions and personal needs on the part of Larry on the one hand and Fred and me on the other. Fred and I wanted more participation by the people in parish decisions and a simpler life style in our community living, both of which Larry found difficult.

At the end of 1972 during a visit to Peru by the new provincial superior Bill Hogan, Larry decided to return to the United States, due probably to problems living and working with Fred and me. That left just Fred and me in Cartavio and Dave and Gonzalo in Chimbote at the beginning of 1973.

One of the reasons we had remained in Cartavio during the changeover to the cooperative system was our desire to accompany the poor, which was a major element in the Medellin documents that the Latin American bishops had drafted to implement Vatican II. Changing our house was for the same reason. We wanted to live more like the poorer people in Cartavio. All our pastoral decisions were based principally on this desire. It caused some divisions, sadly, both in Cartavio society and within the Holy Cross community. We were fully involved in the Theology of Liberation and the work for social justice and the preferential option for the poor. These different opinions about the implementation of Vatican II and Medellin and the Religious life would create tensions several more times during the years. My take on it could be considered a more radical approach, while that of others like Larry might be called a more moderate or prudent approach. All I know is that my way of being often caused friction in the Holy Cross community and sometimes with bishops. I will tell you more about this later in the story.

NEW WINDS

In June 1973, when Gonzalo was planning to leave the Congregation to marry when his temporary vows expired in early 1974, the members of the provincial chapter of the Eastern Province of priests and Brothers of the Congregation of Holy Cross in the United States on which Peru was dependent, hoping that Holy Cross might continue to grow in Peru, requested us, the three remaining Holy Cross men in Peru, Fred Serraino, Dave Farrell (who was still living and working in Chimbote) and I, to find a new place for ministry in that country where the three of us could live and work together and might thus interest other members of the province to come and join us. So, with the support and approval of the provincial superior Bill Hogan, we made the difficult community decision to leave Cartavio.

Cartavio did not offer many possibilities outside of parish ministry for other Holy Cross Religious to come to work there with us. The city of Trujillo where there was a university and a hospital was too distant to commute each day. Cartavio also had by that time a poor reputation with some of the Holy Cross Eastern Province community members because of its early ties to W.R. Grace Company and because of the negative reports by some Holy Cross Religious who had returned to the United States saying that there was nothing to do in Cartavio except parish work. Others who had returned home had had problems with the language or with the Peruvian culture or with the poverty. These difficulties were not favorable for attracting new Holy Cross personnel to come to work with us.

The tough community decision was made (despite my own personal deep sorrow to leave Cartavio) to unite in Chimbote the three of us who made up the small Holy Cross group. There in three parishes we were to create a new beginning for Holy Cross in Peru. It was a good and necessary decision I think if Holy Cross was to survive in that country. To keep the mission open we had to have a place where the three of us could live in community and not as lone rangers. There were delegates to the provincial chapter who were in favor of closing the Peru mission all together if we could not form a viable community other than in Cartavio where no other province member was then willing to go.

Fred and I were interested in the jungle regions of Peru where we thought there was more need for priests than on the Peruvian coast. The jungle was also an area forgotten by the government, so the people there were economically poorer. Fred went to visit the jungle Prelature of Moyobamba where the bishop offered Holy Cross a part of his prelature if Holy Cross would send at least three Religious. But after many meetings and endless discussion among the three of us, and with other people in

Peru like Gustavo Gutierrez and other priests in ONIS, we finally settled on accepting another parish in the diocese of Chimbote, of which I will write more in the next chapter.

I realize now that this decision-making process did not take very much into account the feelings of the people of Cartavio. It was a Holy Cross community decision taken in the interest of strengthening the community life of the Congregation. This was an error that we in Holy Cross would repeat in Peru several more times again in the future. So, I apologize to you the people in Cartavio for this insensitivity on our part, for not including you in the conversation at that time, which left all kinds of erroneous reasoning regarding our sudden departure. Some people in Cartavio still think even today that Archbishop Jurgens threw us out! I think we felt that the people of Cartavio were sufficiently strong and prepared to work with a new priest. And they were in many ways, as I will describe in the next chapter. Thank you, Cartavio, for welcoming us, forming us and then sending us out to the wider Peruvian Church to serve people even more in need than yourselves.

Chimbote was a large, poor urban city with many more spiritual and economic needs than Cartavio had. At that time Dave, Fred and I wanted to be more among the poor of the poor, following Jesus' option for the poor. So, in January 1974, Fred turned off the lights and handed the parish to the new pastor, an Italian diocesan priest named Romano. He had helped out in Cartavio earlier when the Italian Franciscan priests worked there before the arrival of Holy Cross in 1963.

Between 1963-1968 many fine Holy Cross men passed through Cartavio. I will mention just a few. One was George DePrizio who was the Eastern Province provincial superior who made the decision to send men to Cartavio in 1963, and who gave up his job as provincial the following year of 1964 to come to help the struggling new mission. Many Holy Cross men came from the Eastern Province, as well as from the Holy Cross mission in Chile dependent on the Congregation's United States Indiana Province, to help with personnel during those first years when so many came and left as if in a revolving door. Among them was Dan Panchot who will reappear in this memoir later. Thanks to each one, Holy Cross remained in Peru during those first difficult years. Hopefully they will all be remembered in our community history there, for they were the foundation stones on which our presence in Peru is built today. If it were not for them, Holy Cross would not be in Peru at all!

When I visit Cartavio I am always impressed by the way people remember each of the names of these various Holy Cross men who passed through there, even after more than forty-five years out of Cartavio. Each person has his own personal stories and memories about Holy Cross, still remembered there with fondness and gratitude! I suppose we are somewhat like their children, since when we arrived we had to learn so many new things from them about the Peruvian people—their language, their customs, their culture, their way of life and their practice of faith following Jesus. Thank you, friends in Cartavio! I will always remember you.

People are often surprised that I have kept up with so many of my students from the Cartavio days. I think especially of my *compadre* (the father of my godchild Isaac) Felipe Calderon who left Cartavio in December 1972 to join the navy. He and his brother Pablo shared a room in our big house in Calle Real for a few years because the house where they had been living with an aunt and uncle was overcrowded. We have been good friends all those years. I celebrated his marriage in 1979 and am godfather to his firstborn son Isaac Pedro. Felipe and my *comadre* Filomena (Mena) and their family today are my Peruvian family. Felipe even came to visit me here in Florida twice in recent years. The first time, we traveled by car up to Boston to visit Jim Chichetto and back. The second time, in the following year, I drove with him across the country to California and back. Thank you, Felipe, and family! And thank you my good friends Antero Ruiz, Gabi Vega and Iris Vega who always gather all our friends to celebrate our friendship during my visits to Cartavio and Trujillo.

I have visited Cartavio almost every year since I left. Even now six years after leaving Peru I continue to visit. I always tell all of my friends there that I carry Cartavio in a special place in my memories and in my heart! Thank you Cartavio for teaching me so much about Peru. Thank you for receiving me among you and giving me your friendship. Thank you for introducing me to the Peruvian poor, to the Theology of Liberation and to a Church alive and present among the people. What a great experience of Church it was! If only today we could rediscover that we all are the Church, that not only priests and bishops are!

3. CHIMBOTE AND MACATE 1974 - 1980

I was very happy in Cartavio. I enjoyed the work at the school and in the parish, and I had many good friends there. Why would I want to move? The fact is that I did not want to! I was concerned that the large number of foreign-born missionary priests in Chimbote would make us an island amid the Peruvian Church. I had become accustomed to being among mostly Peruvian priests in Trujillo. Yet I knew deep in my heart that it was time to move on.

It was like my decision to go to Peru. I had never wanted to be a missionary when I joined Holy Cross. I did not take the fourth vow, the missionary vow. But I had had the conversation in Rome with Bob Nogosek, the superior of our house there, and suddenly like Saint Paul's experience on the road to Damascus I knew that it was God talking to me through Bob! That event, as I have described, changed the entire direction of my life.

Now once again, it was a moment in my life when I knew that it was what God wanted for me, that it was time to move. I felt that leaving Cartavio for Chimbote for all the reasons I mentioned in the previous chapter was the right decision both for me and for all of us, even though I was attached personally and emotionally to the mission and to my friends in Cartavio. It was time for me to continue the journey with the Lord.

After community discussion between Dave Farrell, Fred Serraino and me, and with our provincial superior Bill Hogan, we decided that the best place to unite Holy Cross into one mission with the few people that we had in Peru would be in Chimbote (rather than in Moyobamba in the jungle of Peru which I suggested in the previous chapter). I personally think that Dave would not have been happy in the jungle. He is too much a city person. So, we agreed on Chimbote which was a new, large coastal city, a three-hour ride to the south of Cartavio. There also was a mountainous area there named Macate where I could minister.

Located not far from Santa, one of the many towns along Peru's coastal desert near rivers that fill with water during the December to March rainy season, Chimbote had been only a small fishing village back in the 1940's, until suddenly there was a demand on the world market for canned anchovies. In addition, guano, the excrement deposited by sea gulls on the nearby islands in the bay of Chimbote, was found to be a great fertilizer, and demand for it also grew on the world market. Then a steel factory was built in Chimbote because it has a very good natural harbor. These factors contributed to a mass influx of people from the mountain villages into Chimbote looking for work in the factories and fishing industry in hope of attaining a better life. It was a time throughout Peru of migration from the rural areas to the large cities on the coast.

Chimbote grew within a few years from a fishing village of a few thousand people to a large industrial city with a population of many thousands. It expanded so quickly that there was little time for city planning, so few houses had water or sewage or electricity. Because of these privations, living conditions there were very poor. Additionally, the earthquake of 1970, which I described in the first chapter, had brought Chimbote to its knees. The epicenter was very close by, in the nearby mountain region of Huaraz and the coastal city of Casma just to the south.

Because Chimbote was a developing city, full of poor working-class people, we felt that it was a perfect place for Holy Cross to begin again as a community embracing the lot of the poor. So we left the Cartavio mission in January 1974 and opened a new mission in Chimbote in an evolving neighborhood named *La Victoria*.

THE MOVE TO CHIMBOTE

As early as 1970 Holy Cross had established a house in Chimbote in a parish named *Santa Cruz* (Holy Cross) located in a neighborhood called *Esperanza Baja*. Santa Cruz parish was established by the American Dominican bishop of Chimbote, James Burke. Dave Farrell first lived there in early 1970 with a Dominican priest Lino Dolan and a St. James priest whose name I have forgotten. They erected a small wooden house of triply with three small bedrooms and a small room to serve as a parish office for receiving people. The toilet was an outhouse. They built a shower lower than ground level with a tank on top that they filled with water purchased from a donkey cart that passed by each day. There was no electricity; light was provided by kerosene lamps or candles. This small original group with Dave disbanded after a year together because their respective Religious communities needed them elsewhere. More recently, at the end of 1973, Dave Farrell was living there with Gonzalo Martin, who had returned to Peru in late 1970 after professing his first vows as a member of Holy Cross, and with a German diocesan priest, Norberto Wassen, who had come to Peru earlier that year.

While I was on vacation visiting my family in the United States from December 1973 until March 1974, Fred took up residence in Chimbote. Before I left, we had moved what little furniture we had in the Cartavio house (a few bunk beds, tables, desks and chairs) to La Victoria parish. Then Fred slept on the floor in the Cartavio house for a month and a half until he could leave when the archbishop found a priest to replace us.

Al Mahoney from the Holy Cross English-Canadian province visited Cartavio during that month of January. He was considering working with us in Peru, but he finally decided in consultation with his provincial superior to go to Chiapas, Mexico, where they felt there was a greater need. He wound up spending twenty years of his life there. Thank you, Al, for your dedicated ministry in Chiapas! Al will reappear in this memoir when I speak about my time in Puno.

Thus, in March 1974 the Holy Cross community was gathered all together in Chimbote, living in two parishes. Bud (Arthur) Colgan, who had spent four years in Chile studying theology, arrived in Peru in January 1974 after his ordination to the priesthood in the United States in the fall of 1973. He lived with Dave, Norbert, and for a brief time with Gonzalo who was awaiting the end of his temporary vows to leave the community to marry.

During the period after Vatican II many Religious left their communities to marry, or for other personal reasons when they discovered they could serve the Church as lay people as well. Gonzalo subsequently worked in Peru for many years as a coordinator for the development projects of the Canadian Bishops' Conference. He eventually divorced and then remarried. He always remained close friends with Dave, and only recently returned with his family to reside in his native Spain.

Gonzalo had helped me a lot personally, both by his tutoring me in Spanish in Rome and by aiding me when I was just beginning in Cartavio. When he left Cartavio in June 1969 to go to the novitiate in the United States, I took over his work in the chapel that he had built with the people in the sector of Cartavio named *Ingenio*. The people there had needed a chapel because the factory separated them from the main church, necessitating a long walk around. They had formed a "small Christian community" with Gonzalo while building their chapel, and I enjoyed working with them all the remaining years until I left Cartavio. Thank you, Gonzalo, and all the people of Ingenio, especially Fernando, Teresa, and Betty, for your friendship during those years!

Fred and I moved into a new parish the bishop had created in La Victoria on the other side of Chimbote from the Santa Cruz parish, in a developing area in the central part of the city. Women in the neighborhood sat all day long in the streets in front of their houses hammering on large rocks to make gravel for the nearby factories. A North American Marianist priest had helped there to build a church, a parish hall and a kindergarten. A small parish community was just beginning to grow. Mass was sparsely attended on Sunday morning, and there was not much activity in the parish. A young woman helped with faith formation for the children preparing for First Communion, and that was about it.

We decided to begin living there in the parish hall. We divided the single, large room with sheets of plywood to make individual bedrooms, a kitchen and office space. The parish hall had no water, electricity or sewage and no bathroom facilities. So, Fred and I had to get used to roughing it after the easier life in Cartavio. But then that was one of the reasons we had decided to leave Cartavio for a new mission in Chimbote. We wanted to live more like the poor. This sounds quite idealistic, and it probably was. We were young and wanted to do all the new things that we thought were so important for the Church.

Bob Baker, who had visited Cartavio in 1971 and helped us out in the parish while studying Spanish, was to arrive in the summer of 1974 to live and work with us as pastor in La Victoria parish. I was still planning to live up in Macate and teach in the high school there and then come down once a month to spend time with the community in Chimbote. Fred would assist Bob in the parish and also work as chaplain in the Chimbote prison and hospitals. However, our plans are not always God's plans.

PASTORAL ZONA NORTE

After Vatican II, the Latin American Church began two types of renewal. One was Liberation Theology which prioritized a pastoral practice of Church based on promoting social justice for the poor rather than the traditional giving out of charity. The other was a charismatic renewal which prioritized a personal renewal of life in the Spirit. Of these two forms of Church renewal, one was more social-action oriented and the other more traditional and personal-oriented, causing them often to be in conflict. Involved were two visions of Church, one that emphasized the documents of Vatican II concerning the Church in the modern world, and the other that focused on a more personal, spiritual development with no direct connection to social action for the poor. They need not have been in conflict, but unfortunately at that time in Chimbote they were. The priests and Religious in each group hardly spoke to one another, and usually did not speak well of each other, either.

Already established in Chimbote when I arrived there was the Northern Pastoral Group (*Pastoral de Zona Norte*) called Zona Norte. A group of priests and Sisters in Chimbote who ministered mainly on the northern side of the city had wanted to work together in a creative pastoral experience with a common pastoral plan. Bishop James Burke supported the group by trying to transfer out of that northern sector of Chimbote pastors who did not want to work that way, moving them to parishes on the southern side, so that all the parishes in the northern zone would have priests who were members of the movement. This decision by the bishop caused an outcry from some of the pastors. It divided the diocese to some degree between those like us who were involved more in Liberation Theology and a common pastoral plan, from those who wanted to continue with their own individual parishes and their own pastoral plans which is the norm even today here in the United States. These parishes were involved more in traditional Church ministry or with the newly formed charismatic renewal. The bishop was caught in the middle, but he came down more on the side of the Zona Norte group. Sad to say, he was pushed out in 1977 when the Peruvian Bishops' Conference began to pull back from its social action commitments, and a new Peruvian bishop was named.

THE MACATE PASTORAL TEAM

From the beginning of the conversation to depart from Cartavio for a new site, I had expressed my interest in working in a rural setting. During the discussion, I discovered that there was a rural parish near Chimbote in the town of Macate, about eighty miles into the mountains. It had a high school where I thought that I could continue in my permanent state teaching position, and possibly live in the town. Macate had a pastoral need; no priest had lived there permanently since the 1940's.

My first visit to the Macate valley was with a friend from Cartavio in April 1974. After reaching one of the villages in the lower valley, we started walking up the mountain on a path which suddenly ended in the middle of nowhere. We continued climbing through the fields on a thick foggy morning without finding any path. We had no idea where we were. Climbing blindly, we occasionally encountered people. Each time we asked where the town was, they would say that it was just a little farther up. I really don't know how we finally found it. The fog was still heavy when we arrived in the town, and the streets were deserted. Eventually we encountered a man who happened to be the person in charge of the church building. We spent an enjoyable day talking and drinking beer with him and some of the other townsmen. They seemed happy that I was thinking of becoming their permanent parish priest. They told me that there was a tiny room, containing two narrow beds, attached to the side of the church for the priest to stay in.

Macate had been without a priest except occasionally in April and August for the fiestas honoring their patron saint, St. Toribio of Mogrevejo, who was one of the first bishops of Peru back in the sixteenth century. Toribio was well known because he did not stay in Lima where most of the Spanish population resided, but he traveled the countryside and into the mountains for years visiting the indigenous population in their villages. He also convoked several councils of the bishops in Latin America to discuss the best ways to evangelize the indigenous peoples. One result was his insistence that all the priests learn the native languages, especially the Quechua language of the majority in Peru. The people in Macate believed that he had visited their valley and performed a miracle making water flow from a rock above their town, thus forming the fertile valley of Macate. For these reasons, I thought that it would be a perfect parish for me to begin my pastoral ministry.

That night I celebrated Mass, and I met the small Christian community in the town. The next morning when we were to begin our two-hour hike back down to the village of Huanroc to board the truck for our return trip, the people gave us a guide so that we would not get lost again on the way down and we would know the route for the walk in the future.

In Huanroc we met some of the village school teachers. They, too, were excited about my new ministry and the prospect of future visits. However, I learned that the school in Macate was not a state school, but was financed by the parents. I could not transfer my teaching post there, because it could be assigned only to a state school. Each one of us at that time lived on our salaries to try to identify more with the working-class people. That required me to change my plans. I also found out about the poor condition of the road to Macate, and how far it was between Chimbote and Macate, and how long it would take to get there on a motorbike, which is how I originally planned to travel. Because that plan was not viable, I opted to live and work instead in La Victoria parish during the week while teaching at one of the state schools in Chimbote, and then to travel to Macate on weekends.

A long bout of hepatitis sidelined me from May to September 1974. Friends from Cartavio had come to visit me in early May, and we had a great weekend together.

When they left, I felt exhausted! I had no energy for anything! I would get up in the morning, then ten minutes later return to bed wiped out! I never before had been sick for such a long period. Sooner or later all the North Americans got the disease, usually from drinking contaminated water. No one in our Holy Cross group escaped! We all got it sometime during our years in Peru.

The four months it took me to recover were like a long retreat for me that gave me considerable opportunity for reading, reflecting and praying. During most of that time, Fred was away at language school in Cochabamba, Bolivia, for a refresher course in Spanish. Bob Baker arrived in August. I finally got better after I went to Lima for the month of August to stay at the Maryknoll Center House where I could really rest. Thank you, Maryknoll, for all your hospitality then and later through all my many years in Peru!

During my time of convalescence, the Zona Norte group with its common pastoral plan formed various work groups. One was of those of us who worked in the rural mountain parishes of the diocese like Macate. When I was well enough in October 1974, I began to visit Macate with two of the Sisters of St. Joseph of Carondelet. They were Sisters Mary Kay Kottenstetter and Elena McLoughlin, who formed the new Macate pastoral team with me. (My father's sister, my aunt, Sister Martina Shea, was a member of that community of Sisters.) We started visiting the various villages, sometimes separately and sometimes together. We organized meetings with the people in each, explaining to them what we would like to do in Macate.

We told them that we would pay our own travel expense on the truck, but that we would need to receive food and lodging from them when we came to their villages. The people were marvelous. They were so happy to have us and readily agreed. They organized themselves into hospitality teams to receive us each time we visited. The public school teachers in these villages also were very helpful to us. Thank you, people of the valley of Macate, for your hospitality all those years!

It was a welcome experience to be working together as a group again in pastoral teams of priests, Religious and lay people as we had done in Trujillo and Cartavio. Sisters Elena, Mary Kay, Anita, Lally, Alma, and Maria Dolores all ministered together with me at one time or another as part of the Macate pastoral team. Several lay friends also helped from time to time, as did a few other Holy Cross priests.

Macate was a small town high in the mountains about a five-hour truck ride eighty miles from Chimbote. The parish included twenty smaller villages (*caseríos*) in its extensive valley rich with fruit trees. Trucks went up daily to bring down the fruit and to supply the people there with public transportation and other services. We rode on top of the cargo in the back of the vehicle for the arduous trip over very narrow dirt roads, first along the river Santa, and then, the air filled with dust, twisting ever higher on closed hairpin curves, all the way up into the rich, fertile valley. The trucks set out from Chimbote around 2:00 am, and traveled until 9:00 am to reach the village of Huanroc where the road ended. There, after unloading their cargo and loading up with fruit from the valley destined for sale, the trucks turned around and returned to the markets of Chimbote.

We usually traveled Saturday, and from the end of the road walked to whatever villages we were planning to visit. The town of Macate was at least a two-hour walk from Huanroc. There was another truck that took a different route directly to Macate, an even steeper climb with more dangerous hairpin curves, but it departed only twice a week on days that usually were not convenient for us because we all taught classes at schools in Chimbote.

Over the years we continued as a team visiting the villages and forming lay leaders among them to participate in assemblies that were held in the village of Huanroc, the most centrally located. The villages that agreed to elect a group of five adults each to take part in the formation process in Huanroc with us would be able to have a priest for their annual religious celebration. Some of the villages were right on the truck route, but others were a considerable walk and usually a steep climb to reach. We could communicate the dates and times of our visits by sending written messages via the truck drivers once they knew us. They gave our letters to passengers going to those villages, to deliver to the people to whom they were addressed. It usually worked out fine.

After our initial and follow-up visits we started the lay leader formation program in Huanroc. We had a very good turn out from each village, and we began to teach the five representatives from each how to do the preparations requisite for Baptism, First Communion, Confirmation, and Marriage, and how to lead Liturgies of the Word in their villages. Afterwards we visited them to observe the results of the formation process. In general it worked very well, and we were quite happy with it. Once people were prepared for one of the sacraments, they received certificates from their village formation team. They could then receive the sacrament in any village where they might encounter us.

Beginning in 1977 the Zona Norte group of mountain parishes began to organize annual assemblies bringing together the various parishes. The fourth one took place in Macate in 1980, and the people there very successfully prepared and conducted the gathering pretty much all by themselves! Even Bishop Bambaren, the new Jesuit bishop of Chimbote who had replaced Bishop Burke in 1978, recognized how well-organized they were. At first, he didn't favor these gatherings because he was somewhat distrustful of the Zona Norte people in his diocese. This assembly was very gratifying for Sister Dolores and me. We got to see the Macate lay leaders take on the entire event and do a great job without depending much on us!

Our new Holy Cross provincial superior at the time, Bill Ribando, traveled to Macate with me on one of his provincial visits. We sometimes forgot how difficult these trips might be for someone from the United States not accustomed to Peru. On that occasion, we took the truck directly up to the town of Macate so that Bill would not have the long, arduous climb. But on the return, after a long two-hour walk down the steep path from Macate to Huanroc, Bill angrily asked me to get him a horse! I had no idea where I could find one. Later, after a good night's rest he apologized. Bill and I would have many good laughs about that trip for years afterwards. Thank you, Bill, for making that trip with me and for all you did for Holy Cross in Peru! May you rest in peace!

In 1980 I began to plan a 1981 year-long sabbatical, and the St. Joseph Sisters were preparing to move from Chimbote to the town of Casma, about an hour's drive south, so all of us on the team knew that we would have to discontinue pastoral work in Macate at the end of that year. Because there was no other Holy Cross priest interested in carrying forward our ministry there, we suggested to Bishop Bambaren that we might be replaced by Carlos, an Italian diocesan priest who was at that time in the rural parish of Santa and who was ready to continue in Macate our pastoral plan of ministry with the lay leadership. The bishop approved, and Carlos agreed to maintain the programs with the lay leaders we had formed in the parish. The people were saddened by our leaving, but were glad to have someone replace us who would continue the collaborative ministry with them. So, I left the Macate parish in December 1980 with my heart happy for that, but with sorrow as well. The people in the Macate valley were delightful people to work with. Thank you one and all!

Macate was one of the few places I did not return to visit with some frequency or keep up contact with friends. I am sorry that I did not, but communication with Macate was not easy. I occasionally saw some of the Macate people on the streets in Chimbote, but I did not return to the town except once in 1984. On that occasion, the four lay leaders of the Esperanza parish traveled with me for a meeting up there planned by Carlos, who was continuing impressively what we had started. He wanted a gathering to share experiences between the lay leaders of the parish teams in Macate with the Santa Cruz parish team in Chimbote where I was working at that time. It was a wonderful re-encounter with the members of our original Macate lay team. It was a gift and blessing for me also to see all the lay leaders who were still actively involved with Carlos after so many years. It was a great day in my life!

I visited with Sister Dolores recently when I visited Tacna where she is living now, and we shared our Macate memories. Thank you, Sister Dolores, and other Sisters of St. Joseph and the people of Macate, for those years of friendship and collaboration in mission together! I will never forget you!

THE SAN PEDRO SCHOOL

Soon after I arrived in Chimbote in 1974, St. Joseph Sister Elena McLoughlin met with me to set up my teaching religion there. She was the director of the Diocesan Office for Christian Education (ODEC) which coordinated between the Church and Peruvian government the teaching of religion in state schools. I had my permanent position with the state, so she explained what I had to do to transfer it from Cartavio to Chimbote. It required my traveling several times to Trujillo and Cartavio during March and April 1974 to do the paperwork. Then I fell sick in Chimbote with hepatitis right afterwards.

In August my Holy Cross provincial superior in the United States, Bill Hogan, received a letter from the archbishop of Trujillo complaining that I was visiting Cartavio every weekend and stirring up the people against the new pastor Romano. Bill wrote back to the archbishop that he did not understand how it could be possible, because I had been sick in bed in Chimbote since early May. What actually happened is that the Cartavio parish council and the people who formed part of the Faith and Social Action (FAS) movement were protesting decisions by the new pastor that undid some of the pastoral changes that Holy Cross had made during our years there. The archbishop could not believe that lay people could speak and act for themselves! So, for him I had to be involved!

Those lay leaders in Cartavio were impressive. They formed themselves into a group called Santa Rosa and asked a lay couple from Trujillo, Miguel and Flor Cabrera, to be their spiritual advisers. The group remained active for many years despite their conflicts with Romano, the following pastors and the archbishop himself. It was a time when some Peruvian bishops had begun to turn away from Vatican II-inspired pastoral changes.

Everything worked out well with my paperwork, so by August my transfer was complete. Elena at first gave me a few hours in several different schools where I began teaching in April. When I got sick, I had to ask others from the Holy Cross community to help. Bud Colgan and Fred and a few lay friends substituted for me until the end of September when I was healthy enough to resume. By that time, Elena had managed to schedule all my hours in one very large and prestigious school called San Pedro, located within walking distance from La Victoria parish.

I taught religion twenty-four hours a week, sixteen in the day session to students in the third and fourth years of high school, and eight in the evening session to young adults who had not finished high school in their youth. In my classes I used picture-book biblical material published by an ecumenical Methodist group called CELADEC (Comisión Evangélica Latinoamericana de Educación Cristiana). Two students sat at each school desk, usually about fifty students in a classroom. I would buy twenty-five copies, which the two or more students at each desk shared, and which I then collected at the end of the class to take to the next one. It was a lot to carry around, but it was very good teaching material.

We would read part of the booklet, and then the students would work in groups on questions directed at understanding Scripture and seeing how we could put it into practice in our daily lives today. All my classes were organized around group work. Both the students and I enjoyed this method recommended in those days by the Peruvian educational authorities, who wanted education to raise the students' consciousness to become creative and critical thinkers.

During school recess, I usually stood outside the classrooms talking with students rather than going to the teachers' staff room. I made friends with the students that way. With some I played basketball at the school on Sunday afternoons, and others, especially some older students from the evening session, accompanied me to Macate. I always was impressed by those evening-session students. They were mostly in their twenties, and had not finished high school when they were young because they had to work to help their families. So now as young adults they worked in the daytime and then came to study from 7:00 to 11:00 pm. They were dedicated students. One mother in her fifties was in my first-year class. I asked her why she came to sit with all these young people in the cold to study at night now. She told me that she had raised and educated her children and was now going to educate herself. What a great lady!

After night school classes I often walked back into town with some of the students to take the *colectivo* (a taxi service transporting several passengers along a set route) that I rode home to Esperanza parish to which I had moved in March 1975. However, the colectivo that went to our house in Esperanza Baja didn't run later than 9:00 pm, so I had to take a different colectivo route that passed close to Esperanza but left me with twenty more blocks to walk to reach home. There was no electricity in those days, so I carried my flashlight to see and to protect myself from the dogs that slept outside their houses and growled and barked at anyone walking by at that hour. That part of the trip I did alone, and I never had any problem with robbers or dogs. Thank God and the flashlight for that!

During all those years, we had a remarkable group of religion teachers in Chimbote. We prepared classes together, and most of us were active in the teachers' union SUTEP. When there were political tensions at San Pedro school and the education authorities arrived to investigate, I often was asked by the other teachers to speak at the school in the name of the teacher's union, since they were afraid they might be fired.

They were exciting years of political change. Some of the students at the school were highly politicized, as well. They wanted to participate in strikes in which their fathers or other family members were involved. I tried to support these students the best I could, inasmuch as the educational authorities said they wanted to form creative, conscientious, critical students. I was involved actively in two four-month national teachers' strikes in 1978 and 1979. It was a time of political unrest. The military government which had ousted President Velasco had replaced him with President Morales Bermudez who was quite dictatorial. With the economy weak and the Peruvian currency devalued considerably, protests and strikes were frequent everywhere.

It was around that time, too, that I decided to apply to become a Peruvian citizen. In our 1978 district chapter, it was agreed that if Americans in the district decided to seek Peruvian citizenship, they would be supported by the district. So, in my youthful enthusiasm I determined to do so. It is interesting that during the process all the Peruvian authorities I dealt with tried to discourage me! In any case, I think my participation in the teachers' strikes and my speaking out for the teachers at San Pedro school became problematic for my petition and may have been a reason it was denied. It probably was for the best, because my mother died in May 1979, and if the process had continued at the usual slow pace I would not have been able to travel to her funeral, since I would have had neither my U.S. passport nor my new Peruvian passport.

YOUTH MINISTRY

In 1974 the Zona Norte group also wanted the membership to create youth groups both in the parishes and in the schools, so I decided to try to start a youth group at the school. Two St. Joseph Sisters, Alma Jones and Lally Leigh, offered to work with me in that enterprise. For our afternoon meetings we obtained permission from the nearby *Virgen de la Puerta* (Our Lady of the Door) parish near San Pedro school to use a small, empty building they owned, and a very nice group of students joined up. We organized a Confirmation group for them, and the confirmations took place at Virgen de la Puerta parish with Bishop James Burke presiding. We continued to use the facility until 1979 when Luis Bambaren the new bishop abruptly gave the site to the Missionary Sisters of Charity, the order founded by Mother Teresa of Calcutta.

Our group formed part of the northern zone pastoral youth organization, so we were able to attend many local and regional assemblies. I am still in touch with several of the young people from these groups. Two among them, Bruno Rojas and Santos Sotelo, later in 1979 would become Holy Cross' first Peruvian postulants when we began our formation program in Lima. Bruno left the program after one year. He studied at the university, and later became a diocesan priest in the Association of Peruvian

Missionaries (APM) and then went on to minister with the Hispanic and Portuguese communities working in Japan, where he remains to today. Santos also left the program after two years with us and now lives as a married layman in the Holy Cross parish in Canto Grande, Lima. Thank you, Sisters Lally and Alma, and thank you, Bruno and Santos and all those involved in this youth ministry! You are all in my memory and in my heart!

During those years, I also began working with the older youths who hung around nights in the plaza in front of our community house in Esperanza. When I got back late from night school classes I often stopped and talked with them. They became interested in forming a youth group, and asked me to help them do it and to accompany them in it. Many in the Holy Cross community thought I was wasting my time with them. For me, it was a great way to get to know them and minister to them, rather like my beach ministry in Cartavio which some Holy Cross members also thought was a waste of time. These young people often talked informally and openly about many of their personal life problems. I felt I could be of some help listening, and encouraging them in their difficult lives.

They did create a cultural and sports youth group, and I enjoyed working with them at least on the cultural side. We became friends, and I think they were appreciative of their new organization and of my presence in it. I enjoyed and still enjoy working with young people like them who often are discarded as not important by society and by some people in the Church. Thank you, young men and women of Esperanza!

During all those years, I continued teaching full-time as before in the San Pedro high school on the other side of Chimbote and working with the youth group there, and I continued traveling to Macate with the team every other weekend. Life was full of ministry and excitement. I helped with weekend Masses in Esperanza parish when I was not up in Macate, but in general, with my school work and youth work and with the Macate parish, I was not very present in the Esperanza parish.

We had with us for a time in Esperanza a young man named Erman Colonia from the mountain parish of Pariacoto. The Sisters there thought it would be good for him to live with Holy Cross as he discerned a vocation. Erman stayed several years before choosing to enter the diocesan seminary. He always considered our house in Esperanza as his home. He was ordained a priest in 1984 but left shortly afterward to marry and to join a group of married priests. He is now a bishop in Chimbote for that organization and is married to a woman priest.

HOLY CROSS

At the end of 1974 we decided as a community that we wanted to write our mission statement for the Congregation, inasmuch as this move to Chimbote had been to strengthen the Holy Cross community presence in Peru by uniting our few members in one area of mission rather than having us spread out in two distant places. We spent several weeks in meetings to talk about the mission statement. We finally all agreed on it and drafted a very good declaration of who we thought we were and what we hoped to accomplish. We wanted to live the preferential option for the poor by living among the poor. We would try to live like them on only our salaries, without requiring money from our province in America, except for our trips back to the United States every three years to visit our families. We wanted to emphasize the prophetic side of our baptism and our religious vows of poverty, chastity, and obedience by a more radical following of Jesus in the Church like St. Francis did in the thirteenth century. So, we proposed some questions to the Congregation about our future in Peru.

The mission statement was written by Dave Farrell, Bob Baker, Fred Serraino, Bud Colgan and me. Norberto Wassen, a German diocesan priest who shared ministry and life with us in La Esperanza parish that year of 1974, also participated. Norberto lived and worked with us until the end of 1977, when in January 1978 he died in an auto accident while on vacation in Germany. Thank you, Norberto, for your years among us. May you rest in peace.

After we wrote the mission statement, the Holy Cross community asked me to go to the United States for two months to rest up from my hepatitis and to visit the schools of the Holy Cross Brothers to invite them to consider joining us in our mission in Peru. I visited almost all the schools in the eastern section of the United States and spoke with the Brothers and their students about our mission in Peru. Unfortunately, no Brothers at that time could come to work with us, due to personnel needs in their schools. As I have mentioned, many Religious were leaving the Congregation at that time when Vatican II had opened the door for new ways for lay people to work in the Church. Only Brother John Benesh arrived later in 1985 from the Holy Cross Midwest Brothers Province to work in schools in Peru. Thank you, Brother John, for coming and staying in Peru even up to today at your age of eighty-five years!

It was when I got back in early 1975 from my visit to the Brothers' schools in America that I was asked to move from La Victoria to the Santa Cruz parish in Esperanza. Fred Serraino had decided to return to ministry in the United States at the end of 1974. Dave Farrell also had just left in January 1975 to go to Chile to be assistant superior of the Holy Cross district there. The Pinochet military takeover in Chile in September 1973, ousting the elected, socialist president Salvador Allende, had weakened that Holy Cross district, because the Pinochet people considered Holy Cross to be Communist-infiltrated. Any group involved with social justice was considered Communist by the military. As a result, many Holy Cross Religious had to flee from Chile or were expelled. Others chose to leave the community for personal reasons. Some of those who had to depart Chile were assigned to Peru, like Bob Plasker, expelled, and Bob Neidhardt who fled. With the arrival of these Religious I moved to Esperanza to live with Bud Colgan and Norberto Wassen. Remaining in La Victoria parish where I had spent my first year were Bob Neidhardt, Bob Plasker and Bob Baker.

In 1975 more Holy Cross priests who had to leave Chile because of the Pinochet takeover began to come to

Peru. After Bob Plasker and Bob Neidhardt arrived, they were followed subsequently by Dan Panchot, Phil Devlin, Mauricio Laborde and Diego Irarrázaval. So, our numbers were up! We began to talk about opening a parish and school in Lima.

Diego, a Chilean Holy Cross Religious who had to flee Chile after the Pinochet take over there, lived with Bud Colgan and Norberto Wassen and me in Esperanza parish when he arrived in Chimbote in 1975. He traveled back and forth to Lima where he worked for two weeks each month in the Bartolome de las Casas Institute founded for Liberation Theology studies and projects by Gustavo Gutierrez and other theologians.

Bob Plasker who had been the religious superior in the district of Chile at the time of the military takeover and expelled by the Pinochet government, was the only other teacher like me. Besides both teaching in the evening session at the San Pedro high school, we also worked together in Macate during 1975, until he went to open the Canto Grande parish in Lima with Bob Baker in 1976. So once again I lost a good community companion and collaborator. Bob Plasker and I used to eat dinner together quite frequently in town before our evening classes at the San Pedro school. Since we were collaborating in Macate too, we had much to talk about. He was a dynamic person with loads of energy and creative ideas.

Bob Plasker and I also worked together on the PILA project which hoped to unite the Holy Cross priests, Brothers, and Sisters working in Peru, Chile, and Brazil into a common apostolate in Peru. This project was fruit of the Holy Cross celebration in 1973 of the one hundred years of our founder Basil Moreau's death. We hoped to start a Holy Cross parish and school in a poor section outside the Peruvian capital of Lima in which one member from each Holy Cross group would participate, hopefully uniting in this way all the Holy Cross entities in Latin America. After initial lively discussions and interest shown by each group, especially during the meeting held in Chimbote in 1975, most felt that they did not have sufficient personnel to free someone for the project at that time. But it did start years of collaboration between the Holy Cross entities in Latin America, and began the process in the Peru district of opening another new mission with a parish, school and formation house in Lima. We now had enough Religious in Peru to spread out from Chimbote. It was an exciting time for developing collaboration among Holy Cross in Latin America!

The provincial chapter of 1976 of the Eastern Province of Priests and Brothers in the United States, which was the founding province for the Peru mission, approved our mission statement and created Peru as a district of the province, which opened for us the possibility of accepting Peruvians into our vocation program. It also was a commitment by the Province to establish Holy Cross permanently in Peru.

When the provincial chapter of the Eastern Province of Holy Cross in 1976 made Holy Cross in Peru a district of the Congregation, this gave us some autonomy in decision making. Bud Colgan was elected our first district superior, and Bob Plasker, Diego Irarrázaval and I were either elected or named to his council. We began making plans for the new Lima parish in Canto Grande which was to start up in late 1976 and the new Fe y Alegría (Faith and Joy) school which we hoped would be opened there in 1977 and administered by Holy Cross.

Canto Grande was a large, new area where poor people in Lima recently had settled, looking to escape crowded conditions in the capital city and seeking a small piece of land on which to build a home for themselves. They lived in straw mat houses without water, sewage or electricity. We were going to put up our own straw mat house to live among the people there.

The Fe y Alegría school system is a Jesuit-founded organization which builds schools in poor areas where there are no state schools or very few of them. The Peruvian government pays the teachers' salaries, so the students are not charged tuition as they are in private schools. The people help to raise funds for the gradual building of the school through a giant national raffle and other fundraising activities during the year. The Jesuits ask Religious communities to administer the schools, and they had invited Holy Cross to participate by administering a school in the newly occupied area of Canto Grande. So, several of the Holy Cross community in Chimbote went to Lima to open this new mission, where Holy Cross still remains.

Our move from Cartavio to Chimbote in 1974 had been to unite the Holy Cross community, and for a while that was the result, I think. We spent time together in community, and that included outings. For example, we went each Sunday as a Holy Cross community to the

81

house of the Incarnate Word Sisters for dinner. One of them, Luisa, was very good friends with Bud Colgan and Dave Farrell. She also worked in the Esperanza parish where they both were involved. The other two Incarnate Word Sisters were Emma who was a nurse in their clinic next to their house and Ester Chavez who was a religion teacher like me and a good friend. When I was sick with hepatitis they also took me into their house for two weeks and cared for me. Thank you Emma, Ester and Luisa! They are all deceased now. May they rest in peace! After Dave left to become assistant superior in the District of Chile in January 1975 and when Luisa left her community, our Sunday dinners soon fell apart.

As time passed, however, due to my teaching schedule I rarely was able to have meals with the community. I was the only teacher in the group. I arrived home late from my morning classes at San Pedro School on the other side of Chimbote, so I usually was not there for lunch when most of the others gathered. Then I was out again in the afternoon, right after my lunch, to go to the new youth group near the San Pedro school in the La Virgen de la Puerta parish building that I mentioned earlier. Afterwards I did not return from evening classes until close to midnight. On weekends I usually was away in the Macate parish. I saw little of the community, except at the occasional meetings of the ONIS priests or the Zona Norte meeting of priests and Sisters.

These were great ministry years for me but the work load with no days off and no community time exhausted me. I became overtired. I probably was a workaholic! I had no close friends in the Holy Cross community since Fred left, and my ministry took me where there were no other members. Community members, though, were supportive of me by helping from time to time in Macate, replacing me when the religious fiestas in the villages fell during the week. They either went up to the village festivals or replaced me at school so that I could travel to the fiesta. I am grateful to the St. Joseph Sisters who had their house in the center of Chimbote during those years. They, as well as the Irish Christian Brothers who resided not far from San Pedro, became my community where I could relax when I had some time free in the evening. Both communities were very welcoming and hospitable. Thank you!

In the next chapter I will move on to my grace-filled sabbatical year of 1981. I also will describe my remaining years in Chimbote, where I continued to teach high school, but also spent more time on the new Esperanza parish team.

4. CHIMBOTE 1982 - 1985

As I begin to write this section Pope Francis is finishing up his pastoral visit to Cuba and the United States. What a witness to Jesus he is! Thank you, Lord, for letting me see a pope who is so much like you! I think of Simeon in the temple saying "Lord, now you can let me depart in peace."

MY SABBATICAL YEAR OF 1981

In 1981 I enjoyed a year of rest, recovery and revitalization away from Peru. I was tired, and quite upset with the direction in which Pope John Paul II, elected in 1978, was leading the institutional Church, and especially with some of the decisions taken by the Peruvian bishops in this new era. It seemed to me that we were returning to a pre-Vatican II, more authoritative Church, fearful of anything new. It appeared that the Church was beginning to turn back in on itself and was more concerned with its clerical power and privilege than with people's suffering. Bishop Bambaren in Chimbote had a great social justice image, but on Church issues he seemed to me to be as conservative and authoritarian as the new pope.

Our pastoral group of Zona Norte, the group of priests and Sisters trying to implement the social justice and religious changes in the documents of Vatican II and the Latin American Bishops Conference at Medellin in 1968 and then again at Puebla, Mexico, in 1979, was continually under attack by Bambaren. The Peruvian bishops in general were clamping down on anyone in any group that they felt was influenced by Liberation Theology, which at that time was encountering opposition at the highest levels in Rome from Joseph Ratzinger (later to be Benedict XVI). Ratzinger believed Liberation Theology depended too much on Marxist thought and that the Church in Latin America was getting too entwined in politics. It was the period immediately following the assassination of Archbishop Oscar Romero in El Salvador by the Salvadorian military and the murder of the four American Religious women there, too. The assassination of Church people, both clerical and lay, was occurring in many Latin American countries.

It appeared to me that Church leadership was pulling back from the "small Christian communities" and from social justice issues. Several priests who were members of the Zona Norte pastoral were expelled from the Chimbote diocese or mistreated and judged harshly by Bambaren. Our little group of Zona Norte that worked in the mountain parishes like Macate were hindered by the bishop while I was working there. He created obstacles to the group's functioning in order to control by himself what went on in the mountain parishes.

He named a very conservative ex-Sister of St. Joseph to head the religion teachers, and she created havoc with arbitrary changes. I had problems with her regarding my class schedule at San Pedro high school when she would not recognize my many years of teaching there. Happily, though, when I spoke personally with Bambaren about it, he listened to me and rectified the injustice she was committing. Our Holy Cross priest Bud Colgan had become Bambaren's vicar (assistant), and so often was caught in the middle, until he finally resigned the position. I was constantly angry at the Church institution, and I was depressed emotionally. So, I was glad that I was going to be away from Chimbote for a while.

My sabbatical year was quite wonderful. I began by traveling to Brazil, to see for myself the growth and functioning of the pastoral system of "small Christian communities" which had been established there to further the faith of the many people in that country who did not have a parish priest—due to the shortage of celibate male priests like me. These "small Christian communities" were little groups of lay men and women who gathered weekly in a home or a church building to celebrate their faith together without a priest. They sang songs and read Scriptures from a one-page sheet that contained the Sunday Mass readings and a Biblical reflection prepared by the Brazilian Bishops Conference. Each year the Brazilian bishops also selected a theme of social justice (e.g., poverty, health care, education) to consider in the Sunday liturgies. They called the gathering a Celebration of the Liturgy of the Word of the Sunday Mass.

I also wanted to acquaint myself with the missions of the Holy Cross Religious in Brazil, so I visited all of them, beginning with the Holy Cross Brothers' school in Santarem located in the jungle on the Amazon river. I spent ten days there and enjoyed the community life and company of the Brothers, particularly my good friend Brother Ronald Hein who was master of novices for the Brothers' district at that time. Then I flew to the city of Belen located near the mouth of the Amazon river in northeastern Brazil. From there I traveled over twenty-four hours by bus to the town of Medina, where I spent several days with the Holy Cross Sisters in their new mountain mission in Minas Gerais. My good friend Sister Josephine Delaney who had come to Peru in 1975 for the meeting of the Holy Cross Religious in Latin America (PILA), which I mentioned in the last chapter, was stationed there. I had an opportunity to visit some of the rural "small Christian communities" with the Sisters, which required riding several hours on horseback. Thank you, Sister Josephine, for that experience.

I continued by bus another eighteen hours to Sao Paolo, the capital city of Brazil, where I spent Holy Week with the Holy Cross Sisters in their home in one of the slums, an opportunity to visit with my friend Sister Ruth. There, too, I had an edifying experience with the "small Christian communities" during Holy Week. Participating with them, I saw how impressively the lay men and women could celebrate their faith together by themselves!

I also visited the Holy Cross priests who have an upper-class school and a working-class parish in Sao Paulo. Then I made a quick visit to our Holy Cross Brothers' upper-class school in the nearby city of Campinas.

Finally, another thirty-hour bus trip brought me to the city of Caxias del Sur in southern Brazil, where I participated in a renewal program, a long retreat of work-shops to help priests, Religious and lay people replenish energy and skills for Church ministry. The program in which I participated was composed of twenty-five Brazilians and twenty-five Spanish-speakers from various South American countries. What a grace-filled experience it was for me! It increased my energy and esteem for my vision of a Vatican II Church as I had experienced it in Cartavio and Chimbote all those years.

As I have said, I was depressed with the pope's and the Peruvian bishops' withdrawal at that time from the documents and previous efforts inspired by Vatican II to renew the Church's mission. They often spoke against the "small Christian communities," afraid that they were becoming too politicized. They feared losing control and power over them. They often referred to them as a parallel Church of the poor, implying one that stood in opposition to the clerical establishment.

The renewal program gave us participants a chance to share our experiences of Church mission and to discover fresh impetus to return to building this new vision of Church in Latin America. Thank you, Caxias, for restoring my energies!

I thank all the people I met during that time in Caxias, especially my Chilean friend who is recently deceased, Hugo Espinoza, a layman who had been arrested during the Pinochet years for his leadership in a workers' union at the factory where he worked. Hugo was an active Christian in the Church in Chile who was fired from his job because of his Christian stand with the poor. His parish sent him to this renewal program. For me he was an excellent example of the type of Christian we were trying to form in the Church of Vatican II. I visited with Hugo several times both in Chile and in Peru throughout the years. We had great discussions during the renewal program, as well as often in the evening when we went out together with other participants for a drink, like Brazilian Sister Maria Hylma Ceva Lopez and American Maryknoll Tom Henehan who worked in Chile. I have stayed in contact with both throughout the years. Thanks to all of you at Caxias for your energizing friendship and our inspiring time together there!

After Caxias, I traveled back to the Brothers' district chapter in Campinas for a few days, and then on to the United States for the second part of my sabbatical year. I began by visiting my father in Albany, New York, and spending some cherished time with him. Afterwards, I had more renewal programs lined up for that summer. One, at the University of Massachusetts at Amherst, was on Reaganomics, questioning President Ronald Reagan's economic programs. My thanks to you, Joe Callahan, Eastern Province provincial at the time, for recommending this excellent program to me!

I attended a conference on the topic of "small Christian communities" held at the Maryknoll Sisters Summer Institute with the Brazilian priest Jose Marins, one of the founders of the "small Christian communities" program in Brazil. It offered me the opportunity to process all my former experiences with the "small Christian communities" and to discover their Biblical roots.

89

After additional vacation time with my father, I began the second part of my sabbatical year in earnest at the renewal program at Maryknoll. It was a perfect continuation of my Caxias experience, adding to the mix more personal items like prayer, healthy communication, and theological updating. Weekends during the session were free, so I had time to spend visiting friends and community members in the New York City area. On one of those occasions I visited my good friend Caroline Nicosia whom I had met years before in Rome where she was working with the Better World Movement.

All these programs re-energized me for my return to ministry in Peru. I remember especially Maryknoll Sister Charlotte Smith who was my spiritual director. She introduced me to The Course on Miracles, a spiritual-psychological program for inner freedom. I still am in contact with the wonderful life-giving people with whom I lived and studied during that year. Thank you, Lord and Holy Cross community, for this renewal time in my life.

Near the end of the Maryknoll program, I was invited to speak by the Holy Childhood Association at their annual conference taking place in New Orleans. I don't think they knew what they were getting into when they invited me. I did tell them beforehand that I was in the Liberation Theology mindset which considered working for social justice and institutional reform a priority for the Church, even as in times of immediate, necessary need we continue to be charitable gift-giving people, too. From my experience in Peru I think most people do not want to live on charity. They want to earn their own keep. They do not want us just to give them food, but rather they want us to teach them and allow them to earn it for themselves. That is basically what I shared with Holy Childhood at their conference, and I think I was able to give them another outlook on Church mission and something new to think about. I enjoyed the trip, finally getting to visit the great jazz city of New Orleans, where I sat at a table of lay leaders in a sea of tables with clerical collars!

ESPERANZA PARISH

After spending Christmas and additional time with my father, family and friends in the Albany area, I returned to Chimbote in March 1982. I immediately resumed my teaching position, from which I had obtained a one-year leave of absence. However, for the day session, instead of going back to the San Pedro high school on the other side of Chimbote where I previously had been, I began teaching at the two smaller grade schools located in our Santa Cruz parish. Each now had a new, recently established high school division attached to it. This made it easier for me to combine my teaching with youth ministry in the parish where I was living.

For just one year in 1982 I continued teaching at the night school at San Pedro. I decided to leave it, however, because there was so much additional evening activity in the Esperanza parish as a result of the new parish plan we were implementing there. After 1982 I accumulated all my class hours exclusively in the day sessions in the schools in Esperanza Baja and La Union. From 1982 to

1985 I taught all my classes in these two schools located within the parish.

I had had great years at the San Pedro school in both the day and night sections. Several of my good friends from the San Pedro night section used to travel to Macate with me from to time. I think of Rafael Tamariz and Domingo Fernandez. Domingo was a painter, and he often spoke to me about wanting go to the United States to live and work. Denied a work visa, he traveled across the Mexican desert to get here, and he eventually achieved legal status. Rafael became a successful married business-man in Chimbote with his own little factory. Sad to say after a few years I lost contact with them, but remember them fondly. Thank you, guys, for your friendship at the night school all that time!

I had many good friends from those school years. Carlos Loli, from the Santa Cruz parish youth group, joined Holy Cross for a few years around 1985, but later in 1990 left the community to marry. He was our second Peruvian to take vows in Holy Cross in 1989.

Friends in the parish were Rosa Torres, Maria Loli, Carmen Rodriguez, Raul Guevara, Felipe Sarmiento and Rogelio Lara. From the JEC group in La Union school, there were Lucho Saravia, Pepe Ballarte, and his sister Anna. And there were Jorge Vera and Pancho Risco from the JEC groups in Chimbote. So many are still good friends. How can I thank them all enough for all those years of friendship and ministry together!

From 1982 on, I ministered full-time in the Santa Cruz parish in Esperanza with Richard Renshaw, who was the new pastor there. He had replaced Bud Colgan who was named pastor of the Canto Grande parish in Lima in January 1982.

Richard, who has been a friend of mine since our years together in Rome, came to Peru in 1979 and worked in the Canto Grande parish in Lima. He was assigned to Chimbote in 1981 to assist Bud Colgan who had been named novice master for the two Holy Cross Peruvian novices. The novitiate had been established at our community residence in the Esperanza parish that year.

While I was away on sabbatical during 1981, many changes took place in Holy Cross in Peru. Our first novitiate experience in Chimbote had concluded with the profession of vows of one of the two Peruvian novices. The newly professed, Miguel Pasache, returned to Lima for his studies, and Bud Colgan was assigned to be pastor there at the relatively new parish in Canto Grande. There was only Richard Renshaw remaining in Chimbote. All of the other Holy Cross men resided then in the two houses in Canto Grande.

I had left the Macate parish. The La Victoria parish had been handed back to the bishop when Bob Neidhardt left the community to marry in 1980. In 1981, Diego had accepted a new position as director of the Institute for Aymaran Studies (IDEA) in the Juli Maryknoll prelature near Puno, about which I will write later.

Richard and I, who both shared the same vision about lay leadership and the importance of "small Christian communities," decided to try to give new life to the Santa Cruz parish. There was no main church, but four chapels located in four contingent neighborhoods, each with its own dynamic. For years, the parish had only been maintained. We Holy Cross priests had done the minimum, hardly more than the Sunday liturgies, because we all had other Church-related occupations during the week which consumed most of our time and energy. Richard and I decided to make the four chapels into "small Christian communities," each with its own leadership and a lay coordinator. The four coordinators would then form the parish council to try to unify the four communities into more of a sense of a single parish.

To begin, we organized a parish-wide assembly of all the lay leaders and participants from each of these four small communities. We presented a parish plan we had drawn up for their comments, suggestions and finally their approval. They did so with enthusiasm, which energized us all the more. It was approved that for the first year Richard and I, with suggestions from each of the "small Christian communities," would name the first coordinators; and then after that the coordinators would be directly elected by their communities. We chose David Cueva for La Union, Gregorio "Goyo" Pastor for La Primavera, Santos Garcia for Esperanza Baja and Jorge Flores for Esperanza Alta after consulting with each small community. Some like Goyo were new faces on the horizon. The others had been helping in the parish for years in different capacities. They formed a great team, and in the first meeting of the new parish council Juan Garcia from the small community of La Primavera was elected to be the coordinator of the parish council.

All of us became very good friends. We often went to Besique beach together on Sunday afternoons, and we celebrated birthday parties once a month with all their families. This new parish council assembled monthly with Richard and me, together with the leaders of the women's groups and parish youth groups and the national movements that were present in the parish. Among these were the Christian Workers (MTC) and the Christian Youth (JEC) and the parish sacramental formation teams that Richard and I recently had created to prepare people for the sacraments of Baptism, First Communion, Confirmation and Marriage. The parish council coordinated activities between all these different groups, planned all-parish events, made decisions concerning the parish, and implemented the parish plan that had been approved at the assembly.

The teams who prepared people for the sacraments encouraged parents who wanted their children baptized to participate in Sunday Mass in their parish chapel. They requested them to attend several times during the weeks leading up to the day of the baptism. During Mass the parents first were introduced to the small community as part of the baptismal celebration. The following week again during Mass they would present their child to the community. Then the third week the Baptism was celebrated during Sunday Mass. The goal was to motivate the family to participate actively in its "small Christian community."

We also instituted in the parish a national program for the preparation for First Communion that was called

Family Catechesis. It involved the parents teaching their own child. First, the parents came to a weekly meeting with the team in charge, and there they studied the lesson for the week in the nationally prepared booklet. Then the parents went home, and during the week were supposed to teach their own child there. At the end of the week the children gathered with a catechist to celebrate together what they had learned at home. In general, the program worked well, except that not many fathers attended because they were busy working long hours to support their families. The mothers' participation, on the other hand, was very good. Quite obviously, one of the aims of this program was to educate the parents in their faith, too.

The Confirmation program was tied to the youth groups with the hope of keeping the young involved in their "small community" after receiving that sacrament. These groups were chapters of the national/international youth movements, of which I have written above, which organized their membership into small local groups within the parishes. They had their own leadership and usually had a priest or Religious as a spiritual adviser. I was the regional, diocesan adviser for the Young Christian Workers (JOC) and the Young Christian Students (JEC) in the Diocese of Chimbote, and Richard was the adviser for the Adult Christian Workers (MTC).

In the summer we sent twenty lay leaders to Lima to participate in a two-week theological program established there by Gustavo Gutierrez and the Catholic University. With other participating parishes we organized fundraising activities during the year to finance the trip. In Lima we slept on the floors of school buildings made available for us and ate together from a common purse in the market place. It was a great experience of community for me. Priests and Sisters from other parishes also accompanied the group. I always felt that it was more important to educate our Christian lay leaders than to invest in church buildings. The people are the living stones of the Church!

The JEC and JOC leadership from the different schools and parishes used to meet monthly at our house in Esperanza. In fact, that was how I met Jorge Izaguirre who was a high school student at the time in the city of Casma, located some fifty miles to the south of Chimbote. Jorge was a member of the JEC movement in the Casma parish where the St. Joseph Sisters had gone to live and work in 1981, and where they were spiritual advisers to the JEC. Jorge often came to our house in Esperanza for the monthly meetings of the JEC's coordinating team with me, their diocesan spiritual adviser. He later joined Holy Cross in 1987, and now is a bishop in the Prelature of Chuquibamba (Camana) which extends from the southern coast of Peru into the mountainous poor areas of the Andes. His name will come up later in this story. I have good memories of so many fine young men and women.

Sisters of the Holy Cross, in Brazil since 1943, came to work with us in the Santa Cruz parish in Chimbote in November 1982. They were Sisters Rose Virginia Burt, Susie Patterson and Patti Dieranger. Patti had participated with me in the Maryknoll renewal program in 1981 as part of her discernment to leave Brazil to work in Peru.

The other two came from different apostolates in the United States. Rose Virginia was a nurse, and Susie was a teacher. They were a great asset to the Church in Chimbote and to the parish. Thank you, Sisters of the Holy Cross!

In 1983 Chimbote and all of Peru suffered a weather crisis caused by the "El Niño" current. The unusually heavy rainfall flooded customarily almost-dry riverbeds and collapsed adobe houses. The parish's Primavera sector, located on low land, was particularly affected when so much rain water collected around the adobe chapel and the adobe houses there. The river's rise badly damaged outlying rural districts along its banks.

The parish had a solidarity group composed of three women, Pancha Vega, Chevita and Gertrudis Lara, who coordinated material aid for the sick and suffering in the parish. After the rains stopped, they stepped in to discover who were the neediest. Sister Patti Dieranger, who had just arrived in the parish, and I began having weekly meetings with the leaders of the numerous rural areas of the parish to discover the extent of the damage in each sector. Sister Patti found her niche in this work. She took over the program and successfully organized these new, rural parish groups to get aid to them. She later became the head of the Caritas program in the Chimbote diocese, and after that in the Chosica diocese in Lima. Caritas is the diocesan office that oversees getting aid to people in need, much as the Catholic Relief Service (CRS) does in the United States. Thank you, Patti, for your many years of service in this pastoral work. You do a great job!

YOUTH GROUP MINISTRY

During those years in Peru, the terrorist movement called the "Shining Path" grew active, mainly in the Ayacucho area in the mountains of southern Peru. However, they began to influence some of the leftist political parties in other parts of the country, who in turn infiltrated the parish youth groups and national youth movements like the JOC and JEC I mentioned earlier. Some of the JOC groups in Chimbote, especially those without a spiritual adviser, became highly politicized, which caused division and tensions in the movement. The politicized youth boasted that the Church prepared the young people and formed the groups but that they then captured them for their cause. Many of these politicized young people I had in class could repeat political phrases that they had learned by rote, but when I asked them to explain the phrases to me in their own words they could not do it. Sad state of affairs! All these young persons were good people even though they often were excessively idealistic and gullible as young people can be. It is amazing how many groups of JEC and JOC we had in the diocese. It was an exciting time for youth ministry. I am so glad that I could be part of it!

I remember especially my friend Sister Ester Chavez whom I mentioned briefly in the previous chapter. She also coordinated a JEC youth group in the neighboring parish of El Carmen. We shared a lot together, since during this time she was named the coordinator of the religion teachers (ODEC), replacing the ex-nun whom the bishop had named after Sister Elena retired and who had caused so many difficulties in the religion teachers group by her authoritarian ways. Ester was a breath of fresh air for all of us religion teachers. Thank you, Ester, for your friendship all those years! She finally returned to the United States after her pastor Miguel Company, a Spaniard from the Island of Mallorca, was shot in the face one evening in 1990 by a group of the Shining Path terrorists as he came out of the El Carmen chapel after celebrating Mass. He survived miraculously and returned to Mallorca. Ester stayed in Chimbote a while longer, but because of the increasing number of attacks by the Shining Path on Church people near Chimbote and elsewhere, she was so traumatized that she decided to return to her Incarnate Word Sisters community in San Antonio, Texas, where she worked in health care with Hispanics for many years, until she recently died. May she rest in peace!

During those years, there were so many other inspiring priests, Sisters, Brothers and lay men and women, particularly religion teachers, who worked with these youth groups as spiritual advisers. Thank you one and all. My memory fails me to mention all your names, but you all are in my heart.

HOLY CROSS

In 1982 the Holy Cross priests and Sisters in Chimbote happily celebrated the beatification that year of now Saint Brother André Bessette. Brother André was a humble Holy Cross Brother in Montreal, Canada, who died in 1937. He was known for his devotion to Saint Joseph and his gift of healing. He was called the Wonder Worker of Montreal.

During those years that Richard and I lived together 1981-1984, we often prayed our Holy Cross community prayers together. That was something I had not been able to do previous years in Chimbote because of my teaching schedule. We also organized quiet retreats in the house for ourselves. Richard was a Holy Cross soul mate for me, something I had not experienced there before 1981.

That we ate our meals together was another aspect of our endeavor to live together as a Holy Cross community of two. We continued to cook our own food as we had been doing in Chimbote since 1975 to live a simpler life style. I cooked—believe it or not!—from Monday to Friday, since my classes were in the afternoon and Richard worked at the jail in the morning. He cooked on weekends. Fortunately through the years we had gained some cooking skills, so our meals were edible. For a while we also participated in a community soup kitchen with about fifteen families from the parish who were suffering economic hardship. We all took turns in groups of four preparing a daily noon meal for all the members. My job was mainly peeling potatoes.

Our local community of two was part of the larger community of all Holy Cross members in Peru. In 1983, Richard and I both endeavored to convince our then superior Dan Panchot of the need for psychological help for everyone. In 1982 our formation program was back to the beginning when our only Peruvian professed member, Miguel Pasache, left the Congregation, and all three postulants also left as well, including my good friend from the Santa Cruz youth group in Esperanza, Alejandro Valerio. A number of us started to throw blame around for all these departures, and we were arguing at community gatherings. Frictions also were arising over theological and ecclesial visions of Church and Religious life that would continue through the following years.

These quarrels mirrored tensions developing in the wider Church during the papacy of John Paul II. With his right-hand Joseph Ratzinger (later Pope Benedict XVI), the pope was appointing more traditional and conservative bishops in Latin America, who went on to persecute Liberation Theology theologians like Gustavo Gutierrez and those who followed them in the spirit of Vatican II. We eight members of the Holy Cross community in Peru at that time had developed some serious communication problems among ourselves. Thank you, Daniel, for agreeing with Richard and me and encouraging the group to participate in sessions promoting community psychological healing.

In March 1984 my father became ill. Coincidentally I was scheduled to travel to the United States to give my first paper on the history of Peru 1963-1983 at the conference of the Holy Cross History Association, an organization that promotes and conserves the mutual history of all the Holy Cross Congregations founded by Basil Moreau in France in 1835. I was able, therefore, to combine that trip with a visit to my father in Albany. It was obvious to my brother and me that Dad could not continue to live alone in his apartment where he had stayed since my mother died in May 1979. After talking with his doctor, I inquired about the nursing home of the Little Sisters of the Poor, where Holy Cross novices did pastoral work, in Latham, New York, near Albany. I phoned the novice master, Brother John Paige, who said he would contact the mother superior. She phoned me back almost immediately, and two weeks later my father was admitted to their residence for the elderly, just a week before I was booked to return to Peru. Thank you, Little Sisters of the Poor for your devoted care for my father in my absence.

When I returned to Chimbote, Marc Cregan, a recently ordained Holy Cross priest, joined Richard and me in the Esperanza parish for six months. He had volunteered to assist for a while in Peru before continuing his studies in the United States. He was a dynamic, hardworking priest and was a great help to us, especially when Richard became ill soon after and had to leave for Lima to rest and recover. Marc later went on to become an immigration lawyer and, from 2000-2014, the president of our Holy Cross Stonehill College in Easton, Massachusetts. Thank you, Marc, for that time with us. I don't know what I would have done if I had been alone then.

The sessions for community psychological healing began in June 1984 and continued through the beginning of 1985 while Richard was living in Lima and I was alone in Chimbote. I took the bus to Lima every Sunday night, a ten-hour trip. Richard and I would meet for dinner with Bob Baker who came into the city from the Canto Grande parish where he was at the time. Afterwards we would meet with the other four from Canto Grande, who arrived after their evening Mass, to begin our session with two gifted women psychologists. Only Diego Irrarázaval who lived far away in Puno did not participate. The sessions were very beneficial. They helped me to learn much about myself and about community/family dynamics, and I do believe they helped everyone else in the group, too, even though some were quite resistant to the process. In our sessions Richard and I encouraged everyone to speak their feelings truly.

I especially want to thank psychologist Ana Maria who remained a friend afterward and helped me in many ways both personally and professionally. She died very suddenly a few years ago from an allergic reaction to shell fish while dining at a restaurant in Lima. May she rest in peace.

In August of 1984 Diego Irarrázaval was ordained a priest. He had lived as a deacon with us in Chimbote from 1975-1981. A theologian, he studied popular religiosity in Peru, and did so while he was with us. Then in 1981 he accepted the invitation of the Maryknoll bishop Alberto Koenigsknecht of the Prelature of Juli, near the city of Puno in the high Andes of southern Peru, to become the Director of the Aymara Institute (IDEA) in the town of Chucuito. There he would research how the Aymara people had incorporated Christian beliefs into their culture, and how the Aymara culture in turn could inculturate their Christian experience as the documents of Vatican II suggested. He had opted to remain a deacon in Holy Cross rather than be ordained a priest because he felt that ordination should not be a personal choice, but rather an invitation by a "Christian community." While living in the town of Chucuito he saw the great need for ordained priests there and felt that the people in a way were asking him to be their priest. And so, he had requested to be ordained. Ten of us from the Chimbote parish traveled by bus and train from the parish in Chimbote to his ordination ceremony in Chucuito. It was an enjoyable ten-day trip together, especially with my friend David Cueva who was at that time the general coordinator of the Santa Cruz parish.

After Marc left in October I was alone in Chimbote. Richard Renshaw was still having personal difficulties and had decided to stay in Lima to live for a while at the Maryknoll Center House there. It is where I myself usually stayed when I visited Lima, because our Canto Grande parish was ten miles outside the central city and very difficult to reach at night. Thank you once again, Richard, for your friendship that goes way back to the days when we studied theology together in the Holy Cross international house in Rome!

LEAVING CHIMBOTE

Since leaving Macate in 1980, I continued to want to transfer to a rural setting in Peru. Diego had been alone in Puno all the years since 1981, but I was told that I was needed in Chimbote and I was asked to wait. Finally, in late 1984 the district superior Dan Panchot decided that I could go to Puno to live and work with Diego. He himself would come to Santa Cruz parish in Chimbote and live and minister there alone until Brother John Benesh, whom I had met at the Holy Cross History Conference in March 1984, arrived to join him in August 1985. Thank you, Dan. So, in early 1985 I was in the process of preparing to leave Chimbote. I had finished organizing everything in the parish for my time away, because there would be a few weeks before Dan arrived when there would be no priest in the parish, when I learned of my father's death in late April 1985.

Before I left for the funeral in the United States, the parish community wanted to celebrate a funeral Mass for my father with me present. I remember their many kind words. I particularly recall those that were spoken by Inocencio Lara, who had been a faithful companion to Holy Cross in the parish from the very beginnings with Dave Farrell back in 1970, and later with Bud Colgan. He said in Spanish, "We do not know your father personally, Tom, but in a way we do know him by knowing you." I have never forgotten those beautiful words which reminded me that it is so true that my father lived on in me in so many ways. Thank you, Mom and Dad, for all that you gave me! Thank you, Inocencio, for reminding me!

So, my departure from Chimbote occurred a few weeks sooner than I had planned. I was off to my father's funeral in Albany, New York, instead of having more time to spend slowly saying my goodbyes to my many friends in Chimbote.

The day after the Mass for my father in the chapel of La Primavera, I left for Lima to fly to the United States. On my return I would go directly to Puno. I remember riding on the *colectivo* from Esperanza into Chimbote with Holy Cross Sister Patti Dieranger who accompanied me to the bus station. I was crying softly after having said my goodbyes to the friends who had come to see me off at the house. I apologized to Patti for my tears, but she responded that it was better to have loved than never to have loved. Thank you, Patti, for those kind words which meant so much to me at that moment because I did love the people in Chimbote, just as I had loved the people in Cartavio and Macate when I left them in 1973 and 1980. And as I cried for my father, I also cried for all these dear friends that I would be leaving behind because I missed them then so much already and still miss them so much today. But I knew once again in my heart that it was time for me to move on from Chimbote, and that the Lord was calling me once again to something new, which I will relate in the next chapter.

5. CHUCUITO (PUNO) 1985 - 1993

When I was leaving Macate in 1980 and going on my 1981 sabbatical, I wanted on my return to Peru to minister somewhere in a rural setting like Macate. I never was interested in working in big cities like Lima, because I felt that the real poor and forgotten in Peru were those who lived in the mountainous regions. In 1980 our Holy Cross district chapter had recommended we look for a new location for rural ministry in the future.

As I have related, Diego Irarrázaval was invited in late 1980 by Alberto Koenigsknecht, Maryknoll bishop of the Prelature of Juli, to come to Chucuito to accept the position of Director of the Institute for Aymara Studies (IDEA) located in that town. IDEA had been founded a few years earlier by a Maryknoll priest to teach the Aymaran language and culture to Maryknoll's North American members and others who came to work in the prelature. The Aymara Institute (IDEA) also investigated how the Aymaran culture had assimilated Christianity into its cultural and religious world view. It hoped to help with inculturating Aymaran cultural symbols into the Roman liturgy as had been recommended by the documents of Vatican II.

The Prelature of Juli was formed in 1957 by partitioning off a section of the very large Diocese of Puno with the hope that one day that area would reach diocesan stature. All the Aymara-speaking towns and villages located around Lake Titicaca, the highest lake in the world, were included in it. The Prelature of Juli was entrusted by the Vatican to the North American Maryknoll Missionary Congregation which had been working in the Puno Diocese since 1942.

In early 1981 Diego accepted the position of Director of IDEA. Before that, he had worked for several years in the Bartolome de Las Casas Institute in Lima which had been founded by the Peruvian Liberation theologian Gustavo Gutierrez to study the popular religiosity (the Christian beliefs and devotions) of the Peruvian people. Diego conducted a study with interviews in Chimbote on that theme while he was still living with us there, and he wrote a book based on the results of his investigation. Afterwards he authored several more books and articles and became well known in theological circles in Peru and worldwide.

On arriving in the Prelature in early 1981 Diego took up residence in the town of Ilave in a house of formation for aspirants to the diocesan priesthood. The several priests there and young Aymaran men training to be priests gave him a community to live among. The downside was a twenty-five-mile drive in a tiny Volkswagen each day to the town of Chucuito where the IDEA offices were located, about fifteen miles from the large city of Puno.

I visited Diego in Puno in 1983 to see the prelature, with the possibility in mind that I might be interested in working there in the future. However, I was told at that time by the Holy Cross superior Dan Panchot that I still was needed in Chimbote, so I would not be able to join Diego quite yet. In August 1984, as I recounted earlier, a group of us from the Chimbote parish traveled to Diego's ordination to the priesthood in Chucuito. Shortly after that trip, I was told that I could join Diego in August 1985 when Dan, the superior of the district, would himself move to Chimbote. So, when my father died in April 1985, I was ready to transfer from Chimbote to Chucuito.

At the time when I returned to Peru in August 1985, Alan Garcia had been elected President of Peru, replacing Fernando Belaunde who had held that office since 1980, after the end of the military dictatorship. Peru was in serious financial difficulty, even as it had to contend with the growing presence since 1980 of the terrorist group *Sendero Luminoso* (Shining Path).

ARRIVAL IN CHUCUITO

I traveled directly to Puno. On my arrival, Diego met me at the airport with Ursina, a woman who worked with him in IDEA. I settled into the Prelature retreat house located in Chucuito while we both looked for a place where we could live together. At the time, Diego resided in a small room in a house with a family on the outskirts of Chucuito. He had moved there from Ilave in 1984 shortly before his ordination to the priesthood. The family did not have a second room for me, so we needed to look for another place. We found one in early September not far from where Diego was living. However, it was very, very small, and the owner's wife preferred not to rent it to us because she used one of the rooms to store her potato crop. She may also have held an Aymaran cultural belief—often used to defend themselves against foreigners—that Diego and I were *kharisiri*, white men, usually priests, who sucked the fat from persons' bodies causing sickness or death. But the opinion of her husband prevailed. I moved into the one small room that was available right away. Diego was to move in after the potato crop was transferred out in December. Once I put my small single bed into the room there was not much space for anything else. Diego came for meals with me in our very tiny kitchen, where only one person could stand at a time, and I practically had to bend in two to get through the low door. Diego who was short loved the place. Of course, I had another opinion! After two months the owner returned to say that his wife did not want to give up the whole house, so I would have to move out. I was very grateful to her.

With luck, we found another, larger house down the main road about a mile more from the town of Chucuito. It was a simple adobe building on a hill overlooking Lake Titicaca with a beautiful view! At first Diego thought that the house was too big and that the two-mile walk from the town was a bit too far, but we finally decided to rent it anyway because it was our only real option at the time. We moved into the adobe house in early January 1986.

From my experience in Chimbote where we did not have electricity or water most of the time, I was quite used to lighting with kerosene lamps and candles. We had to fetch our own water from a well, but at least it was on the same level as the house, so we did not have to drag it up the hill. Living at twelve thousand feet as we were made us consider little seemingly unimportant things like that.

I was very happy to have much larger kitchen area, a bedroom big enough for more than a bed, and a door frame high enough that I would not bang my head so frequently. In my bedroom, there was a table and a stool, a bookcase of planks and bricks, and a portable plastic closet for hanging my clothes. The view of the countryside and the lake from my three windows was breathtaking. I even had a bed for guests on the far side of my small room.

On the far side of his room, Diego created a little chapel. The house also had a tiny back room without windows where the owners probably stored potatoes. We had to use an outhouse, but that also had been the case in Chimbote. After settling in, both Diego and I realized what a great house it was. We were very happy with our little house, where we lived for almost fifteen years and where we received many guests. Thank you, Alejandro and Sofia for renting it to us. For just three dollars a month!

THE MOBILE PASTORAL TEAM

During the months that I was getting acclimated to the twelve-thousand-foot altitude and looking at ministry possibilities, Bishop Alberto asked me to consider accompanying his mobile pastoral team that trained lay community leaders as catechists. Relatively new, it was established in 1981 by the bishop after an assembly with all the priests, Brothers, Sisters, and lay people working then in the prelature. He wanted to enlist lay people in the farming communities who could serve the needs of the Catholic community, because many Protestant evangelicals were entering those communities, and Catholics were joining them for lack of a priest. In this way he hoped to create a Catholic presence among each of them.

As many as several hundred farming communities formed part of a large parish. If the parish was one of the fortunate ones, it might have a priest and a small parish team to visit the farming communities from time to time to provide for their spiritual needs. One parish where there were priests and a parish team was that of Ilave, where Diego lived when he first arrived in the prelature. Its parish boundaries encompassed a large town plus over two hundred-fifty farming communities. Of six people on the parish team, two were priests.

Most parishes in fact did not have a priest. An example was the Chucuito parish, which included a small town and about twenty-five farming communities spread out in all directions at a distance from the town. Diego began to serve this parish of Chucuito first as a deacon from Ilave. In 1984 when he saw that the people needed a priest he asked to be ordained.

The layman Marcos Asqui, who lived with his family in Chucuito, was the director of this Mobile Pastoral Lay Formation team whose office was in the retreat house where I first stayed on my arrival in Chucuito. I accepted to accompany Marcos on the team even though I spoke no Aymara, the local indigenous language of the people in the prelature. Most adults in the farming communities spoke more Aymara than Spanish.

Sister Barbara Kavanaugh, a Sister of Mercy who lived in the nearby town of Acora, had a program for the formation of lay women. So, Marcos and I invited her and some of the laywomen who worked with her to join us to create one lay formation team for the training of both men and women leaders for the prelature. We decided that the new team would visit all the parishes in the entire prelature to talk with the pastors and the parish teams to learn what they already were doing about lay formation, to find out what they would like to do about it in the future, and how they thought the mobile lay formation team might be able to help them.

We prepared a leadership training program that included basic Bible studies and theology training in the context of Peru's socio-political situation, particularly that of the Andean region at the time. It included courses in basic health and natural medicine, women's rights, and courses training lay persons to lead liturgical celebrations and to prepare people for the sacraments using Aymaran cultural symbols. We created it to be a well-rounded program that would benefit all the members of the farming community and not just a few religious leaders. And off we went visiting all the parishes during the last months of 1985 and the beginning of 1986.

Sometimes we got effusive welcomes. Other times the pastor, Religious or lay leader in charge of the parish was not interested in our help. Many teams, especially those with Religious Sisters in charge, told us that they preferred to do their own formation programs and would not need our help. Others though, especially those with lay leaders in charge of a parish without a priest, were very grateful for our offer. These visits gave us a sense of where the prelature stood regarding the formation of lay leaders, both men and women, in the farming communities.

What I personally discovered during the visits was the need to speak Aymara to communicate effectively in these communities. Marcos, the director of the lay formation team, was an excellent Aymara leader and teacher. Sister Barbara, a nurse, could speak Aymara somewhat, and the Aymaran women on her team, of course, were fluent. I was the only member who could not speak it. So, at the same time as I worked with them, I began studying the language at the Aymara Institute (IDEA). I realized that being able to speak Aymara was absolutely necessary if I was to continue doing ministry among the farming communities. At first learning the language seemed easy, but as time progressed it became more difficult. My ear is not good at languages, so I never got a good grasp of it. I did finish the whole course, though, and I could celebrate the Mass in Aymara. Thank you, Santiago Mendoza and Juan Mallea, my Aymara teachers at IDEA, for all those Aymara classes and for your patience with me.

I spent most of my morning hours during that first year in Chucuito in those language classes. However, even as I did so, I sensed that I was not needed on the mobile team except perhaps as a support for Marcos. I also discovered that Marcos and many of the Aymaran men were not good at working as equals with women. This was particularly true when they were dealing with strong North American women like Sister Barbara and some of the other Sisters in charge of parishes in the prelature. These Sisters often found the male lay leaders too clerical and authoritative. The Sisters wanted to organize the lay leadership more in a circular fashion, rather than top-down. Marcos was great with the men, however, and he proved to be a natural leader for them. This issue of gender created considerable internal tension in the team, as well as in the prelature.

It all came to a head after Bishop Alberto died in a car accident in the spring of 1986. Mike Briggs, a young Maryknoll priest, was named Diocesan Administrator. He was a very good friend of some of the Maryknoll Sisters who like Sister Barbara were strong women. They did not feel that the mobile lay formation team ministry was necessary in the prelature. They believed it was outdated and that each parish should do lay-leader formation as it wished. So, in the August 1986 prelature assembly, after a lively debate of the ministry's pros and cons, it was decided to terminate it. I still believe that this decision was a big mistake, because many parishes as a result simply did nothing to form leaders or catechists. I believed that the formation of lay Christian leaders was important because they were the ones who would remain with their people when the Sisters and I someday would move on.

Afterwards Marcos joined the Chucuito parish team, and Sister Barbara went back to ministry with women in

Acora. During those brief months, however, I was able to learn a great deal about the area and the Aymaran people, as well as the internal dynamics within the prelature. Thank you, Marcos, and thank you Sister Barbara. It was an important year of introduction for me into life in the Altiplano (the high plain) in the south Andean part of the Peruvian Church.

MY TEACHING POSITION

After arriving in the prelature, I thought about giving up my government permanent teaching position, but the bishop wanted me to keep it. So I spoke with the public school principal in Chucuito, Gladys Malaga. She scheduled me to teach twenty-four hours of religion, including a few hours of philosophy, in the coming year beginning March 1986. So I began the long, complicated process once again of moving my permanent teaching position from Chimbote to Puno, much the same as I had in 1974 when I moved it from Cartavio to Chimbote. Thank you, Gladys, for that offer. And may you rest in peace.

In all of Peru religion is taught in the state schools at all levels according to a diplomatic agreement between the Peruvian government and the Vatican. The teaching of these religion classes is coordinated in each diocese by an office called by its acronym ODEC. At that time the ODEC-PUNO office served the Prelature of Juli, because the latter did not have its own ODEC-JULI office. Almost immediately after my arrival in August 1985 I was invited by the ODEC-PUNO team to help them give formation workshops to the lay religion teachers. I was glad to have this opportunity to teach Bible and methodology courses to the grade school teachers in the farming communities and towns in the prelature. I always enjoyed teaching, and particularly in this instance because the teaching was not in Aymara but in Spanish.

I enjoyed working with the Dominican Sisters who constituted the ODEC-PUNO. They encouraged me to speak with Bishop Alberto about forming an ODEC office for the Juli prelature, because they had more than enough work in the Puno diocese. I did so at the end of 1985. I thought that I might be able to transfer my permanent teaching position from Chimbote to this new office, instead of to the Chucuito high school. Bishop Alberto spoke with the Peruvian president Alan Garcia while the latter was visiting the Peruvian Bishops Conference during their annual meeting in Lima in early February 1986. Bishop Alberto asked the president for two permanent teaching positions to establish an ODEC-JULI office for the Prelature of Juli, and the president immediately signed the request. A week later near Acora Bishop Alberto died in a car accident after falling asleep at the wheel. I thought that ended any possibility for an ODEC-JULI office, but when the newly appointed administrator of the Prelature Maryknoll priest Mike Briggs and I went to visit the educational authorities in Puno in early March 1986, they told us that they had the two permanent teaching positions waiting to be filled for the newly established ODEC-JULI office. I always felt that this was Bishop Alberto's first miracle! He was a great pastoral bishop. People used to say that his car was his office because he was always visiting the farming communities. Thank you, Bishop Alberto, and may you rest in peace.

Mike Briggs immediately proposed me, and Sister Vilda Zamalloa, a Dominican Sister who had recently lost her teaching job in the town of Pomata high school and so was available. Consequently, in March 1986 I took up my teaching position as Director of the new ODEC-JULI office.

Sister Vilda and I began to plan for the new office. It would be located in Chucuito, since that town was the most centrally located in the prelature. I moved from the Mobile Lay Formation office which I shared with Marcos in the retreat house to the new ODEC-JULI office in the Aymara Institute (IDEA) building next to the sixteenth-century church in the main square of Chucuito. This move facilitated my Aymara classes, my Chucuito parish ministry and my new ODEC ministry with the lay religion teachers. It had me interacting with more people, so I could practice my Aymara. I had been rather lonely down in the lay formation team office, because Marcos frequently was away on leadership courses in the farming communities. It all worked out providentially.

THE CHURCH IN THE HIGH ANDES OF PERU

I had to get used to the way the Church was organized in the Peruvian high Andes. The pastoral ministry of the dioceses and prelatures of the southern Andes was coordinated in the Andean Pastoral Institute (IPA). This interconnection between ecclesiastical jurisdictions was a legacy of the early 1970's when the Peruvian Bishops Conference decided to group diocesan bishops into regional areas, so they could organize among themselves a common pastoral plan to deal with the socio-political situation and the religious needs in their common geographical area. It was a major national project to unify the bishops and their dioceses with their parishes and other institutions into a unified regional Church structure. The move was inspired by reflection on the documents of Vatican II and by the Latin American Bishops Conference at Medellin that I have mentioned earlier.

Following the election of Pope John Paul II in 1978, however, the winds of change in the Church began to shift back to a pre-Vatican II stance. Almost immediately some of the bishops grew fearful of this new, more circular structuring of the Church. I believe they thought it gave too much decision-making power to their lay people and Religious and priests. So, the regional plan was rejected by all the Peruvian bishops except those in the southern Andes where it was working well, thanks to the exceptional bishops we had at the time who favored collaborating with one another and with their people. Thank you, Bishop Alberto, and all the bishops of the southern Andes.

Each year the IPA organized a six-week program for new missionaries coming either from outside Peru or from the Peruvian coast to minister in the region. We learned about the history, culture and religiosity of the Aymara- and Quechua-speaking people who lived there since before the arrival of the Spanish. The program also helped us to get to know one another. I participated in April-May 1986 amidst all my other activities.

THE JULI PRELATURE

As I have described, the Prelature of Juli was organized around pastoral teams of priests, Religious and lay people working together. Many parishes in the prelature did not have priests. The parish in Moho, for example, was tended by the St. Joseph Sisters, with whom I had worked in Chimbote and Macate. The Sisters celebrated what we called mini-Masses. These consisted of the first part of the Mass, the liturgy of the Word, with Communion which the Sisters obtained from the priest in the neighboring parish. Doing that was common practice in the prelature, since most of the parishes had a parish team with either a Sister or a lay person in charge, but no priest.

Diego and I were occupied full time in IDEA and ODEC, so in the Chucuito parish we were mainly Eucharistic ministers for the parish team. The other team members did most of the leg work in the twenty-five farming communities located either on the peninsula, along the main road, or up in the hills above the town. Some of these communities were a considerable distance away. To go from the town of Chucuito to the peninsula required traveling across the lake for an hour in a small launch, because the rains usually made the only road impassable, and there was no public transportation. After debarking from the launch one had still had to walk miles farther to reach the various communities. Maryknoll Sister Jaruko Doi, Mercy Sister Martha Larson (a Maryknoll Associate) and Mercy Sister Deborah Watson were all members of the Chucuito parish team during these years. They lived in a small house in one of the nearby farming communities on the other side of Chucuito from where we lived. They were dedicated workers in an often very difficult situation. Most of the people, and especially the women, in the farming communities spoke mainly Aymara and knew very little Spanish. Inasmuch as the Sisters did not speak Aymara, communication was difficult for them. I myself had learned that lesson when I worked with Marcos Asqui and the mobile pastoral team. These Sisters devoted a great deal of time to catechesis, and performed emergency social aid work as well, especially when the people lost their potato crop to flooding. Thank you, Sisters, for all you did.

While I was engaged in other more specialized ministries, I aided the Chucuito parish team where Diego was pastor. He and I celebrated Mass on Saturdays only if there were weddings scheduled. Sunday was the day on which we focused, with a community Mass for everything. We felt that this pastoral approach of combining weekly Sunday Mass with sacraments like Baptism and Marriage created a more communitarian atmosphere, celebrating life's stages in the context of community.

Diego and I also were busy during the year with the annual fiesta Masses in each of the twenty-five farming communities that formed the parish. Chucuito, founded by the Spanish in 1563, had two major fiestas each year, the Feast of Our Lady of the Assumption in August and the Feast of Our Lady of the Rosary in October. These were week-long celebrations with community dancing and food and drink for which family members gathered from all parts of Peru. I loved those fiestas!

Then we had the beautiful Holy Week processions organized by the people. I learned so much about the faith of the Aymaran people in these celebrations which went on with or without a priest. The images of Jesus and Mary were decorated beautifully with flowers and candles by the families in charge. Walking behind them in silence through the dark, muddy, unpaved streets of Chucuito, often with rain pouring down on us, reminded me that our faith is all about following Jesus in life's difficult personal and social situations.

Another major celebration in the Chucuito parish was the Celebration of the Holy Cross in the month of May on top of nearby hills that were sacred to the farming communities. Since before the arrival of the Spanish and Christianity, the Aymaran people considered their hills to be sacred places, much as the ancient Hebrews had. For me these great celebrations were an example of the inculturation of Jesus into the Aymaran religious and cultural belief system.

In later years, the climb up the hills could be a little difficult for me, but then I would see an elderly woman climbing with three cases of beer on her back. That encouraged me to keep going, as I huffed and puffed along the way. Thank you, Lord, for those great days with a dedicated parish team and an effective diocesan and inter-diocesan collaborative ministry. Hopefully someday the Church institution will adopt more of these participative, creative, refreshing and uplifting celebrations.

As I mentioned earlier, Marcos Asqui became a lay member of the Chucuito parish team in late 1986 after the mobile pastoral program was abandoned in the prelature to allow each parish to organize its own lay formation program. During those subsequent years Marcos was very helpful in forming the lay Aymaran leadership in the Chucuito parish because he spoke Aymara.

Victor Barrientos, the parish secretary for years, also was a member of the team. He dealt mainly with daily administration in the parish office. I became very good friends with Victor, his wife Jacoba and their daughters Princesa and Carmen Rosa. Victor and I would enjoy an Arequipena beer during my Aymara class recess with my teachers Santiago Mendoza and Juan Mallea.

I also became friends with Estanislao Cruz, a high school senior and the night watchman for the historic church building in Chucuito which is a national monument. Estanislao was an orphan and the younger half-brother of Marcos Asqui. In the afternoons after work all of us often played volleyball and had a very good time together. Thank you, Victor, Marcos, and Estanislao, for a great job on the Chucuito parish team and for your friendship during all my years in Chucuito.

When I arrived in the prelature, there were few youth groups in the parishes. So, in late 1985 several of us in the prelature decided to make a major effort to organize them, and we did. During the early years in the Chucuito parish Ursina, Diego's secretary in the Aymara Institute (IDEA), worked with me to form a youth group called "Cultural Roots." We got ten young persons to join, and with them we went to the youth assemblies organized in the prelature. Then all the parish youth groups in the prelature decided to join the Young Agrarian Christian Youth (JARC) national movement, which resembles the Young Christian Workers (JOC) and the Young Christian Students (JEC) movements I described in an earlier chapter. Their national leaders came up from Lima to talk to us and to the young people about the movement, and then we voted to join. I remember all the young persons, especially Blas Tintaya from Yunguyo, Artemio Huarachi and Wilber Mamani Cotillo from Chucuito and many more. Thank you, all.

So, within a year I was doing sacramental parish ministry, youth ministry in the Chucuito parish with the JARC movement, studying Aymara full-time, supporting the mobile pastoral leadership team by trying to keep it alive with Aymara-speaking lay people, and founding the ODEC-JULI office for ministry with the religion teachers in all the state schools in the prelature. My brief work with the mobile team had prepared me quite well for the work with teachers, because our visits to the parish teams in 1985 introduced me to the entire prelature. I was well settled into my new ministry in Chucuito in the prelature of Juli, and thereby in the pastoral ministry of the Church in the southern Andes of Peru.

HOLY CROSS PERUVIAN VOCATIONS

During 1985 the Eastern Province of Holy Cross, on which the Peru district depended, had a provincial chapter in the United States that made several important decisions for the future of Holy Cross in Peru. Some in the province thought that we should pull out of Peru because we had no vocations (applicants to join our Congregation of Holy Cross) there at the time. Vocations in the Eastern Province also were declining, which was causing a growing concern about the future of the province in the United States. Thanks to the provincial superior, Joe Callahan who had visited Peru often, we managed to regain the confidence of the Eastern Province membership.

The chapter formed the Peru Solidarity Committee which organized trips to Peru so that the membership could see firsthand what we were doing. In the following years, we had visitors twice a year from the Holy Cross Eastern Province; they came in small groups of five or six persons. Besides boosting our morale with these community visits, the visitors personally learned a lot about our ministry in Peru and returned to describe it to others in the province, which gained support for us. The visits were a great success. Subsequently we had much more backing from the province, and most of the previous tensions disappeared. Thank you to the twenty or so men who came down to us during those years! You all lifted our spirits. Thank you, Joe Callahan, for all that you did for us!

In 1985 we had had a very important district chapter which turned our Peru formation program around again by re-establishing vocation and formation programs which had been dormant since 1982. At that chapter in a very much contested election Dan Panchot was re-elected district superior. Some in the Peru Holy Cross district found him disorganized and difficult to work with, but I did not.

Before coming to Peru Dan had labored many years in Chile. He was arrested after the Pinochet coup there in 1973 by the military government. He was tortured, and then had to leave Chile. He came to Peru in 1977 and worked in the then recently founded Canto Grande parish developing a new school for handicapped children called in Quechua *Yancana Huasi* (House of Work).

After the chapter, Dan named Richard Renshaw to be Director of Formation in the district, replacing Bud Colgan. During the chapter, we had voted to open a new formation house in Canto Grande rather than have the formation program continue functioning in the parish house there. Dan also named me Director of Vocations and Bob Baker to be Head of Studies. Richard, Bob and I worked well together as a team to organize a live-in discernment program which would allow seven young men that we knew from Chimbote and from Canto Grande to live in community to consider the possibility of Religious life. Bob Baker oversaw that program in a rented house in the parish of Canto Grande.

Carlos Loli from Chimbote was the only one out of the seven who finished the two-year discernment program. He then asked to become a postulant in 1987 and a novice in Chile in 1988. He was professed in 1989 just one year before leaving. All during his formation Carlos had been honest with us about his doubts whether he could live life-long celibacy. He later married and had children. He is currently a religious education teacher in the public schools in Lima. Thank you, Carlos, for getting our new vocation program off the ground and for always being honest with us about your doubts.

Many others who left the discernment program also became good Christian laymen. Several continue working in Church lay ministries even today. I always believed that our Holy Cross formation programs should be oriented toward forming Christian leaders both lay and Religious.

I have stayed in contact with several of these young men all the years even up to today. Thank you especially, Hector Nicho from the Canto Grande parish, with whom I am still good friends. Hector was one of the men who left the discernment program, but who has continued to work as a layman in the Canto Grande parish and in the Fe y Alegría school all these years.

Thank you also, Richard Renshaw. Richard was far ahead of his time in many ways. He guided us through difficult community decisions about formation during those years when the Holy Cross community was beginning to debate very differing views on Religious life and Church.

At that time we also tried to establish a Holy Cross Lay Association with lay men and women from Chimbote and the Canto Grande parish. Bud Colgan, then the new pastor in Canto Grande, with a few others from the Canto Grande parish thought that this would be divisive for the laity. We had a great weekend meeting in Canto Grande with some of the lay leaders from both parishes. The lay people wrote up a beautiful mission statement which included helping Holy Cross with Peruvian vocations and living in the Holy Cross spirituality. Sad to say the Lay Association was never established.

Our first vocation who came from the Puno area was Jorge Mallea whom I met in early 1986 when I was traveling with Marcos Asqui and the prelature mobile pastoral team for the formation of lay leadership and we visited the Moho parish team on the northern side of Lake Titicaca. The large town of Moho was the most distant from Chucuito and was in an area of the prelature that was suffering from flooding caused by the *el niño* weather phenomenon which sometimes brought heavy rains. We had to go a good part of the way in a small motorboat because all the roads had been washed out by the floods. There I met Jorge Mallea, who was one of the diocesan seminarians working at the time with the St. Joseph Sisters in the parish of Moho for the summer.

I am reminded again how important the St. Joseph Sisters have been in my life. As I have said, my father's sister, Sister Martina, was a St. Joseph Sister and is one of the pillars of my vocation. I also worked with these Sisters in Chimbote and Macate. In the prelature of Juli they were the leaders in the Moho parish where there was no priest. As usual, I invited the diocesan seminarians in Moho to visit Diego and me in Chucuito any time they might wish, since we had room for two guests and we enjoyed visitors. Jorge arrived at our house a few days later, and afterwards he visited us almost monthly. He even spent a semester break with us in August 1986 helping

Marcos with the mobile pastoral team and working in the Chucuito parish.

Since my arrival in August 1985, I had been teaching in the pre-seminary program in Ilave, where Diego had lived. Then in 1986 I also began teaching Bible classes at the regional diocesan seminary in the city of Juliaca, where Diego already taught classes, about an hour and a half away by bus from Chucuito. I would stay overnight in both places, so I got to know many of the seminarians well. I often saw Jorge in my classes. He asked to work again with Holy Cross for the longer summer break in 1987, and during that time he spoke with Diego and me about switching from the diocesan seminary program to Holy Cross. We told him that he would have to work all that out with his spiritual director and with the diocese, because I did not want it to look like Holy Cross was stealing people from the diocesan program. Jorge spoke with the seminary rector, Maryknoll priest Ray Finch, who was also his spiritual director. Ray was very supportive of Jorge's desire. He knew that Jorge had been interested in Religious life since the beginning of his vocation discernment back in 1983, but since there were no Religious communities in the prelature at that time, he had joined the diocese. Thank you, Ray, for that support!

It was decided that Jorge would transfer to Holy Cross in March 1988 and have a year off from the diocese to discern better his vocation to Religious life. Jorge stayed with Holy Cross and became our first Holy Cross Peruvian priest, taking his first vows in February 1990 and his final vows in February 1993, and ordained a priest in

November 1994. I think that Jorge probably suffered somewhat during his formation years, since as North Americans we were still learning how to adapt Holy Cross to Peruvian ways of doing things; but he finally became our first Peruvian as well as our first Aymaran Religious! Thank you, Jorge, for coming with us and staying with us all these years!

My teaching at the diocesan seminaries in Juliaca and in Ilave ended in 1988 after Jorge left the diocesan seminary program to join Holy Cross. Some people in the prelature felt that I had stolen him. That is often the way with misunderstandings and unfounded suspicions that are part of life even in the Church! I missed the teaching there, but then what could I do?

Jorge Izaguirre from Casma near Chimbote, of whom I have written in previous chapters, also entered Holy Cross as a postulant in 1988 after a pre-postulant year in the formation program in Canto Grande. He spent three summers in Chucuito, studying at the school in Puno for training lay religion teachers (ESER), from which he graduated in 1990.

As well in 1990, the year I replaced Diego as pastor on the Chucuito parish team, Fidel Ticona from a farming community near the town of Ilave also became a postulant with Holy Cross. Fidel continued on as had Jorge Mallea, and in 2000 in Chucuito he became the second Aymaran to be ordained in Holy Cross. During those years, the Holy Cross postulants usually spent their summers in Chucuito with Diego and me, working mainly in our summer school programs for children and young people organized by the parish team. I thank all these men for joining Holy Cross and bringing their many talents to serve their people through our Congregation.

In 1991 Jim Phalan arrived from the United States to live and work with Diego and me in Chucuito. At that time, Jim was a Holy Cross deacon. After spending his diaconate year with us, he was ordained a priest in Chucuito in February 1992. Jim devoted most of his time to visiting the farming communities on the peninsula.

I celebrated my fiftieth birthday in June 1991, enjoying festivities with compadres, godchildren, other friends, and my Holy Cross community in Chucuito.

HOLY CROSS COLLABORATION

As part of my assignment as Peru Director of Vocations, the district superior Dan Panchot in 1985 asked me to write to all the Holy Cross Brothers' provinces and to the other two congregations of Holy Cross Sisters to invite them to consider collaborating with us in the Peru ministry. The Sisters of the Holy Cross were already present in Chimbote, and had been since 1982. The district had invited them to join us there after being in contact with them since 1975 when we had had the first gathering of all Holy Cross personnel in Latin America known as the PILA project, of which I wrote in an earlier chapter.

In June 1986, the Sisters of Holy Cross, the French-Canadian branch of the Holy Cross Sisters with headquarters in Montreal, responded by sending Sisters to consider ministering with us in the Prelature of Juli. Sisters

Marguerite Gravel, Frances Savoie, Lia Finnerty and their assistant superior general Sister Laura arrived for a two-week visit. They investigated ministry possibilities for their congregation in Juli with the administrator of the prelature, Maryknoll priest Mike Briggs. The Sisters were enthused, and in April 1987 Lia, Frances and Marguerite arrived in Lima to attend language school. They came up to the prelature in September 1987 to begin their ministry, living with Mercy Sister Barbara Cavanaugh in the neighboring parish of Acora. Sister Marie Pilon arrived from Canada to work with them in 1988. She began using her nursing skills in the communities where the Sisters lived, first near Acora and later in Mocachi. This was the beginning of a long collaboration between Holy Cross congregations in the prelature of Juli. Thank you, Sisters of Holy Cross.

Almost immediately Sister Marguerite had trouble living at the altitude, so the Sisters decided to open another house in the Holy Cross Canto Grande parish in Lima, thanks to the invitation of the superior Dan Panchot. Sister Marguerite went there. At the same time the Sisters of the Holy Cross who had been in Chimbote since 1982 also decided to open a new house in the Holy Cross parish in Canto Grande, after also being invited to do so by Dan. Sister Vivian Coulon of the Holy Cross Marianite congregation also came to visit during that time, but could not stay since she had no Marianite Sister companion from her congregation to live with her. The Marianites were trying to find Sisters for their recently founded mission with Holy Cross in Chile. So, in 1987 three of the four

Holy Cross congregations were present in Peru. Thank you, dear Sisters, and thank you Dan Panchot for making possible all that collaboration.

In August 1985 Brother John Benesh accepted an invitation I had offered him at the Holy Cross History Conference in March 1984. He came to work in the district in August 1985, joining Dan Panchot in Chimbote and teaching math and chemistry at a Fe y Alegría school there. Thank you, John, for giving the Holy Cross Brothers a presence in Peru.

I felt that such a Holy Cross collaboration was very important for the Peru mission. We began to cooperate not only in ministry together, but also in vocation work and in holding community assemblies as the family of Holy Cross. This was the dream of our common founder Blessed Basil Moreau who always sent the Sisters, Brothers and priests out in mission together, even when a bishop asked for only one of the three groups. Many of the older Peruvian members of our congregations often say today that their initial attraction to Holy Cross was this collaborative spirit between the men and women, clerical and lay Religious.

Thus, beginning in 1988 we were doing vocation ministry together with the Sisters. Each year after that a large group of young men and women who discerned a vocation to Religious life participated in a monthly meeting we held at the parish in Chucuito. As the director of vocation ministry I also traveled with some frequency to Lima and Chimbote to help organize vocation encounters there. I remained the vocation director in the Puno area for many years and the national director, as well, excepting only 1988-1991.

In addition, Bob Plasker, whom I wrote about in an earlier chapter on Chimbote, organized two six-week renewal programs for the Holy Cross priests, Brothers and Sisters working in Latin America, in which I participated when I could. These were a continuation of the collaboration begun in 1974 at the PILA meeting in Peru.

ODEC-JULI

In 1988 Holy Cross Sister Frances Savoie began to collaborate with me on the lay religion teachers training team in the prelature (ODEC-JULI) which was expanding thanks to financial help from Adveniat, a German Catholic organization that funded Church programs in poor areas of Latin America and elsewhere. Before receiving that help I had managed to keep the work going with the one hundred twenty-five dollars that for years Jim and Marcie Wilson sent me each month. Jim had been a Holy Cross Brother until he left to marry in 1980. I had lived with him in Rome, and his parents and mine came one year to visit us while we both were there. Thank you, Jim and Marcie, for your generosity, solidarity and friendship.

In 1986 two young men, Rudi (Rudolph) Cutipa and Wilber Mamani Cotillo, began to assist me from time to time as secretaries in the ODEC when I had to travel to distant schools for workshops with the teachers. They prepared the certificates of participation for those in attendance while I and the others taught the teachers. Later when I received more financial aid from Adveniat, I hired Rudi to be the office secretary. In 1987 Sister Vilda, who had begun with me in the ODEC in 1986, was moved out of Yunguyo by her congregation, and so Dominican Sister Maria Gabriela Hurtado from Yunguyo took her place on the team. Then Narciso Valencia, a recently ordained Aymaran diocesan priest, joined the ODEC team in 1991. Frances, Maria Gabriela, Rudi, Narciso and I organized workshops for grade school teachers throughout the extensive area of the prelature.

Besides the difficulty of travel on the dirt roads, we had to deal with many different educational authorities who were not always the most cooperative with us, since they thought religious education was not all that important. They had not had an office like ours to deal with before, and so were not used to collaborating with the Church on these issues. Since the ODEC-JULI was new, we had to start from scratch to get the high school teachers to come to our workshops. Most of them had no formal training in religious education, and some used their class time to teach something else. It often was a discouraging battle, but little by little we gained ground, and each year we had better participation. It was a learning experience for all of us. It could be very frustrating when we traveled a long distance for a workshop only to find when we arrived that the educational authorities had not even informed the teachers about it, or had not given the teachers the necessary permission to cancel their classes that day to come to it. Even when we supplied paper for them to print the invitations, they often would not distribute them, or worse still, they would use the paper for their own purposes. My Irish temper rose in those situations.

Rudi was a lifeline for me when there were problems, because being Peruvian and Aymaran he could deal with the authorities more effectively than those of us who were not Peruvian. Wilber continued to help from time to time when we went to areas where there was a large group of teachers and we needed more typists for the teachers' certificates. Thank you, Rudi and Wilber.

Because I enjoyed the teaching opportunities it gave me beyond the administrative aspects, I stayed with the ODEC-JULI team many years. I am a teacher at heart, and I joined Holy Cross to teach. I missed the classroom, but I believed that I could do more good forming lay teachers in their faith with Bible studies and instructing them in the life-giving methodology of linking faith with real life issues. The teachers themselves seemed to appreciate the workshops, and when many of the educational authorities got to know us better, they began to appreciate them, too. Hopefully everyone learned things to help them be better educators in the faith.

Meanwhile the terrorist group Shining Path, present in Peru since 1980, became more active in the Puno area. Several Church institutions, particularly those dedicated to helping people in need like the Agricultural Center in Ayaviri and the social aid institution of Caritas in Puno, were attacked by the terrorists and burned down or bombed. The town of Moho where the St. Joseph Sisters lived was attacked, and the Sisters had to hide during the violence. The ODEC team's travel and workshops were impeded by Shining Path's continuing escalation in the Puno region. Many teachers were sympathetic to the terrorist group which was using fear and violence to fight for more social justice and equality in Peru. We had to find ways to respond to the new reality of living with terror. The prelature formed a human rights team headed by Maryknoll Sister Pat Ryan which was very helpful, encouraging us to persevere with our workshops in the outlying areas of the prelature.

Each January all those years, I also taught courses in the summer school that trained lay religion teachers (ESER) for the entire south Andean area. The teachers attended this summer program during January for three years, after which they received official recognition from the Peruvian educational authorities and from the Church to teach religious education in the state schools. My aim in the ODEC-JULI was to assure that only trained teachers, with official certificates in religious education, taught in the state high schools. It was a battle sometimes with school directors and others, both in state and Church positions, who were accustomed to using religion classes to give teaching jobs to their friends. It especially bothered me when priests and Sisters would ask me to give positions to their friends or to persons in formation who had no teaching certificate or little training. I think in the end we won the struggle to some degree.

In the summer school (ESER) I usually taught Bible, History of the Church in Latin America, and Methodology for Religious Education. Sister Alma Jones, from the Moho St. Joseph Sisters team and with whom I had engaged in youth ministry in Chimbote, also helped me one year. We team taught a class on Bible, each one taking a day. I thought it went very well, but a few students found it confusing. Holy Cross Sister Frances Savoie and I also team taught a class on Methodology. Thank you, Alma, for the years we shared ministry together both in Chimbote and in the prelature.

I enjoyed that month of teaching immensely, during which I usually stayed in Puno weekdays at the Maryknoll Center House. It is the same place where over the years I also went for relaxation and reflection on my days off. Thank you, Maryknoll, for the hospitality at your home in Puno. It resulted in my being absent from our house in Chucuito, but it was a very life-giving month for me. We taught teachers and sometime lay leaders (catechists) from the three neighboring Prelatures of Sicuani, Ayaviri, and Juli, as well as the Diocese of Puno. By staying in Puno, I got to know many of these lay teachers and lay leaders. The summer school had an impressive staff of teachers, all of whom were committed to the vision of a Church incarnate in the southern Andean culture and in the life situations of the people.

In general I enjoyed those first years in the prelature, as well as the collaboration between the four ecclesiastical jurisdictions of Puno, Sicuani, Ayaviri and Juli that formed what we called the South Andean Church. Our assemblies usually were held at the retreat house in Chucuito with priests, Sisters and lay persons sitting down together for ten days with the four bishops to discuss, reflect upon and plan a common Church strategy for the South Andean area. Unfortunately this collaboration between lay and clerical Church members and between four bishops in their jurisdictions with a common pastoral plan was not always supported by other Peruvian bishops at that time or by the Vatican. But it worked well for us, and we were happy in it; and this collaboration continued to grow despite obstacles from those who did not like it. I think that we followed Jesus' way of identifying with the problems of the poor and trying to accompany them in their hardships by finding ways to stand with them in their struggles and by defending them when necessary by making their voices heard. And really for me that is what following Jesus is all about.

A VIOLENCE OF ACCIDENTS

Along with the violence of the terrorist groups in the Puno area, we also endured a number of serious accidents during those years. In May 1988 I was driving our Volkswagen bug with Jim Mulligan, my novitiate class-mate who was visiting me, Jorge's brother Juan Mallea, who worked with Diego in the Aymara Institute (IDEA), and Richard Renshaw, the director of the Holy Cross formation program in Canto Grande where Jorge was now a postulant. We were returning to Chucuito after visiting Jorge Mallea's family, who lived in a farming community just outside the town of Juli. I rammed our car into the back of a large truck that had stopped on the two-lane highway without any lights on. Jim Mulligan suffered the severest injuries, with a broken leg, a broken foot, and his hip out of joint. I had a large head wound that needed thirty-five stitches. The other two in the back seat of our car, Richard Renshaw and Juan Mallea, had only minor cuts and bruises. We all survived, thank God. We were about forty miles from the Puno hospital when the accident occurred. Luckily a pickup truck behind us stopped and took us to the hospital in Puno, where we received good care. The next day Jim was flown back to Lima and then on to Canada for more surgery on his foot. Today he still walks with a limp. Thank you, Jim, for your friendship since 1960, our Holy Cross novitiate days in Bennington, Vermont. And thank you again, Richard, for your friendship through the years since our days together in Rome.

A special thanks to Juan Mallea who probably saved my life that night by putting his shirt around my head to stop my bleeding. Shortly before the accident Juan had asked me to be godfather for his recently-born son Daniel. In Peru a godfather is like a second father to the child being baptized. The practice has considerable cultural and religious significance for the people. The godfather is expected to help the child with advice, and perhaps with financial assistance for education or emergencies if need be. The godfather becomes a second father to his godson or goddaughter and a member of their extended family. I was putting Juan off, as I usually did when people asked me to be godfather, because as a Religious I had no personal monies and so could not help with the cultural financial expectation. But considering what Juan had done for me after the accident, I wanted to be his *compadre* (co-father), and *padrino* (godfather) of his son Daniel, and so become part of Juan's family. Thank you, Juan, for saving my life, for helping all of us that night of the accident, for inviting me into your extended family, and for being such a great compadre and friend all these years.

A few days afterwards I went with Juan to the place of the accident and drank a tea mixed with a bit of the earth from the scene. It is an Aymaran custom based on the belief that the evil spirits in the earth sometimes try to grab people driving on deserted parts of a road. When you drink the earth, the evil spirit enters you as well, and so will not try to do it again. Maybe it is thought to work like a vaccine. It may also derive from a sense that all creation is one, and that somehow everything is interconnected. I became compadre with Juan and Isabel in December 1988 in the presence of Juan's brother Jorge, who was on vacation in Chucuito at the time.

A surprise ending to this story occurred a few years later in 1991 while Juan Mallea and I were visiting my friends Jaime and Lois Pino in Tacna. Jaime who had been a deacon in the Prelature of Juli and Lois who had been a Maryknoll Sister had both worked in the Puno area back in the 1970's, and then had left and married. They were living in the United States near my hometown of Albany, New York, when I visited them in 1981 while on my sabbatical. Ten years later, in 1991, I encountered them again in Tacna for the funeral of Jaime's mother. That is when I learned that members of Jaime Pino's family were driving the pickup truck that rescued us the night of the accident. What a small world!

The same year as the car accident, in the fall of 1988 Holy Cross Sister Frances Savoie survived the air crash of the Aeroperú flight from Juliaca to Lima as it took off from the airport in Juliaca. Frances was one of the few who walked away from the crash with just a slight shoulder injury. Another miracle? Later Sister Frances developed serious traumatic aftereffects that made it difficult for her to fly, and it took her years before she could board an airplane again. She returned to Canada in 1990 for several years to deal with that health issue. We missed her on the religion teachers' training team (ODEC).

In 1992, Paul Farber, a priest from the Holy Cross Eastern Province, visited Peru. He had been asked by the provincial Dave Farrell to be the province's new Peru Solidarity Coordinator in the United States. When he arrived in Puno in August 1992 he developed serious altitude sickness, apparently complicated by his high blood pressure medicine. He died in our car on the way to the Juliaca airport. May he rest in peace.

Shortly after that, in late August 1992, the religion teachers training team (ODEC), traveling by car to give a teachers' workshop, struck and killed a little five-year old girl who was crossing the main highway on her way to school. Her older sister had left her behind. Afterwards, Rudi who had been driving the car in that accident and I went to La Paz, Bolivia, a four-hour bus ride from Chucuito, for ten days to calm our nerves. A few months later the whole team traveled there for a few days to rest.

All of us were kept on edge during those years by the constant presence of the terrorist movement Shining Path which attacked the town of Moho where the St. Joseph Sisters were living. All of us who decided to stay lived with that terror threat. It was not until years later that I fully realized how much tension wrapped our lives.

A NEW BISHOP

The Juli Prelature had been without a bishop since February 1986 when Bishop Alberto died in a car accident. After a three-year delay, in 1989 Rome finally named a new bishop, Raimundo Reveredo, a Vincentian Peruvian priest from Lima who had been working for many years in Santiago, Chile. I, as well as many others, had hoped that the new bishop would be an Aymaran who could speak the language of most of the people and understand their culture better, so we were disappointed. Most of us in the Juli Prelature were concerned because we felt Rome was naming bishops in those days whose style and ways would create more tension than relief to most of us ministering in that region. It seemed to many of us in the prelature that there was pressure on the new bishop from the Peruvian episcopate and from Rome to change the collaborative style that had been the norm in the southern Andean Church for so long. As a consequence, there was a build up of internal and external tension among Church members those last years.

I was grateful for the offer of a sabbatical year in 1993. Bud Colgan, the district superior, and his council felt that I should examine my beer consumption. So, off I went in February 1993 for a life-giving sabbatical year.

6. THE WONDER YEAR 1993

It was in 1993 that I completed twenty-five years of living and working in Peru. Thank you, Lord, for those years, and thank you for 1993, a year that renewed my vitality in so many ways with spiritual energy that continues to invigorate my life's journey even today!

In late 1991 some of the community leadership believed that I might have a problem with alcohol, because it seemed to them that I was drinking too much. The district superior, Bud Colgan, who lived in Canto Grande at the time, confronted me one day saying that he and his district council thought that I should look for professional help during my upcoming sabbatical year. I told him I was surprised that he and the others on his council had never thought it might be good to speak with me personally about it, as the gospel recommends, before forming such an opinion. However, I was not resistant to their concern, since I knew I was drinking more than I wanted to, and I was willing to look at it with professional help.

Thinking about beer in my life takes me back to my childhood years. One of the pillars of my vocation was my Aunt Julia, my father's sister who became Sister Martina with the St. Joseph of Carondelet Sisters. I have an early memory of her coming to visit my family at our house at Christmas time and asking my dad for a large glass of beer. I was sitting on her lap when she got it, and I took a sip of the foam on top. It reminded me of soap suds. After that I never tasted beer again until my teenage years when once while playing poker I had to drink a full glass straight down for losing, and I threw up all over the cards. What a sight and surprise for my high school friends! I felt so lousy I just wanted to sleep. I stayed away from beer after that until I attended religious fiestas in Macate where all the men stood around and drank socially. I poured only a little into my glass as the glass followed the bottle around the circle in the Peruvian manner. It was a very communitarian way of celebrating friendship. That was the beginning of my beer drinking in Peru.

I was always a group drinker. I never looked for beer or alcohol when I was alone. So, I knew that my problem with drinking too much was somehow tied up more with my social relationships with the men in the group rather than with the beer itself.

When Dave Farrell the Eastern Province provincial superior at the time came for his visit to Chucuito in early 1992, he and Bud spoke with me again about it. They both repeated that they wanted me to get professional help during the 1993 sabbatical year that I already was planning. I had no problem with asking myself why I was drinking so much. So, I accepted their proposal and decided to look for an additional program for that year, one that would help me examine any addiction I might have.

My good Aymaran friend Jorge Mallea was to pronounce his final vows in the month of February 1993, and he had asked me to be his official witness, so I did not want to leave on my sabbatical until after that. The problem was finding a renewal program in the United States that would begin in March, since most started in January. I spoke with my Maryknoll priest friend Mike Briggs, and he told me about a program in which he and others from Maryknoll had participated that took place in Attleboro, Massachusetts. When I wrote for information from the organizers, Formation Consultation Services, I discovered that they did have a ten-week program beginning in mid-March. It was perfect timing and another sign for me that God was leading me there.

When I learned that this program was to be held in a building at the La Salette Shrine in Attleboro, I considered this yet another sign from God, since a second pillar of my vocation was my cousin Jack Barnes on my mother's side of the family, a La Salette priest who died very young when I was in high school. He had taught me not to be afraid in the water and how to swim. Thank you, Jack.

Both Jack and Sister Martina were so happy in their respective vocations. I always wanted to be like both of them. That's why I felt now that this program was God's will for me. I have always believed in strong signs from God to lead me in making decisions in my life.

I wrote to the provincial superior Dave Farrell about the program, telling him that I liked the looks of it, but that it was expensive because it was led by professional therapists. Dave wrote back that I was worth the cost of it. Thank you, Dave, for those kind words and for letting me participate in this life-giving experience.

A prerequisite of the Attleboro program was that I write an autobiography beforehand, divided into fifteen chapters, each about an aspect of my family life story. So I undertook to do it in 1992 while I was still in Chucuito, on an old-fashioned Olivetti typewriter with my terrible typing skills. There were specific questions required to be answered in each chapter, but then I could add anything else that I remembered and felt was important to mention. Thanks to this experience of writing my life story, I had an opportunity to learn much about myself that I had not previously recognized and a chance to delve deeper into some of the questions about my life experiences that I had not understood so well before. It was the beginning of an intense inner journey for me.

At the end of 1992 I arranged for Rudi Cutipa who worked with me on the religion teachers training team (ODEC) to take over, with the help of the Sisters, as head of the team during my absence in 1993. Jim Phalan would replace me as pastor on the Chucuito parish team, which was being coordinated by the layman Marcos Asqui that year. So, I was free to go!

Dan Kayajan, a Holy Cross seminarian from the United States who was spending a pastoral year in Peru in 1992, came to Chucuito in December of that year to celebrate with me my twenty-fifth anniversary of priesthood. He was scheduled to work with us in the parish summer school program for three months, but unfortunately became ill with hepatitis in early January and had to return to Canto Grande. Thank you, Dan, for that time with us in Peru and for your friendship throughout the years.

As usual I taught during the month of January 1993 in the religion teachers training summer school (ESER) in

Puno. Then in February I went to Lima, together with Jorge Mallea's father and brothers, to participate in Jorge's final vows ceremony. February saw several more celebrations of my twenty-fifth anniversary, in Canto Grande, Chimbote, and Cartavio/Trujillo, before my departure from Peru for my sabbatical. Thank you everyone for those commemorations of our years of friendship!

One day in late February 1993, summertime in Peru, Jorge Mallea and Jorge Izaguirre accompanied me to the Lima airport. It was difficult for me to say goodbye to Peru for a whole year, and I was nervous about what the future might hold.

My sabbatical year was set to begin at Holy Cross' community residence in Cocoa Beach, Florida, meeting there my brother Bud and my sister-in-law Jo for a week-long vacation together. The trip back to the United States was uneventful until I found my flight between Miami and Orlando cancelled. I had to take a long bus trip in a freezing air-conditioned van from which I got a stomach cold, of course, and was awake all night! My brother Bud met me at the Orlando airport. During the following days we had a quite wonderful family visit. We went to Universal Studios to see the "I Love Lucy" exhibit, visited Jo's brother Charlie Alfano who was living then in West Palm Beach, and spent some time in the Cocoa Beach area which I had never visited before.

At the end of that week, I flew north to Providence, Rhode Island, on what became a stormy, snowy day. I was met at the airport and driven to Attleboro on snow-laden, slippery roads.

The following morning I met with a therapist named Ed. He accompanied me in the autobiography that I had written by reading it back to me. It was a moving experience to hear my story related to me that way, and simply by listening I discovered so much about my life. I was amazed when Ed told me he had had some similar experiences in his own life.

Afterwards, another therapist, Bob, led me through psychological testing to introduce me to my unique personality. Then another therapist, Jim Stone, who would later become my primary therapist during the program, interviewed me about my drinking and possible addiction. Jim was a recovering alcoholic. He restated what I already believed about myself. If I had been drinking too much, it was not because alcohol was a primary problem or addiction for me. It was just the red flag for other addictions in my life which I slowly would discover during the ten-week program. Thank you, Jim, Ed, Bob, and all the other therapists at Attleboro.

After that initial preparatory week at Attleboro, I went to our provincial house in Bridgeport, Connecticut, traveling by train with a large suitcase on another very snowy day. The airports were closed, so the train arriving in Providence from Boston was crowded, and I wound up sitting on my suitcase in the space between train cars for a four-hour trip. Jim Preskenis, the assistant provincial, was waiting for me at the station. The following day, after a conversation with Dave Farrell the provincial superior, I drove up to Albany and spent a week with Bud and Jo. Then I drove back to Attleboro with my nephew Patrick who at that time was in his freshman year studying at nearby Stonehill College, my Alma Mater.

THE SABBATH PROGRAM

I began the ten-week program at Attleboro in mid-March. It opened late because of another heavy snow storm on the east coast and the difficulty it caused for some of the participants to travel. When it finally started, we formed a sacred circle with incense and candles.

I had resolved beforehand I would share honestly a lot about my life during this program, but that I would not tell all. But once the staff shared their own life stories in front of us on the opening day, I decided that for once I would tell all as it is. The experience was so freeing! I did not have to pretend or put on a happy face. I did not have to wear any masks. I could just be me as God created me.

I had decided that I wanted these ten weeks to be like another novitiate experience for me. My novitiate year in 1960 in Bennington, Vermont, had been special in my Holy Cross formation. During that year, we novices lived a monastic life without many outside distractions. I decided that during the ten-week program I would not go out much. I wanted to stay more to myself.

The group preceding us had been a rather social one, but thankfully most of the eight in my group were looking for quieter times. We decided that Friday night would be a social night for us with a movie in the house, and week-ends would be free to do something together or not. That worked out perfectly for me. I had brought with me from

Peru a lot of old letters, papers and notebooks, memories from my life all these past fifty-two years. So, I slowly read them and then either threw them out, or saved them for the Holy Cross archives if they described my life during my formation years, or saved them for family history purposes. I listened to many good tapes and read many books from the program library. I was in heaven with all my time for reading and to just be me. I took long walks in the budding New England springtime to pray and reflect on my life journey.

The seven other men in the program with me included a Religious Brother, a Maryknoll lay missionary, two diocesan priests, one Maryknoll priest and two other Religious priests. I bonded quickly with Leo and Paul, two of the Religious priest participants who were also missionaries. We went together for a swim at the YMCA three mornings a week at 6:00 am. I had a car to take us. I can't believe I got up that early! Swimming came back into my life.

The program contained many new experiences for me. The bioenergetic exercise classes, the personality study groups, and massage therapy offered me a whole new attitude towards my body. In my youth I often had been ashamed, because I thought my body was too thin, weak-looking, not muscular enough. The spiritual therapy sessions enabled me to examine my spiritual journey and to underscore in the group work that God is my friend. Then the twelve-step spirituality program helped me to recognize the addictions in my life and to find ways to free myself from them. Mandala art therapy classes led me to penetrate deeper into my life story as it was reflected in the creative freedom of personal color and design. I also had three individual therapy sessions each week with my primary therapist, Jim Stone. He was my guide and companion on the life journey. Thank you, Jim, for being such a guide for me! And thank you therapists Clare, Ed, and Jackie for being there for me, too. I will never forget you!

I will not delve now into all that I learned about myself at the time. Let me only point out that reconnecting with my body, spirit and emotions, and stepping a bit outside my controlling mind was a blessed, liberating experience for me that would influence me considerably during the following years.

Within the group at Attleboro we shared our stories, through childhood and adolescence to the present. It was amazing how similar some of these were. I learned so much about myself from listening to the others, especially the Irish-born Redemptorist priest Paul who was finishing up years of ministry in Brazil. We had a lot in common. Thank you, Paul. It was so freeing for me to tell my story, too, without avoiding anything. Weeping, embraced by Paul and Jim at one moment during my telling, all signified so much to me. Such life-giving memories give me new energy even today.

I was planning to leave the program early to go to Notre Dame for the Holy Cross community celebration of the anniversaries of priestly ordinations. But after a while in this program I decided that I wanted to stay in Attleboro for the closing of the program with the others.

So, I did not go to Notre Dame. I am so glad that I stayed until the end.

On the last day, we formed the sacred circle again as we had formed it at the beginning of the program. I thought the circle would be broken at the end, but to my surprise it was not. The circle was expanded in a symbolic way so that wherever I might be in the world I could tap into the new life-giving energy that I had found during these ten weeks. Paul, my new-found Irish friend from Brazil gave each of us a wooden ring to wear. All I needed to do was to touch it when I felt that I needed the strength of the group. For me it was great symbolism. I have lost the ring, but I still feel the strength of the group even today, particularly when I sense I need it. I left the program at the end of May on a real high. I thank Holy Cross for giving me this opportunity. It was a grace-filled experience for me.

A few months later, in mid-July, I went back to Attleboro for another week of therapy as recommended by the program therapists. It was a reinforcing experience to continue to share my story and to free myself even more. Once again, a great group of men walked with me during that week. Thank you one and all for sharing your life stories.

As Religious men, we have so much in common when we remove our masks. I remember especially one Jesuit priest in this week-long program who seemed to have had the exact same parents as I did. We both discovered that our parents acted almost exactly the same way and spoke the same words to each of us.

THE SUMMER

I spent June and July with the Holy Cross Brothers at Valatie, New York, near my hometown of Albany. It was the first time I stayed there. After my parents died, when I was on home leave from Peru every three years, visiting family and friends in Albany for three months, I had stayed at the Holy Cross interprovincial novitiate in Waterford, New York. Valatie was a new community experience for me. There were several Holy Cross Brothers living there who had been my teachers at Vincentian Institute High School in Albany.

In June I celebrated my twenty-fifth anniversary of priesthood with the Holy Cross Eastern Province at our community center at Stonehill College in North Easton, Massachusetts, with my classmates and with my family, several cousins and close friends. Afterwards I traveled to St. Edward's University in Austin, Texas, to present a paper on the Spirituality of Holy Cross in Peru. This was my third history paper there on Peru in ten years' time.

In the latter part of June, my brother Bud and his family organized a twenty-fifth anniversary celebration for me at Valatie. More than one hundred of my friends and family gathered for Mass and afterwards for brunch at a nearby restaurant. This was an opportunity for me to thank in my homily all my family and friends for their presence in my life's journey. Thank you, Bud and Jo, for organizing that celebration, and thank you to all who participated.

I visited family and friends until early August, when I set out for Ireland for the second part of my sabbatical year. First, I visited Roger and Josie Masters, my English friends whom I met in 1967, my diaconate year, during a summer program in Aldershot, Hants, England. They visited me in Peru several times beginning in 1987. In 1991 they came back to Peru to live for a year with their entire family of more than nine adopted children.

After spending some days with Roger and Josie, I made my first visit to our new Chucuito sister parish in Karlsruhe, Germany. I followed that with a trip to Rome where I revisited memories of studying theology for four years 1964-1968 during the Second Vatican Council. On this occasion in 1993, I stayed at the Holy Cross Generalate. In the heat of an August day I walked by my old haunts, including the Gregorian University where I had attended courses and the Trevi Fountain close by, into which I had thrown a coin in 1968 in hope of returning one day.

I continued on to France to visit Louie Lemeur, a Holy Cross classmate in Rome from that country. He was now working in western France in a parish near where Holy Cross was founded back in 1835. I still remember a homily Louie gave while I was there. He reminded us that we owe gratitude to the institutional Church for handing the gospels down to us. Something positive to remember about the Church institution!

From there I went back to my friends in England and then on to Dublin, Ireland, for the Faith and Mission sixteen-week renewal program in Dalgan Park at the Columban Missionary Priests' Center just outside the city.

THE FAITH AND MISSION PROGRAM

The Faith and Mission program, like Attleboro, was designed to open all of us up to new life. We were twenty-five men and twenty-five women participants, mostly priests and Sisters. Almost all of us were working outside our native cultures. I chose this particular program from among many others because I wanted to share my life experiences with a group of missionaries who would understand them. A participant was Sister Maureen Lynch from the Sisters of Charity of Halifax, the same congregation of Sisters as my friends, Sisters Zelma and Kay, whom I knew from my Cartavio days in Peru. She and I were the only American-born participants. We both lived and worked in Peru, so we had a lot to share. Thank you, Maureen, for your friendship. May you rest in peace.

Other participants were Columban priest Paul and Mercy Sister Jackie both of whom also ministered in Peru. They, too, had just completed the Attleboro program, in the session following mine. So, we had lots to share, too. We even practiced the bioenergetic exercises together.

Once a week the participants met in small groups for more personal sharing. My group helped me to look ever more deeply into my life's journey.

Part of this program was a directed eight-day retreat. It centered around what was going on in one's own life rather than focusing solely on religious themes or Christian virtues. I had never done a retreat like that one before. It reminded me of the spirituality that I had discovered in Peru working with Catholic Action groups like the Young Christian Workers (JOC) which looked at real life issues and then used the Sacred Scriptures to reflect on them. The Scriptures were not the starting point, but were rather the light or guide for living through present-day difficulties. Irish Columban Sister Redempta was my spiritual director during the retreat. Thank you for your insightful spiritual guidance, Redempta.

After the retreat, we had a five-day vacation break. Since seeing the movie "Brigadoon" as a child, I had always wanted to visit Scotland. Roger Masters, my English friend who had come to Peru with his entire family in 1991, met me in Glasgow. While waiting for him on the first floor of the hotel, my hotel room on an upper floor was robbed. Fortunately I did not lose anything of importance. The theft reminded me once again that I was not in control and that I had to keep letting go of things in my life. Roger and I visited Oban, Inverness and Edinburgh on a train that offered a free same-day return ticket. Thank you, Roger, for your friendship and that sunny vacation in Scotland in chilly November 1993.

During my time at Dalgan Park, I went twice to visit Bart Salter's cousins in Skibbereen near Cork. Bart was a Holy Cross priest friend of mine, originally from Ireland, with whom I studied in the seminary at Stonehill College. I had visited his cousins, Denis and Mary O'Shea, on my way back from Rome in 1968. It was enjoyable to renew friendship with them after twenty-five years.

A special week-long program to help us deal with authority issues in our lives was part of the second half of Dalgan Park. These sessions helped me to understand my own personal dynamic with authority. During that week, we were encouraged to do some role playing by trying out different styles of responding to authoritative persons, as a way to get to know ourselves better. Little did I know at the time that this workshop would be very helpful to me in the upcoming years when I had several conflicts with ecclesiastical and civil educational authorities.

Thank you to all at the Dalgan Park program, both co-journeyers and staff, for those life-giving sixteen weeks expanding me in so many facets of my life.

Near the end of my time in the program I received a letter from the Peru district superior, Bud Colgan, assigning me on my return to my former ministries in Chucuito. Of course, I was delighted. Thank you, Bud.

All good things finally come to an end. In mid-December I returned to England for a few days of Christmas cheer with Roger and Josie Masters and their family and with a few other English friends like Chris Mann whom I also knew from my diaconate summer of 1967 in Aldershot. Chris had visited my dad and me in Albany, New York, during the summer of 1981 when I was on my first sabbatical. Thank you, my dear English friends, for being an important part of my life.

Just before Christmas I returned to the United States renewed and refreshed. Dalgan Park was a perfect sequel to the Attleboro program.

THE WINTER

I spent Christmas with my brother Bud and his wife Jo and their family. It was my second time in Albany for the holidays since 1977, just before my mother died in 1979. I spent January visiting family and friends in the Albany area, and I participated in the annual Holy Cross community winter gathering at King's College in Wilkes-Barre, Pennsylvania. It was a cold, snowy winter. The car that the province loaned me broke down several times with a weak battery.

Thank you to all who received me in their homes during that life-giving year and during all the years I visited from Peru. In my 25th celebration homily, I said I am who I am thanks to all the wonderful people who have been part of my life. We are each one the fruit of family and friends and life experiences. Thank you, Lord, for placing such marvelous people on my path.

In late February 1994 I set out for my return trip to Lima. It would again be via Cocoa Beach where my brother Bud would meet me. However, the day I was to fly out of New York City there was a heavy snow storm. La Guardia Airport had just been shut down when I arrived there, so I had to return to Bridgeport on the same shuttle van that I had come on. What had been a one-hour trip getting to the airport became a six-hour trip going back. The provincial treasurer who was a classmate of mine, Brad Beaupre, met me at the shuttle stop. The next day I returned to the airport in New York and managed to get out on a flight. My brother Bud had made it to Orlando from Albany the previous day, barely managing to beat the snowstorm in the Albany area. After several days together at the Holy Cross residence in Cocoa Beach, Bud with his brother-in-law Charlie Alfano drove me to the Miami airport for my flight to Peru. It was the end of a great year and the beginning of a new adventure in Peru.

In February 1994 I returned to my previous assignments in Chucuito strengthened by this wonderful sabbatical which I will never forget.

7. CHUCUITO (PUNO) 1994 - 2000

As I continue recording my memories, I am amazed once more how God works in my life. I seem to be supported by Him in this effort of mine to share my life story. I recently attended a diocesan day of reflection for older priests in Orlando, Florida, where the speaker, a psychologist from St. Louis, talked about the importance of living our elder years in a healthy and fulfilling way. He said that one means is to mentor others by sharing the wisdom of our life stories. That, too, is one of my motives for writing these memories. Besides the sheer joy of reliving my Peru days again by recalling them in this manner, I also feel impelled to share my journey with the young.

I want to share the joyful and the sorrowful, the light and the dark, the love and the sin—of lacking love—in this life of mine. It was not all roses. As you read this, you will observe occasions when I was weak and faltered. I am not proud of those times in my life, but they are a part of me. The year 1993 helped me to get in touch with the history of my life and own up to it, and discover that my loving and merciful God was walking with me all the time. Thank you, Lord, for your presence even in the dark and difficult days of my life's journey.

I resume now my memories of Peru, beginning in February 1994 when I returned, re-energized by my sabbatical year, a time of reflection, a pivotal year in my life.

I was overjoyed that the provincial superior in the United States, Dave Farrell, and the district superior in Peru, Bud Colgan, had asked me to return to Peru and to go back to my beloved mission among the Aymaran people in Chucuito in the Prelature of Juli on the shores of Lake Titicaca. Honestly, I had been afraid either of them might assign me elsewhere. Therefore, once again I thank you both, Dave and Bud.

Peru was a changed country now that the leader of the terrorist group Shining Path, Abimael Guzman, was in jail and the movement was mostly dispersed. President Alberto Fujimori, who had been elected in 1990 to replace Alan Garcia, also was bringing the country back from financial collapse. The environment was less tense, more relaxed. Tourism which is so important economically for Peru had returned, and so had foreign investors.

THE RETURN TO CHUCUITO

I had been back only a few weeks when in mid-April Marcos Asqui Chambi, my friend and member of the parish team, died suddenly of pancreatic cancer. I went with him to the Juliaca airport to see him off the day that the hospital in Puno sent him to Arequipa for an emergency operation. Sadly, he died during the operation. I was grateful that the parish could send both his wife Hilda and his brother Estanislao to accompany him to Arequipa. You will recall how important Marcos was during my first days in the Prelature of Juli back in 1985 when I worked with him on the team he led for the formation of lay leaders in the farming communities. Marcos had been a good friend, and he was an impressive lay leader for the Church. His death came as a shock to us all. We gave him a great send off in Chucuito. Bishop Raimondo who had been named in 1989 the new Bishop of the Prelature of Juli came to celebrate the funeral Mass, and I eulogized him in the homily. We later named the parish hall in Chucuito in his memory.

On my return from the sabbatical year I was planning to suggest to the Chucuito parish team that Marcos become the lay administrator of the Chucuito parish. That would have freed me up to dedicate more time to the formation team for the training of lay religion teachers in the state schools (ODEC). That was the ministry I enjoyed most and the one where I felt I could make better use of my teaching talents. The idea died with the death of Marcos. Our plans are not always God's plans. However, something positive did come of his death.

Marcos' younger brother Estanislao Cruz, who had been the night watchman in the historic old parish church for years, was invited to join the parish team. He became very involved in preparing people to receive the Sacraments in the farming communities of the parish. Over the years Estanislao grew as a person. He was elected the coordinator of the Chucuito parish team in 1995 and accompanied me all during my years as pastor in Chucuito parish until 2001 when Diego replaced me. More recently, in 2012 Estanislao was elected mayor of the district and town of Chucuito. Congratulations, Estanislao. Thank you for your friendship and our ministry together.

Estanislao began a whole new approach to preparation for the Sacraments in the farming communities on the distant peninsula and the upper regions of the parish. He would travel to them with a team each week and offer the sacramental preparation there on location. Diego or I would follow afterwards to celebrate the Sacraments, especially First Communion, Confirmation and Marriage. Estanislao also accompanied the Aymaran religious lay leaders who had been formed previously by his brother Marcos and who normally would celebrate the sacrament of Baptism. Estanislao and his lay team entered the communities easily because they spoke the Aymaran language and were well-known to the people. Through them the parish attained a greater presence in those communities.

The composition of the parish team changed during these years, too. Having gotten past the terrorism threat that ended with the capture of its leader Abimael Guzman in September 1992, many Church people were now having pastoral difficulties with Bishop Raimundo Reveredo. Several of the Sisters who previously had been on the team left the prelature. Sisters Martha Larson, Debora Watson, Jaruko Doi, and Marisa Hanahoe, who had joined the team in 1992, all left. Holy Cross Jim Phalan was transferred by the district superior Bud Colgan to our house of formation in Canto Grande.

The Sisters of Holy Cross who had been ministering in the parish in Acora decided to move their community residence to the farming community of Mocachi which was located midway between the Acora and Chucuito parishes. They asked to become members of the Chucuito parish team in 1994. Holy Cross Sisters Frances Savoie, Blanche Lemarre, Raquel Laramie, and Marie Pilon all began to work with the Chucuito team. Thank you, Sisters, for all those years of collaborative ministry.

I never wanted to be a parish priest. I joined Holy Cross because of its unique founding gift, that its members were educators in the faith. However, in Peru because of the dire need for parish priests, I always wound up performing much of that function. I did not particularly care for it, and I avoided it when I could. I was much more interested in the ODEC team, and so gave it much more time and energy. I am grateful to the many lay people and religious Sisters who kept the parish going so well.

Fortunately, being pastor was less of a burden in the prelature because we functioned in a more circular fashion with parish pastoral teams. To me that was a great model for Church, more community-oriented than top-down. Hopefully the Church will move increasingly towards the community-based decision-making style of leadership that I experienced during those years in Peru. Lord, thank you for my years in this life-giving, circular Church where all peoples' gifts are cherished and used.

Thank you, Diego, for the years we shared together in community and ministry in the Chucuito parish where we alternated as pastor. Thank you for your friendship and support and respect. We have different personalities, but we managed to honor one another and our individual gifts and differences during all those years.

I mentioned in the last chapter that during my sabbatical year I visited our new sister parish of St. Hedwig in

Karlsruhe, Germany, on my way to the renewal program in Ireland. The Chucuito parish team in 1991 had requested membership in the Partnerschaft program of sister parishes between Peru and the Diocese of Freiburg in Germany. Before I left on my sabbatical, Chucuito parish had been accepted by the St. Hedwig parish. So, I stopped for a few days to visit the pastor Bruno Hill and the parish team there, and was received very graciously. Bruno Hill came to visit Chucuito parish in September 1994 with Brigitte Beer, the coordinator of their One World parish committee. They had the opportunity to see the needs of the Chucuito parish as we got to know one another better.

In June 1995 they invited me with Estanislao who by then was our parish team coordinator to visit their parish in Germany. We made a whirlwind two-week trip to the parish in Karlsruhe and shared a lot with the people there. On our way back, Estanislao and I visited the Masters family in England of whom I spoke in the last chapter. Then in 1996 Brigitte, with Hermann her husband, came for a two-week visit to Chucuito. In subsequent years, others of the parish team, Sister Francis and Aymaran Mercy Sister Carmen Rosa Callomamani and Holy Cross Sister Blanche Lemarre, as well as layman Roberto Ari, also went to visit the parish in Germany. We had very good relations with the German parish, exchanging news through letters and reinforcing our connection through these visits by parish team members.

The St. Hedwig parish helped the Chucuito parish financially, especially funding our January parish summer school programs each year. It also contributed to the construction of a parish library and youth center, and a parish volley ball court. Thank you, Bruno and Brigitte and all the others in the Karlsruhe parish for your friendship, generosity and solidarity with us all those years. Our friendship endures to today. I know that they continue to help the projects of the Sisters of Holy Cross in Peru, and in particular the health mission of Sister Marie Pilon in Mocachi.

ODEC

In 1994 when I returned from my sabbatical year to the ODEC team, there were some changes on it, as well. Sister Frances had come back from Canada and the United States where she had gone to recover from the trauma of the Aeroperú plane crash in 1988 at the Juliaca airport. At the same time Dominican Sister Maria Gabriela from Yunguyo was having health problems due to the altitude, and her community wanted her to go down to Lima to work. St. Joseph Sister Carmen Carrion who lived with her community in Moho on the northern side of Lake Titicaca had joined the ODEC team back in 1991 when it needed someone living in that area of the prelature, since there was a six- to eight-hour ride between Chucuito and Moho. Rodolfo (Rudi) Cutipa had grown into his job during my absence, so he was taking on a lot more of the administrative work outside the office, as well as helping with the youth group in the Chucuito parish. We decided to hire another person to be secretary in the office in Chucuito, so that Rudi would have more time for his work outside the office, visiting religion teachers, school principals and other educational authorities.

Each year the ODEC team would prioritize what we wanted to do with the teachers. One year it might be workshops with the grade school teachers, then other years workshops with the high school teachers. One year we prepared a new high school/grade school curriculum and updated programs for students and teachers.

The primary school workshops required considerable traveling, since the prelature was very extensive and many of the farming communities were not located near main roads. As I described earlier, a difficulty was that the education authorities often would not give their respective permissions for the teachers to attend the workshops, or they would not tell the teachers about them. It could be quite frustrating. We would travel three or four hours over bumpy dirt roads, and when we arrived we would find no one there to greet us. Other times it worked out well, and the teachers were happy and grateful to see us. Often, they would invite us to lunch afterward and tell us that we were the first education people to come to visit their schools and that they wanted us to return as soon as possible because they had learned so much. It was very reassuring to hear things like that. Thank you, grade school teachers.

We organized two workshops for the high school teachers each year, usually near Chucuito which was the most centrally located town in the prelature. For three consecutive years, we invited the Pastoral Bible lay team of women from Chimbote, which had been founded by Holy

Cross priest Gerry Barmasse. They had developed a number of very good, easy to understand Bible formation programs with a very active, dynamic methodology. The lay teachers loved these five-day Bible workshops, and about two hundred usually participated. These events boosted our morale, too; our influence was apparent. I always felt that an important factor of these workshops was that the lay teachers could see lay people and especially lay women just like themselves doing a great job of evangelization without a priest or Sister telling them what to do. I hoped that would inspire them in their ministry as lay religious educators in the Peruvian public school system. Thank you especially to Teresa and Alita, who usually came to run these workshops, for your friendship and witness to how lay people can minister in the Church.

We also included in these workshops courses in education methodology. We wanted the lay teachers not only to teach doctrine or prayers, but also to learn to relate the Scriptures to the cultural, political, and social realities in which the students were living. We taught them to use the Christian social action methodology of "*See* the reality, *Reflect* on it using the Bible, *Act* to better the reality, and then *Celebrate* that we are participating in making a better world." This was the same methodology that social action groups like the Young Christian Students (JEC), the Young Christian Workers (JOC), the Young Rural Christian Workers (JARC) and the Adult Christian Workers (MTC) used in their meetings.

I have mentioned earlier that the religion teacher training team (ODEC) and the Chucuito parish team functioned financially with the help of grants received from Adveniat in Germany. They were aided by yearly grants from The Koch Foundation in Gainesville, Florida, as well. Both were organized to financially help Church programs for lay leadership. They gave us financial help annually with the approval of the local bishop. Other help for the religion teacher training team (ODEC) continued to come from Jim and Marcie Wilson's monthly donation. It was thanks to these gifts that I expanded the teacher training ministry (ODEC) during all those years. Thank you to all.

One year our teacher training for lay religion teachers team (ODEC) joined together with the other ODEC teams from Ayaviri, Sicuani and Puno in the South Andes region to create new programs for religious education in the public high school system. We wanted the programs to reflect the lived reality of the Andean people. It was for me another important experience of collaboration. Each one of the teacher training teams took one of the five-year programs to develop. Our team from the Prelature of Juli which was the largest, undertook the programs for two of the years. When each team had prepared its assigned program, we all met to fine-tune them until we all were satisfied with all of them. I must say the result was impressive. When we presented the final product to our four bishops, they readily approved it.

I might add here that despite the difficulties that many in the Prelature felt with Raimundo Reveredo our Juli bishop, he was a strong supporter of our teacher training team (ODEC). He sometimes accompanied us when we had problems with the education authorities, and he would sit there with us and say to the authorities that he had come to support his team because "what they want I want!" He was our great defender, and we usually got what we needed.

When Bishop Raimundo came to speak with the high school religion teachers during their workshops, he always told them and us that for him, after the seminary our training team for lay religion teachers was the most important ministry in his prelature. He was very good listening to the teachers. He would tell them that he had come to hear what they had to say rather than to give a talk. He wanted to answer their questions and respond to their problems. Thank you, Bishop Raimundo Reveredo. You encouraged our ODEC team several times when we were most in need of it and when we were ready to give up on administrative difficulties.

Another example of Bishop Raimundo's great commitment to the prelature occurred when the Shining Path terrorist group entered one of the towns and killed several of the town's local civil authorities, including the mayor. Bishop Raimundo traveled immediately to the town to offer help, not concerned about his own personal safety.

VOCATION MINISTRY

As I mentioned earlier, I was named national vocation director for Holy Cross from 1985 to 1988, and then again in 1991 when Bud Colgan was re-elected district superior. (Bud was the first Holy Cross district superior

1976-1980.) In 1994 Bud called on me once again to be Director of Vocations for the district, as well as in charge locally in the Puno area. Jorge Mallea was appointed to be in charge in Lima. Various members of the Congregation were chosen to handle vocations in the Chimbote area, depending on the changing yearly assignments there. We had a good vocation ministry team, made more effective by our collaboration with the two congregations of Holy Cross Sisters who had been with us in the three Peruvian areas since 1987. We organized vocation encounters together with the Sisters, and both the young men and the young women who participated seemed to find this collaboration a plus for Holy Cross.

At the end of each year we invited young men in our areas interested in becoming postulants in the Congregation to participate in a retreat in Lima organized by the Peruvian Conference for Religious. That retreat allowed the three of us on the vocation team to get to know each of the candidates. Afterwards we met together, decided which of the group we thought were ready for the postulant program, and sent those names to the district superior and his council for approval. We felt this selection system worked well for us. We usually had about six men accepted as postulants each year, most of them usually poor Aymaran youth from the Puno area where I lived. We developed a wall calendar with photos of us and our ministries and contact information. Later we added book-size calendars. We did not have a large budget, so we were limited.

Beginning in 1996, however, some of the Peruvians who had entered during those years and who were now studying in Chile where there were no Holy Cross Sisters working, began to request that our Peruvian vocation material be exclusively about the men as it was in Chile. This exclusion of the Holy Cross women bothered me.

Some in Holy Cross began to question the academic quality of the young men joining up, saying that we should not be accepting candidates from low-income families because they considered them not well enough educated. They felt that we should look for vocations to Holy Cross only from the better-educated, higher social classes with better family backgrounds. However, all our ministries were with the poor! How were we to tap these upper social classes?

Increasingly I found myself in so much disagreement with those attitudes that leading the vocation ministry for the Peru district became a burden, rather than the joy it had been for me previously. It seemed to me that many, or at least the most vocal, in the community were unhappy with my leadership.

I began to have a repeating dream that I had left a suitcase in the Lima airport. When I shared the dream with Sister Frances, she thought it might mean that I needed to drop whatever in my life was burdening me. I realized immediately that it was the vocation ministry. So, in 1995 I had a long conversation with district superior Bud Colgan about my feelings, telling him I felt a lack of support from many in the Holy Cross community, and I asked him to relieve me of being district vocation director. I was willing to continue vocation work in Puno with the Sisters there.

Bud felt that I was being overly sensitive to the opinions of others and asked me to reconsider, but I said that I thought that Jorge Mallea, who was the member of the vocation team in Lima, could do the job very well. He even lived and worked in Canto Grande. Bud finally approved Jorge as the new district vocation director. I remained on the team with Jorge, together with a Peruvian from the Chimbote area. We continued to attract five or six candidates for the postulant program each year, right to the year 2000 when a new vocation team was named. Jorge recently reminded me that the first six professed Peruvians in the Peru district all joined Holy Cross during our time as the vocation directors in the district. Thank you, Jorge! I enjoyed working with you all those years. I also enjoyed the vocation ministry in Puno with the Holy Cross Sisters. Thank you, Holy Cross women.

NEW WINDS IN HOLY CROSS

Bud Colgan had a difficult re-election as district superior in the 1997 chapter of the Holy Cross District of Peru. It seemed that some of the young Peruvians who had a vote, along with others, wanted a change of leadership. I also thought a change would be good, since Bud had been superior since 1991. The other candidate was Bill Persia who was just beginning a sabbatical year in New York. I would have liked Bill to be superior, but I did not want to make him give up his sabbatical year which he had just begun with studies at Fordham University in New York City; so I voted for Bud. After the election, Bud proposed that in the next election only two Peruvians in temporary vows be allowed to vote. Though many of us were against that proposal, it passed by a slight majority. For some reason after that election, Bud always seemed to think that I was behind his difficult re-election. It may be because Diego and I in Chucuito often were outspoken and critical of some things in the district under his leadership.

A few years before, in 1995, Dave Farrell had returned to Peru, to Canto Grande, after having been out of the country for twenty years. He had left in 1974 to be assistant district superior in Chile following the Pinochet military coup. After six years in Chile he went to England for further studies, and then engaged in social work in Central America. In 1986 he was asked by Joe Callahan the Eastern Province provincial superior to be the assistant provincial, and then in the chapter of 1988 he was elected provincial superior of the Eastern Province until 1994. In late 1995, after a year with Holy Cross Family Ministries in the United States, he decided to return to Peru.

During the district chapter of 1997, Dave and Bud proposed to institute Holy Cross Family Ministries in Peru. It was a new Holy Cross initiative, an offshoot of Family Rosary founded by Holy Cross Patrick Peyton in the 1940's in Albany, New York. Family Ministries attempted to update Family Rosary by dealing with broader family life issues. In Peru it also could provide North American-level salaries to some of the Religious, and so would bring considerable financial assistance with it.

Dave, who recently had been made pastor of the Canto Grande parish in Lima, was now named by Bud also to be the director of this newly founded Institute of Family Ministries based in Canto Grande. By that time, Canto Grande had grown into a very big parish covering an extensive area with a population of about 250,000. The parish consisted of nineteen chapels, each large enough to be a parish here in the United States. The Fe y Alegría school there had grown to more than 2,000 students in both grade and high school. There was a school for handicapped children called Yancana Huasi (House of Work) founded by Dan Panchot. So, Holy Cross now had several large institutions located in the Canto Grande area.

I offered to participate in Chucuito in this new Family Ministries Institute by developing two projects, one a parish project led by Holy Cross Sister Blanche Lemarre, and the other, an ODEC project with Rudi and me doing workshops in the public schools. Both dealt with education around family issues, such as violence, self-esteem, communication difficulties and gender issues in the Andean family. Some of the religion teachers in the public school system were very enthused about the workshops, and they helped us to be invited into their schools. The workshops were popular and successful. There was a lot of interest in those years, particularly regarding problems of self-esteem and family violence. We received many invitations from the public schools.

In 1997 Al Mahoney arrived to join Diego and me in the Chucuito parish. Al, who was from the English-Canadian province of Holy Cross, had worked previously in Chiapas, Mexico, for twenty years before he was expelled by the Mexican government in 1993. The government did not want foreign-born clergy ministering in that area any longer, because there was so much political unrest there. Along with other things he undertook, Al began to help Sister Blanche with her Family Ministries project, organizing small Andean family Christian community workshops in the Chucuito parish. The Family Ministries brought a lot of new activity to both the Chucuito parish and to the religion teachers training team (ODEC) during those years.

ODEC AND THE PRELATURE

In June 1999 Raimundo Reveredo the Bishop of Juli retired because of health issues. The new administrator named provisionally to lead the Prelature of Juli was diocesan Aymaran priest Pedro Siguayro. I always considered Pedro a friend, since the time I arrived in the prelature in 1985, even though during prelature assemblies he often became very critical of Religious communities because he claimed we "robbed the prelature of leadership people."

The day after Raimundo resigned Pedro told me that the Human Rights Solidarity Team in the prelature wanted to have a meeting with me. He did not tell me what it was about. When I went to the meeting the following day, I discovered that Pedro had invited the entire ODEC team except Rudi Cutipa. Pedro was initiating an investigation into the ODEC-JULI team, claiming there were serious complaints and accusations by some of the lay religion teachers as well as by some of the priests, Sisters and lay leaders of the prelature parishes against Rudi, who was, under my direction, the lay administrator of ODEC.

Rudi recently had separated from his wife Marisol, and she was going about the prelature complaining about him. I was godfather of their marriage back in 1989, and I had been present at many of their reconciliations during the years, so I knew the complexities of their marital relationship. I personally felt that Rudi's marital relationship should not be confused with his performance at his job. Some in the prelature seemed to think differently.

At the meeting the members of the Human Rights Solidarity team informed me that some of the lay religion teachers had verbally accused Rudi of corruption, of asking for and accepting bribe money from them when they wished to get a teaching assignment to a particular school. I had personally seen no indication of that, but I agreed to a full investigation of the accusations. I told them that I would collaborate fully with them in any way that might be helpful, and would accept their findings and take what action they recommended. However, I also told them that I was disappointed that the only person on the religion teacher training team (ODEC) who had not been invited to this first meeting was Rudi, the one being accused. I felt that he had a right to be at the meeting and that his side of the story should be heard by them.

At first the names of the teachers making the accusations were not revealed to me. I was told that they had a right to anonymity. How was I, the director of the team, to judge what was going on unless I knew who was involved? I knew that like all of us Rudi had some personality traits and weaknesses that bothered some of the people in the prelature. He could be haughty, sometimes putting on airs of superiority; but I also thought that he was a good, hard-working, and dedicated member of ODEC, trying to do his best in often very difficult situations with the educational and school authorities.

I had never seen or personally heard of any instance of corruption or misuse by Rudi of his authority. It also did not make sense that teachers would give money to Rudi, since all the appointments for teaching jobs in all the schools had to be approved personally by me after a meeting of the entire team. I suspected that there might be some jealousy or anger against him by those who had not been given jobs, especially by friends or family members of the prelature Religious and lay leaders. I myself was the object of some of those verbal or written attacks when in the past I would not give positions to people who were not certified teachers and who had no preparation for teaching religious education in the public school system, even if they had strong letters of recommendation from a priest, Sister or lay leader in the prelature. So, I felt that the discontent might lie more with me than with Rudi, and that people in the prelature might find it easier to attack my policies through Rudi than by directly attacking me.

The Human Rights team carried out the investigation over several months. They never called Rudi to talk with him directly. During the investigation, they could find no real proof of anything improper. The teachers who were accusing Rudi would not put in writing their accusations and would not meet with the investigating team. I finally discovered through the grape vine who some of the teachers were who had made the accusations. I knew these teachers from my own experience with them, and I knew in my heart that most of them were lying, because I had had problems before with the same people myself. The conclusion reached after two months of investigation was that there was no clear proof against Rudi, but that the Human Rights Solidarity team still felt that there were some indications of guilt. Pedro still wanted Rudi out of the job. I told Pedro that I would not fire Rudi since there was no proof of wrongdoing, but that he, as administrator of the Prelature and my actual superior in this case, could fire Rudi himself if he wanted to. However, for some reason Pedro did not fire him then and there.

Afterwards I and the rest of the lay religion teachers training team (ODEC) spoke with Rudi about curtailing some of his personal ways that might be making some waves in the prelature. Then we set down new internal regulations to avoid any future misunderstanding among the teachers, establishing a clear point system for the conditions necessary for obtaining religion teaching positions.

I was deeply saddened by the fact that some of the priests and Sisters and committed lay people in the prelature were involved in these accusations. I thank God for my Holy Cross local community composed at that time of Al Mahoney, Diego Irarrázaval and Fidel Ticona, and for the Holy Cross Sisters, all of whom were a great support to me, giving me good advice during that difficult period.

Fidel Ticona, a young Aymaran from Ilave who had joined the community in 1990 and was ordained deacon in 1999, was now living and working in the Juli prelature with us. Besides helping out with the Chucuito parish ministry, especially with the youth and women's groups and Family Ministries, Fidel worked with Victor Maqque, the head of the pastoral team at the University in Puno. Thank you, Fidel, for choosing to be with us in Chucuito.

Having four Holy Cross Religious, Diego, Al, Fidel and me, living together made community life more enjoyable for me. Our house, rented since 1985 on the hill in Cusipata overlooking Lake Titicaca, was small, but it was great, simple country-living. Thank you, Sofia, for renting us your home for so many years.

MY PERUVIAN FAMILY

During my many years in Peru I accepted several times to be godfather at baptisms and at marriages. By becoming a godfather at baptism, I assumed the role of *padrino*, "second father," to my godchild and *compadre*, "co-parent," with the child's parents. As was the Peruvian custom, my godchild was expected to respect me always, visit me often, and help me when I needed. As godfather, I was expected to care for my godchild spiritually, and financially when possible. For me, this was a very serious responsibility that I did not want to accept lightly, since I was not Peruvian or Aymaran, and I did not know how long I would be in Peru. Also, as a Religious I did not have financial resources at my disposal to help a godchild.

A godfather in marriage carried similar responsibility. As godfather, I became a second parent to the married couple. When they had marital problems, they came to me as their godfather rather than to their own birth parents. In both cases I became part of their extended family.

At the beginning of my time in Peru back in 1968 I had decided not to accept any of these invitations, because I felt that my circumstances prevented me from assuming the cultural and economic responsibilities that were expected of a godfather. I changed my mind in 1979 when my friend Felipe Calderon, who had lived together with his brother Pablo in our house in Cartavio, asked me in 1978 to celebrate his marriage in Callao near Lima in the navy chapel, and then later asked me to be his *compadre*, godfather, to his first son Isaac Pedro born in 1979. I accepted because of the long friendship that we had. When I traveled to Lima after Felipe moved there in 1972, I visited him often, and we stayed close friends. I never regretted that decision. Ever since, Felipe and his wife Mena have been my extended family in Peru. Thank you, Felipe and Mena, for inviting me into your family. I could not have asked for a better one.

Ten years later I had a similar experience with Juan Mallea in Chucuito. He is the brother of Holy Cross priest Jorge Mallea. One day when I met Juan in his home town of Juli, I told him about a position open to teach Aymara with Diego in the Aymara Institute (IDEA). He went to Diego, applied for the job, and eventually got it. He was so happy. He rented a room in Chucuito during the week, going home to his family in Cutina Capilla, a farming community near Juli, on weekends. He used to come to eat frequently with Diego and me and sometimes spent the night in our house in Cusipata. He later moved his family to Chucuito. One evening he asked me to be *compadre*, godfather for his recently born son Daniel. I said I would think about it, but I really was planning to say no. Then a few months later I had the auto accident I described earlier, and Juan was the person who probably saved my life. After that I said yes to him and his wife Isabel, and I am glad that I did. Juan and Isabel have been great *compadres*. I feel I am part of their family. Juan and Isabel, thank you.

Shortly after that my friend from my days in Chimbote, Goyo Pastor and his wife Francie asked me to be *compadre*, godfather of their two sons, Lucho who is mentally handicapped, and Junior Teófilo. Since I had known Goyo for so many years I accepted. Maria Jose Masters from England became *comadre*, godmother with me for Junior, and Santos Garcia was *comadre* for Luchito. From the beginning, I tried to insist that at least the godmother be a Peruvian just in case I did not stay in Peru, but I lost that battle with Junior. Thank you, Goyo and Francie, for being my family in Chimbote. And may you, Francie, rest in peace.

Around 1990 Estanislao Cruz and his wife Leonor asked me to be godfather to their son Willie, who is pictured with me on the cover of this book. Once again, I accepted, since I had known them for five years. Then Juan Anchapuri, Juan Mallea's brother-in-law, and his wife Carmen Rosa Barrientos asked me to be godfather to their daughter Vanessa. Juan had been a candidate for Holy Cross in 1990 and Carmen was the daughter of my good friends Victor and Jacoba Barrientos. So, once again I accepted. And finally Salvador Asqui and his wife Candi invited me to be godfather to their son Nilto. I accepted once again because Salvador was the brother of the deceased Marcos Asqui, and Estanislao Cruz was his younger brother. So thank you, Estanislao and Leonor, Juan and Carmen and Salvador and Candi, for inviting me into your families.

While I was living in Chimbote, I also accepted the invitation to be godfather (second parent) in the marriage of Juan Garcia and his wife Pancha Vega. They wanted a Catholic wedding to bless their civil marriage of twenty-five years. With Holy Cross Sister Patti Dieranger I agreed to their request inasmuch as the ceremony would be a simple, almost private celebration in La Primavera chapel in Esperanza. Thank you, Juan and Pancha, for that invitation.

Later in Chucuito in 1988 I accepted to be godfather to the marriage of Rudi Cutipa, who worked with me on the teacher training team (ODEC), and Marisol. I would not have accepted if doing so had entailed all the traditional expense that a godfather usually incurred with the three-day cultural celebration in the Aymaran tradition. However, Rudi and Marisol were already living together and had a child and wanted to get married in a simple, quiet ceremony, since neither of their families were very keen on the marriage. After much thought, I finally acquiesced, together with Holy Cross Sister Lia Finnerty as godmother. My *compadres* Felipe and Mena came up from Lima, as well as my *compadres* Goyo and Francie from Chimbote for this celebration. They both had been invited to be godparents for Rudi and Marisol's first child Heidi. It was a joyful three-day celebration of friendship. A few years later in 1994 I accepted, almost at the last minute, to be godfather to Rudi and Marisol's son Junior, together with Holy Cross Sister Frances Savoie as the godmother. Sadly, their marriage broke up in 1998. Thank you, Rudi and Marisol, for that invitation into your extended family during your years together.

My last acceptance was in 1997 when my good friend Wilber Mamani Cotillo and his wife Juana asked me to be godfather to their marriage. I had known Wilber since my arrival in Chucuito in 1985 when he joined the youth group there and began to help me in ODEC. We have been very good friends all these years. They, too, were going to have a simple family celebration of their marriage, so I accepted once again. Thank you, Wilber and Juana, for inviting me into your family and for your friendship all this time.

In the year 2000 I decided to close my godfather book because of my age, even though there were some invitations afterward like that of Percy Malaga and his wife Marlene, the sister of Wilber, that I was very tempted to accept. Sorry about that, Percy and Marlene.

So, this is my great extended family in Peru. I am happy with all of them and proud of each one of them. Most of my godchildren by Baptism are now married and have their own children. I have tried my best to be a good godfather, and I believe that I have your love and respect, and that is enough for me.

THE NEW CENTURY

For years, my good friend Jorge Mallea and I would take vacations together, usually right after Christmas when Jorge came to visit his family in Cutina Capilla in Juli. To welcome the New Year 2000, we decided to travel down to Tacna and then on to Arica, Chile. We went by Tacna because I wanted to speak with the bishop there, Hugo Garaycoa, who was one of the few progressive bishops still left in Peru. I wanted to know if he would be interested in having someone like me, and perhaps some others of the Holy Cross community, in his diocese in the future. It was a moment in time when I was not sure that I wanted to remain working in the Juli prelature, even though I loved the Aymaran people. I was feeling a lot of tension from the difficulties that the teacher training team (ODEC) was having with the temporary administrator, Pedro Siguayro and some of the other, younger diocesan priests. I was angry about accusations brought against the ODEC team by Pedro's new administration, that I considered unjust and without foundation. I planned, therefore, to plant the seed at the Holy Cross community district chapter in February 2000 for the possibility of a new mission in Tacna.

My idea at the time was that Holy Cross might form two local communities in the region, the one already established in Chucuito along with a new one in Tacna, each with two members. These in turn would constitute a regional community of four that could gather together for community time every month or two for a few days. A new paved road between Tacna and Puno shortened the usual twelve-hour bus trip to eight hours. Additionally, the Holy Cross Sisters were about to open a new mission in Tacna in March 2000, and Al Mahoney and I thought that a Holy Cross mission for the men in Tacna would be a good way to continue to collaborate with them. Usually the Sisters followed the Holy Cross men, so this would be the reverse for a change.

The meeting with Bishop Hugo was very informative, and he seemed enthused about the possibility of Holy Cross coming to his diocese in the future. Jorge and I also visited with the Maryknoll Sisters and priests working in Tacna, and with my good friends ever since Cartavio days, Sisters Zelma and Kay, who were now working in Ilo in the diocese of Tacna. Then Jorge and I went over to Arica to bring in the New Year 2000! There were three celebrations there, each corresponding to the time zones in Bolivia, Peru and Chile.

The year 2000 began with a month-long summer pastoral program in the parish in Acora involving all the Peruvian men and women in Holy Cross formation. It was organized principally by Fidel and Al, since Diego and I were teaching as usual at the ESER in Puno during that month of January. Then in early February practically all the Peruvian members of Holy Cross, together with most of the Holy Cross community from Canto Grande and Chimbote attended the joyful three-day celebration of the ordination to the priesthood of Aymaran Fidel Ticona. Fidel invited me to be his *padrino* (godfather) at his ordination, as Jorge Mallea had done. Thank you, Fidel, for your friendship all these years.

At the Holy Cross district chapter held in Lima in February 2000, Al Mahoney and I suggested that the district look at the possibility of opening a new mission in Tacna with the Holy Cross Sisters. After discussion, the members of the Chapter voted to begin a search for a new place of ministry, looking especially at Tacna where there was the progressive Bishop Hugo Garaycoa and where the Holy Cross Sisters were about to open a new mission.

This was good news. I was experiencing so much tension with Pedro and a few others in the Prelature of Juli that I felt an urgency to move on elsewhere. I reached the point even of considering returning to the United States, although I loved Peru with all my heart. Fortunately my good friend Fred Serraino, who had just arrived back in Peru in 1998, was elected district superior at the end of 1999. With his encouragement and support I decided to go on a mini-sabbatical, a thirty-day retreat, something I had never done before.

In June 2000, thanks to Fred, I left for the United States for such a retreat at Eastern Point Jesuit Retreat House in Gloucester, Massachusetts. It would be for me another pivotal, personal, spiritual experience of God's guiding hand in my life journey.

8. CHUCUITO (PUNO) 2000 - 2004

My thirty-day retreat took place during the month of
July 2000 at the Eastern Point Jesuit Retreat House in
Gloucester, Massachusetts. Jesuit priest Frank Belcher
was my spiritual guide. I went into the retreat pretty
much convinced that it was time for me to leave the mission in the Prelature of Juli to move on to something new.
I was still feeling so much tension with Pedro, the prelature administrator, and with my godchildren by marriage
Rudi and Marisol Cutipa, who had separated in October
1998 after many years of marital problems. Their separa-
tion had created strain not only between the ODEC team
and some in the prelature of Juli, but also between some of
my other friendships in Chucuito.

During the course of the retreat, I had a strange experience on the tenth day when we had a half-day off. I
rode the train to Boston that afternoon with Doug Perlitz,
a layman on the retreat who worked with street children
in Haiti. We each wanted to spend the day mostly alone,
but we planned to meet later in the evening for dinner
together before returning to Gloucester. I had no more
than reached the city when suddenly I experienced a panic
attack. I grew dizzy, nauseous and sick. There was nowhere for me to go, and it would be several hours before
the next train back to the retreat house. I wandered
around Boston Common all afternoon fretting and anx-

ious, then took the first train possible back to Gloucester. As soon as I got into my car I had left at the Gloucester train station, the panic attack subsided completely. It is very difficult for me to explain this experience which I interpreted as a sign from God. I like to control everything and everybody in my life, and I felt that God was telling me that He is in control and that I need not worry. I could trust Him. I could surrender control to Him.

That is the issue I had been dealing with during the first ten days of the retreat, that I wanted to be in control of my life! I wanted to control the lives of others, too. That experience was foundational for me to see that I am in God's hands like it or not, and that God is my friend and will take good care of me through it all, no matter what.

I was very happy that we had three days at the end of the retreat to share among the thirty of us there. We all had had strange, spiritual experiences. I was enthused to return to my life in Chucuito and to continue forward, because I knew now that God was leading, guiding, and supporting me through all the difficulties there. God's message to me was to go back to ministry in Chucuito and to trust that He was with me through it all! Thank you, Jesuit Frank Belcher, my spiritual director. You understood me from the start, having had your own mission experience in Iraq. You guided me so well during those thirty days. May you rest in peace.

I returned to Peru in August 2000 after some time in the United States visiting my family, the Holy Cross community, and friends. My British friends, Chris and

Moira Mann, who had visited me back in 1996 while I was in the United States on vacation from Peru, came to see me again. I have known Chris since the summer of 1967 when I worked as a deacon in his parish in Aldershot, England. We stayed in touch all those years. He came to Albany in 1981 and stayed with my father and me for a month, and I visited him during my 1993 sabbatical year. Thank you, Chris and Moira, for your long friendship.

ODEC

On returning to my work on the teacher training team (ODEC) in September 2000, I immediately encountered a new conflict between the diocesan administrator Pedro Siguayro and Rudi Cutipa. The diocesan administrator was furious with Rudi, because while I was in the United States an article had appeared in the Puno newspaper criticizing the Juli Prelature for the way it was assigning the lay religion teachers for the teaching positions in the state schools. As I mentioned earlier, the ODEC team had recently established a strict point-system to evaluate the teachers asking for jobs. On the day the educational authorities were assigning teaching positions in a public forum, a teacher without the necessary points, and who knew it, accepted a position to which she had no right. When Rudi showed up with a teacher with the necessary ranking who was being assigned to that school by the ODEC, he discovered what had happened; so he insisted that the job be given to the teacher with the correct ranking who had just arrived with him. The Puno newspaper had printed the ensuing verbal exchange that occurred between Rudi, the teachers involved, and the educational authorities. Pedro was angry at what he considered bad press for the Church. I could not find any fault in what Rudi had done. He had reacted just as I would have. He insisted on justice being done for the teacher with the correct ranking. The diocesan administrator could see it only as a scandal for the Church!

Shortly afterwards Pedro called a meeting of our religion teacher training team (ODEC) and told me in front of everyone that I had to fire Rudi. I told him that in conscience I could not do it. So finally, Pedro fired Rudi in front of us all. I felt that if Rudi was considered unjust in his actions, then I as his supervisor was guilty, too. So, I immediately offered my resignation to Pedro, to be effective in April 2001, when I would complete thirty years of service to the Peruvian educational system and would be eligible for a small pension from the Peruvian government.

Holy Cross Sister Frances Savoie also offered her resignation. She was tired of the internal bickering and wanted the more peaceful task of helping Sister Blanche with the new Family Institute project in the Chucuito parish. Saint Joseph Sister Carmen Carrion, the other team member from Moho, told Pedro that she would like to stay on and continue with the new teacher training team, but the administrator did not encourage her or respond with any affirmative answer, which deeply disappointed her. Sadly, she took sick a month later, was diagnosed with pancreatic cancer, and was dead within the year. May she rest in peace. She was a great lady! Thank you, Sisters Carmen and Frances, for all your support, and for our many years of ministry together! They were great years!

So, in April 2001 the end of an era came for my work with the lay religion teacher training team (ODEC) which I had founded for the Prelature of Juli back in 1986. Believe it or not, I felt relieved and glad to end that ministry. I thought I would miss it, but I did not.

THE HOLY CROSS FAMILY INSTITUTE

After the meeting with Pedro, I became involved almost immediately in advancing the Family Institute workshops which we had begun as part of ODEC in 1997. Since Rudi had obtained a permanent teaching position with the education authorities back in 1996 thanks to Bishop Raimundo, and he was assigned to education work in another area of Puno, I formed a new team for the Family Institute project. In place of Rudi I invited my godson Wilber Mamani Cotillo together with his brother-in-law Percy Malaga to participate. They were great to work with, because they were full of energy and creative ideas. We found so much to do so quickly that I also invited Marlene Cespedes, wife of Percy and sister of Wilber, to join us. Marlene, a social worker, helped us with the feminine side of the family violence issues. So, new life for me grew out of all the previous pain and infighting.

This new team created many workshops dealing with the issues of family violence and self-esteem during those years. Some were organized close to Chucuito, and others were provided in more distant places like La Paz in Bolivia, and Tacna and Ilo on the southern coast of Peru, and Puerto Maldonado in the Peruvian jungle. We also organized workshops to help men look at their childhood wounds and discover the cultural, social and religious constraints put on them, just as often happens with women. I felt that both sexes needed liberation. Since there were many women's groups in the prelature already helping women, I felt that we needed to dedicate more time to the men who often could not understand the new stance of women in Andean culture.

In 2001 when Alfredo Hernandez and Cesar Ramos, two of the young Holy Cross Religious in formation, were spending a pastoral year in Chimbote, they told me about an evangelical Christian group in Lima that had a school approved by the government for training and certifying family counselors. Students could do the studies from home, and both Alfredo and Cesar were at that time enrolled in this family counseling program with a study group in Chimbote. So, my next time in Lima I went to visit the headquarters of the family counseling school there. I thought that our Family Institute team could easily organize a study program in Chucuito just like the one existing in Chimbote. The directors of the school Luis Guizada and his wife Pilar Cuadros were enthusiastic about the possibility.

After talking over this program with the new team in Chucuito, we decided that we would launch the school right away in June 2001. We announced the news on the radio, and soon to our surprise we had more than two hundred people signed up for the family counseling school program. This was a much larger number of students than we had anticipated, so we needed to recruit more people to run the smaller study groups which were an essential part of the program.

The students each received a text book, which they studied at home during the week. Then once a week they met in small groups of about twenty to share together what they had learned and to hand in their weekly exam. When they finished the one-year program, they received an official certificate awarded by the government. This certificate allowed them to work as family counselors or to open their own counseling service. It was a very useful document for teachers, police, healthcare workers, and social workers to have.

The social service program at the University of Puno enrolled all its students to participate, since the University's program did not give much attention to the problems facing the Andean family in these changing times. When the students finished the basic one-year program, if they wished they could continue studies in a specialized area of family counseling, such as women, children, addictions or human sexuality.

We began by organizing the weekly study groups of about twenty students, taking into consideration their various geographical areas and work schedules. About one hundred twenty of the two hundred participants who began the program that first year finished it. We repeated it each year afterwards, although with fewer students.

I, myself, and the other members of the Holy Cross Family Institute team also studied in the program, and we all learned much for our own personal lives, as well as for our work on the team. Thank you, Luis Guizada and wife Pilar Cuadros in Lima, for creating these programs for us and for offering them to people in remote parts of Peru like Puno. Thank you also, all who traveled long distances weekly to assist us by accompanying the study groups.

The Family Institute team also organized a program on self-parenting for persons who had suffered from dysfunctional families. Lasting ten weeks, it helped to reprogram the messages received as a child from parents and other adults that were neither true nor helpful in developing a healthy self-esteem. This program, recommended to us by a Puno-born psychologist who now lived in Lima, was a very popular one, too. Another well-liked program that I found in a book on forgiveness offered steps that people could follow to enable them to forgive others who had offended them during their lifetime. All in all, these programs were life-giving for me and for the team, as well as for all who participated in them.

THE CHUCUITO PARISH TEAM

Recently-ordained Fidel Ticona began a new Family Institute project in the Chucuito parish that included organized retreats and leadership programs for the youth and the women's groups. He also organized a computer center in the parish for the Chucuito high school students to use. Few families had home computers at that time.

Most had had to travel all the way to the city of Puno to access the Internet centers there.

Shortly afterwards I also started another Family Institute project for the Chucuito parish to train lay leaders in the farming communities how to prepare their people for the sacraments without being dependent on visits from the members of the Chucuito parish team. This program was like the one I had developed in Macate. At the same time, these leaders were trained in the use of herbs and plants for the health needs of their communities, which often were distant from the state-run clinics. My compadre Juan Mallea was in charge of this new health program. He also conducted the parish Confirmation program in Chucuito.

After Sister Blanche went to Lima to be mistress of novices for her community, Sister Frances continued the Family Institute program that Sister Blanche had begun in 1997, developing it even further with the use of a local radio station to educate women about family issues. She also set up workshops addressing family problems in the farming communities near where the Holy Cross Sisters lived in Mocachi.

During the summers, we always sent some of the people who worked with the Family Institute to Lima to participate in a two-week leadership program organized by the Bartolome de Las Casas Institute. It replaced for us the summer theological reflection program that had been organized by the Catholic University in Lima for more than twenty-five years, in which Jorge Mallea and I participated and to which we used to send our lay leadership.

The University event had been discontinued by the Opus Dei Cardinal Archbishop of Lima Luis Cipriani, who would not give permission for it in his archdiocese.

All this activity was the upside of the Family Institute programs. The downside was the continual difficulty we experienced to obtain our tri-monthly financing from Dave Farrell, the national director of the Family Institute in Canto Grande. Fidel, Sister Frances and I often grew quite frustrated waiting for it. The bank transfers tended to arrive into our accounts in Puno more than a month and a half after the dates Dave had established he would deposit them. When we phoned his office to ask about them, we were criticized for being overly interested in money. We finally had no choice but to adapt to the late financing. Thank you, Sister Frances, for being such a great help keeping track of the various accounts in the Family Institute, in ODEC, and in the Chucuito parish all those years. Thank you for your diligence in double-checking our spending, and for sending on to Dave all the receipts with our financial reports every three months as he required.

Dave never visited our projects and rarely wrote about them in his annual report to the district. He was focused on his own Family Institute programs in Canto Grande. Thank you, Fidel and Sister Frances, for your collaborative support and ministry during those years. I think we did a great job and we can be proud of it.

THE NEW HOUSE

Since 1999, Diego, Fidel, Al and I had frequently discussed, both among the four of us and with the district superior Bud Colgan and his council, the need for a new residence for us in Chucuito. In 2000 before I left for my retreat in the United States, there were differences of opinion about whether we needed a new house, where the new house should be located, its size, and whether it should be built with bricks or adobe. The four of us living in Chucuito at that time wanted a simple house like we had in Cusipata, but one that would be larger and more agreeable to the younger Peruvian members of the Holy Cross community who might consider working in Chucuito in the future. Sadly, many of the Peruvians who joined Holy Cross because they were impressed by our simple living, now had become accustomed to more ample lodgings during their theology formation in Santiago, Chile.

Our major point of discussion was whether it should be a traditional Aymaran one-story adobe house or, instead, a two-story brick house as the Aymaras were beginning to build. Diego, who was heavy into respecting the traditional Aymaran ways, insisted on adobe and one-story. In the final construction we compromised. Most of the house was a brick two-story, but Diego's bedroom stood alone, a one-story built of adobe.

Our new house was to be in the town of Chucuito on prelature land located behind the church and parish hall. We had an understanding that the house would be ours until Holy Cross might leave, at which time ownership would pass to the prelature.

While I was on retreat, Fred, the new district superior, and the district council in Lima approved this final plan for the house. When I returned from the United States in August 2000, construction was begun under the watchful eye of Juan Mallea who was chosen to supervise it. We moved into the new house in December 2000 in time for Christmas when the one-story adobe room was finished for Diego and the first-story brick community room, kitchen and chapel were ready. For the moment, Fidel used the room designated for the chapel as his bedroom, and I set up a bed in my former ODEC office which I was vacating in the IDEA building next door, since the new director was moving the ODEC offices to Puno. In March 2001, the two-story brick house with four bedrooms was finished. Fidel and I moved into the two bedrooms on the top floor of the structure, with a great view of the lake from our bedroom windows. That view was the one thing that I had insisted on. The two bedrooms on the ground floor were for guests.

THE NEW BISHOP

At that time Peru was in crisis. After re-election to a third term, President Alberto Fujimori had fled the country to escape claims of corruption. His departure left the country in political chaos. In July 2001 Alejandro Toledo, an economist who had been living in the United States for several years, was elected the new president.

We also had a new bishop. In June 2001 Rome appointed Salesian Elio Perez to become bishop of the Prelature of Juli. Elio was a very simple and humble man, from a large family in a farming community in northern Peru. He rode the public bus just like anyone else. He was a big change from the former bishop Raimondo who often tended to be somewhat pompous. Bishop Elio was open to listening and learning from the Aymaran people and from those of us who had been ministering in the area for years.

To me Bishop Elio was a breath of fresh air, particularly after the experience I had had regarding the religion teacher training team (ODEC) with the interim diocesan administrator Pedro. I and others wondered how Elio had fallen through the cracks, since most episcopal appointments by Rome in the recent years had not been favorable for the south Andean Church. It had seemed that the Papal nuncio and the Peruvian Bishops Conference in Peru wanted to break the unity and pastoral collaboration between the Diocese of Puno and the three Prelatures of Sicuani, Ayaviri and Juli that had been going on since the early 1970s. But Bishop Elio was into keeping the collaboration going.

There are many stories about him, like that of his playing his harmonica for the Pope on his first visit to the Vatican after his consecration as bishop. There is another story that he spent all the night in a train station studying Aymara after he had been taken off a European train for not having the correct visa.

Shortly after Bishop Elio's arrival, Holy Cross Sister Frances Savoie, who had worked with me on the religion teacher training team (ODEC), and I went to speak with him about what had happened to Rudi in ODEC. The new ODEC director, a layman appointed by Pedro to replace me, was still making life difficult for Rudi in his job as religion teacher in one of the state high schools in Ilave, where he had been assigned by the educational authorities. Rudi was there due to the permanent teaching position he had attained thanks to Bishop Raimundo back in 1996. At our meeting with Bishop Elio, I told him that I had given all the pertinent documentation about Rudi to Pedro before leaving my ODEC position, and that I had written to Pedro at the time specifically requesting that he place it all in the prelature archives in case the new bishop might need it. Bishop Elio told Sister Frances and me that he had looked in the archives, but could not find any of that documentation in the ODEC folder! Fortunately I had kept copies of it all, which I gave to the bishop. Soon afterwards Rudi was left in peace. Thank you, Bishop Elio, for listening to Sister Frances and me and for being such an uplifting presence.

HOLY CROSS

In 2002 the district superior Fred Serraino suggested to Diego that he go on a sabbatical year to refresh himself and to renew his energies. Diego was not happy about it. He blamed me for influencing Fred to make him take a year of rest at a time when he did not want to. I must admit that as local superior I thought Diego could use a change of scenery for a while, and I had shared that opinion with Fred.

There seemed to me to be a lot of tension in our local community in Chucuito since Al Mahoney decided not to continue working with us. Al went back to Canada in June 2000 to coordinate the Holy Cross General Administration's new Justice and Peace ministry. That left only Diego, the young Peruvian Fidel, and me in Chucuito. Ever since the move into the new house Diego always seemed to be at odds with Fidel over lifestyle. Fidel wanted a cell phone. Diego thought we as Religious should not have personal cell phones. Fidel wanted comfortable furniture. Diego wanted simple living. As local superior I often was caught in the middle, and I needed some space and fresh air for myself. To me, Fidel represented the thinking of the young men in Holy Cross, and like it or not they were the future of the Chucuito mission. I felt that even though I might agree in principle with a lot of what Diego thought, he and I needed to let go of our ways of doing things and adapt to the young Holy Cross men. After I shared that preoccupation of mine with Fred, he made the final decision about Diego's year away. In the end, Diego enjoyed the year and came back refreshed. Thank you, Diego.

After my nine years as pastor, Diego became pastor on the Chucuito parish team once again in 2001. Fidel and I would cover the sacramental side for 2002 while he was away. On the parish team, Estanislao Cruz had been replaced as coordinator by Roberto Ari, a young Aymaran layman from one of the peninsula farming communities who worked with Estanislao for years in the sacrament preparation programs. Fidel really did most of the sacramental work in the parish that year, since I was away on my home leave in the United States for three months from May to August 2002, and then I traveled for the Family Institute to other parts of Peru, as, for example, to the coastal city of Ilo for a month-long series of workshops in October.

After Christmas that year Jorge Mallea and I took a ten-day bus trip to visit Argentina via Chile. Since my time in Puno we had a tradition of vacationing together. Thank you, Jorge, for those vacations over the years. As I recounted earlier, we spent New Year 2000 in Arica where there were three celebrations, one each for the Bolivian, Chilean and Peruvian time zones. Other years we went as far south in Chile as the cities of Antofagasta and Iquique, which before the 1880 Chilean war had belonged one to Bolivia and the other to Peru. We also took vacations within Peru, one time flying north to the city of Tumbes on the Ecuadorian border, then working our way slowly down by bus through the other northern coastal cities. We often vacationed at Huanchaco Beach close to the city of Trujillo, enabling me to visit my friends in Cartavio. Huanchaco had been a Holy Cross parish in the Cartavio years. In the late '90's we visited Chimbote together, since Jorge had spent his diaconate year there, and I had many friends there, too.

Jorge and I made two major bus trips to Argentina in 2002 and 2003 when prices had dropped. On the first, we traveled from Arica down to Santiago, Chile, then over the Andes to the beautiful Argentinian wine center of Mendoza, one of my favorite cities with its five public squares and a street lined with outdoor restaurants, where we sat to eat and to enjoy the scenery. We traveled on to Buenos Aires, then down to beautiful Bariloche, and across the Andes again to the Chilean southern coastal city of Valdivia with its many lakes and rivers.

The final leg of the trip took us up the Chilean coast, first to the capital Santiago where we met up with two friends of mine for a quick visit in the bus station. One was Sergio Concha whom I knew from my studies in Rome and who recently had left Holy Cross and was then a human rights lawyer in Santiago. Hugo Espinoza was the other, with whom I studied in Caxias do Sur in Brazil during my 1981 sabbatical year. How wonderful it was to encounter these good friends!

Then Jorge and I headed back to up to Arica. We accomplished the whole trip in less than two weeks with very little expense. As usual we shared the cost together from our community vacation budgets. However, this vacation did raise some eyebrows with commentary during the Holy Cross district chapter in Lima in 2003. Many of the Holy Cross men did not take vacations.

In 2003 Jorge and I crossed Bolivia by bus into northern Argentina where we got to know and appreciate the Aymaran southern high plain that Argentina shares with Chile, Bolivia and Peru. This had once all been the Aymara nation before the Europeans arrived in the early sixteenth century.

Thank You, Jorge, for your friendship all these years!

THE 2003 HOLY CROSS DISTRICT CHAPTER

When we returned from the 2002 trip, in January 2003 Fidel and Jorge Mallea organized a summer ministry in Chucuito for all the young men in formation in Holy Cross, as had been done in 2000 by Diego, Al and Fidel in Acora. It was great to have the young men around, and we had lively discussions in preparation for the district chapter in February. As usual in January, I spent most of the month in Puno teaching at the ESER school for teachers.

At the Holy Cross 2003 district chapter, the mission committee headed by Dave Farrell presented legislation that would require the presence of at least three Holy Cross Religious working in a mission as a necessary prerequisite to having the mission recognized as a Holy Cross community commitment, even though the Eastern Province provincial chapter documentation on which the Peru district depended recognized communities with just two Religious. The provincial chapter legislation had been the norm for the Peru district all these years. Both Chimbote and Chucuito often were communities of two Religious due to lack of personnel. The idea of having more Religious in a community was a very good one for community life, but I felt that with our small numbers this new legislation could easily be used in the future to justify closing a mission. However, Dave Farrell, whose committee was presenting this change to the chapter, assured me that that never would be the case. He maintained that the committee was interested only in ensuring a good, healthy community life in each mission. I agreed with that point, but I still felt that with our few members this legislation could cause problems, especially for the Chimbote and Chucuito missions in the future.

The mission committee also presented legislation to make the Canto Grande parish a permanent Holy Cross commitment. Dave declared that Norberto Strotmann, the Bishop of Chosica where the Canto Grande parish was located in Lima, was requesting that Holy Cross assume the Canto Grande parish in perpetuity. For me that signaled that the Canto Grande parish, the Fe y Alegría school, Yancana Huasi, the specialized school for the handicapped, and the headquarters for the Holy Cross Family Institute, all located in Canto Grande, would become the center piece of the district with everything else becoming expendable.

After much discussion and debate, the chapter voted to close the mission in Chimbote at the end of 2003 after more than thirty years of Holy Cross presence there, for lack of three Religious interested in working there.

Next the chapter voted on the request of the Bishop of Chosica. That issue was heavily debated and was passed by only a small margin of the fourteen-member chapter, with several no-votes and abstentions. Some of us, including the outgoing district superior Fred Serraino, felt there was no need to tie the Congregation down to one parish forever, even if it was at the time a great mission among the poor. All things change, and Canto Grande would change, too, over the years, and with time would no longer be a place where the poor lived. I felt we should be freer to move on to other areas in Peru that would have more need in the future, but most of the Religious who worked and lived in Canto Grande wanted a permanent mission, like Notre Dame University in South Bend, Indiana, that the members of Holy Cross could point to and call our own.

CHANGES IN THE AIR

During those years, Rome was naming some very tradition-minded, quite pre-Vatican II bishops, including men from very conservative Church groups like Opus Dei. Holy Cross, too, both in Peru and elsewhere seemed to me to be turning in that pre-Vatican II direction. The Congregation appeared to be focusing more on maintaining our own Holy Cross traditional institutions than on responding with new ministries to the lived, suffering, real needs of the poor. I felt we were retreating from some of the more prophetic stances we had taken in our mission priority statement of 1974, when we called on the Church institution to make necessary changes, like addressing the shortage of priests by empowering lay people in areas like Puno. Now we in Holy Cross were, instead, adopting the old clerical way of being Church, the in-thing now with most newly appointed Peruvian bishops. The singing of Latin hymns was brought back into community celebrations. Some priests began to wear the clerical Roman collar again. Holy Cross appeared more concerned about its relationships with these new bishops, who suspected Liberation Theology's view of Church, than with being the prophets that Vatican II had asked us to be.

In the Peru District, I felt that we were moving away from a collaborative model of Holy Cross toward a more authoritative model. Dave Farrell, especially, seemed to me to insist on a more top-down military style of organization. I frequently had disagreements with him, and I became the object of angry outbursts on his part in our community meetings. During our twice-yearly assemblies, Dave habitually would say regarding important matters that there was no need for a lot of community discussion, because the superior of the district and his council should decide them, and once they were decided there should be no questioning the decision. They should just be obeyed. I remember the anxiety I felt as the time for these assemblies approached, because I was never sure what was going to happen between Dave and me. It could enrage him when I asked him or the superior a question. I also felt that Bud Colgan, both when he was district superior and then as provincial superior after his election in 2000, seemed to agree with Dave's opinions, either openly or by his silence.

Other members seemed also to favor the Holy-Cross-run institutions in the district, especially those in Canto Grande in Lima rather than the auxiliary ministries in Chimbote and in Chucuito. The institutions in Canto Grande were becoming the priority for use of donations and the assignment of Holy Cross personnel. It seemed increasingly that our Holy Cross presence in Chimbote and in Chucuito was losing importance in the larger plan of the district. I myself believed that both, serving our Holy Cross institutions in Canto Grande and doing more auxiliary ministry, should be equally important. I opposed locking ourselves into one place like Canto Grande and into our Holy Cross institutions there. I felt we needed to be free to respond to new needs among the poor in Peru.

Those of us like Diego and me who were used to engaging in a more collaborative style of ministry with others in the Prelature of Juli became considered by some in the district to be "doing their own thing" for not contributing to brick and mortar Holy Cross institutions in Peru. I have always recognized that auxiliary ministry was part of Blessed Basil Moreau's, our founder's, original plan for our Congregation. The founding documents state that Holy Cross priests, as well as engaging in education, were established to be auxiliaries to the diocesan priests in the country parishes by conducting missions and retreats. I perceived increasingly there were two different visions taking hold in Holy Cross in Peru, between those working in Lima on one hand, and those of us working in Puno and Chimbote at that time on the other.

THE VISIT

During Holy Week in 2003 we were visited by two of the Holy Cross general assistants from Rome, Father Arulraj Gali of India and Brother Joseph Kofi Tsiquaye of Ghana. They were able to participate on Monday, Tuesday and Wednesday nights of Holy Week in the Chucuito parish processions, all organized by the people.

I have always enjoyed those processions in a special way. In the cold of the dark night, often in the rain, we walked through the muddy streets of Chucuito in candlelight, recalling the suffering of Jesus and his mother Mary.

For me it was always a very moving experience, as were the fiestas of the Cross on the tops of the parish hills in May. There is so much spiritual wisdom among the Aymara people that is not present in our western, more cerebral religious rituals. During the fiestas in August in honor of the Assumption and in October in honor of Our Lady of the Rosary, dancing also is an important expression of devotion for the Aymara. They celebrate their fraternal community during these seven-day religious fiestas by eating and drinking together. Throughout the year each town and village also has its own particular religious fiestas, celebrating in community its faith story, expressing its belief in Jesus, and simply enjoying life together.

Like many Holy Cross community visitors in the past, Father Arulraj and Brother Joseph had difficulty comprehending why there was a difference between a Peruvian coastal parish like Canto Grande and a parish in the small towns of the Andean Aymara people. A parish in the Andes was not a central place for gathering as it was on the Peruvian coast. For the Andean people their many, scattered, farming communities were their places for gathering, celebrating in each one their fiestas with dance and music. Each local farming community was individually more important to its occupants than the parish which extended very widely across them all. The Andean parish was more on the periphery of their daily lives, quite the opposite of the fixed place and center of focus it was for the people on the coast. So, the organization of the parish, the services provided by the priest and expected by the people also were quite different.

During all my years in Chucuito I remember countless times that Diego and I tried to explain these differences to district chapters and to Holy Cross visitors alike, usually without much success. Some people tend to think that a parish should be the same everywhere, no matter in what country or culture it is located, and that we should all be doing the same things. That was the centralized way Rome was looking at the Church in those days. I remember that once when I worked in Cartavio a priest recently arrived from Ireland said at a meeting about new forms of Baptismal preparation in the Diocese of Trujillo that "if it worked in Ireland it should work anywhere." That, in my opinion, was just not true. There are cultural differences between people. And there is still a great need to inculturate Christianity into the different cultures of our world. Unity does not depend on uniformity.

In their report to the district council after visiting us, Father Arulraj and Brother Joseph were critical of us in Chucuito. They thought that each of us three priests should have been celebrating the Roman liturgy for Good Friday in different villages rather than all together in Chucuito. They did not understand that on Good Friday in the Andes the people organize processions, a type of stations of the cross, climbing to the top of their sacred hills and spending the day there in prayer.

I was especially surprised by their lack of understanding about this pastoral difference, because on a personal level, when I spoke to them privately about community-life difficulties in Holy Cross with some of those in Canto Grande, they had responded that each one of us has had different life experiences, which often makes community life and a common vision difficult. So I thought they comprehended the same rationale on a pastoral level when they left us, but they obviously had not, since their final report criticized our ministry in Chucuito in that respect. Their criticism was not a propitious omen for Diego and my continuing in the Prelature of Juli, since some in Canto Grande already considered our presence in Chucuito as our individual, personal ministry rather than as an auxiliary Holy Cross district mission inserted into the wider Andean way of being Church.

Since the Prelature was organized on a collaborative auxiliary model of Church, no Religious congregation in the Prelature had its own parish. We all collaborated in a common pastoral plan, and even the Maryknoll priests and Sisters who were the founding congregation of the Prelature did not claim any one parish as their own. Repeatedly in district chapters Diego and I tried to explain this pastoral way of being Church in the Andes to get the official recognition of Chucuito as a Holy Cross community mission. We were opposed by those who preferred to look at it as though Diego and I were doing our own thing in Chucuito and that the community had no formal responsibility to assign people there. The strong difference between pastoral views on ways of being Church divided the district those years.

There seemed to me to be exaggerated emphasis on our Holy Cross institutions in Canto Grande. It was back to the times of the pre-Vatican II Church when each congregation had its own parishes, schools and territories and were in constant competition with one another over which was the best, the largest, or the most important. For me this way of being Church separates us from others rather than unites us. It was a very different model of Church from the one I had experienced during my life in Cartavio, Macate and Chimbote up to this time and especially now in the southern Andes Church. So, in Holy Cross we were at odds between what it meant to be Church in Chucuito and the southern Andes of Peru and what it meant to be Church in a coastal parish in Lima like Canto Grande. The criticism of Father Arulraj and Brother Joseph once again brought that difference among us to the fore.

CLOSING

In Holy Cross, each level of the Congregation has an authority structure. The smallest unit is the local community house. The next larger unit is the district which forms part of a larger structure called a province on which a district depends for approval of some major decisions. The district has an elected superior and a four-man council. Two of the councilors are elected by the membership of the district, and two are appointed by the district superior with the approval of the provincial. The provincial also has a council, and they are dependent to some degree on a Superior General who presides over his own council and who is head of the whole congregation world-wide.

Bill Persia replaced Fred Serraino as district superior in February 2003. Bill had been in Peru since 1986, working both in Chimbote and Canto Grande at different times. He had been pastor of the Chimbote parish and principal of the Fe y Alegría school in Canto Grande. He had been a candidate for the Peru district superior position during both the 1997 and 2000 district chapters, and in December 2002 he was elected unanimously. He took over at the end of the chapter in February 2003.

Eight months later, in October 2003, during the Our Lady of the Rosary fiesta, Bill came to Chucuito for the annual district superior's visit to our Holy Cross local community. In our meetings, Diego, Fidel and I discussed with him the future of the Chucuito mission and the continuing presence of Holy Cross in the Prelature of Juli. Bill told us that the community plan was for Fidel to go to Lima in January 2004 to begin studies to become the new person in charge of the district formation program in Canto Grande in 2005.

Realizing that Fidel's departure would reduce us from a community of three persons, the number recommended by the chapter, to two, Fidel, Diego and I described to Bill the interest in working in Chucuito expressed to us by numerous Peruvian and Aymaran men in formation now finishing their theology studies in our formation house in Santiago, Chile. I knew as well, however, that many of those from the Prelature were not interested in returning to work in the place of their birth for a long period. Diego and I reasoned that with the decision to close the mission in Chimbote taken during the last chapter, there would be more young men available, and so at least one could be assigned to Chucuito each year for a shorter period. That way we could have a community of three as the chapter desired.

Bill told us that he was excited about the possibility of a new mission somewhere else in Peru. He spoke of a school in the jungle area that was being offered to Holy Cross. There was, however, no mention of a new mission in Tacna, nor was there any talk about a possible closure of the Chucuito mission.

One month later, in November 2003, Diego was in Canada on one of his speaking engagements for the Third World Theologians. During all those years in Chucuito, Diego, by then a well-known theologian, was often invited to speak in different parts of the world. As a result, he often was away from the parish for weeks at a time giving talks in various countries around the globe. During his sabbatical year in 2002 he had been elected president of the Third World Theologians. What a recognition and honor!

During that same month of November, I was sent by the Holy Cross Peru district to represent it at the Holy Cross International Justice and Peace Conference organized in Dhaka, Bangladesh by Jim Mulligan, now a general assistant in Rome, and Al Mahoney who had left Chucuito in June 2000 to take up this work of Justice and Peace ministry for the Congregation.

While both Diego and I were out of Peru we each received from the district superior Bill Persia a general email sent to all the members of the district, notifying everyone that he and his council had voted unanimously to close immediately both the mission in Chimbote (a decision that had been voted on and approved in the district chapter of 2003) and the mission in Chucuito (even though the closing of the Chucuito mission had never been discussed or voted on during the chapter). Bill's district council at that time was composed of assistant district superior Jorge Izaguirre, elected councilors Bob Baker and Fidel Ticona, and appointed councilor Dave Farrell.

Bill wrote that by leaving the two missions at the same time the district would be able to free up enough personnel for a new mission which he and his council chose to be in Tacna, since we had spoken about the possibility of Tacna in previous district chapters. He and the assistant superior Jorge Izaguirre were going to travel to Tacna immediately to discuss with the bishop there the possibility of Holy Cross taking over a parish in March 2004. Bill informed us that the Eastern Province superior Bud Colgan and his provincial council already had approved this plan unanimously and that Bill already had informed the respective bishops in Chimbote and in the Prelature of Juli that we would be leaving Chimbote and Chucuito parishes at the beginning of 2004. Bill himself would be the new pastor, and Diego, I and Jorge Mallea, who was being taken from his permanent teaching position at our Fe y Alegría School in Canto Grande, were being assigned to this new mission in Tacna.

When I received this email I was on my way back from the meeting in Bangladesh and visiting my English and German friends in Europe. I had no one with whom I could share my anger and frustration. As usual when I was in high-stress situations like this one I came down with a very bad attack of bronchial asthma and rhinitis, from which I had been suffering increasingly during the recent years. I was so sick that when I got back to Lima I was ordered by the doctor to stay in Lima for a week until my condition cleared up.

It was early December 2003, consequently, before I returned to Chucuito. As local superior I immediately called a meeting of the local Holy Cross community to discuss all that had happened. Diego and I were both angry that the decision had been made without any input from us, and without a discussion and a full vote of all the members of the district. We felt that the district superior Bill Persia and his council had taken on themselves decisions that should have been left up to the whole group gathered in assembly or in chapter.

Fidel who was a member of Bill's district council told us that he had not voted for the closure even though both Bill and Bud Colgan, the district and provincial superiors, insisted in their letters to the community that the vote had been unanimous. I thought at first that Fidel might be trying to play both sides of the fence. As time went on I began to believe him, since Bud in the past often had written in his reports that votes were unanimous when they were not, as was the case with the vote to make Canto Grande a parish in perpetuity.

Diego, Fidel and I decided at this meeting that we would send a letter to the district superior Bill Persia respectfully asking for a reconsideration of the decision to close the Chucuito mission and requesting him to postpone the decision until the entire Holy Cross community could meet in the annual assembly in February 2004, only two months away, to discuss it further with the input of all the district membership.

Diego, Fidel and I wrote in our letter to him that we believed that although during the 2003 district chapter there was a lengthy discussion about communities of three, in the actual district legislation there was no mention of that number. We argued that two Religious were allowed to form a local community under the Eastern Province provincial chapter legislation, and that since the district always followed province legislation unless the district explicitly legislated otherwise in a chapter, this should be taken into consideration. We also wrote that during that same district chapter there had been no discussion of starting a new mission in Tacna.

In his reply, Bill explained that Fidel had to go to Lima in March 2004 to begin studies in preparation for being the director of the district formation ministry in the future. That would leave only Diego and me in Chucuito. He cited 2003 district chapter legislation that recommended that only viable communities of three Religious should be maintained. Thus, he and his council had to close the Chucuito mission down, because there was no other Religious available or interested, inasmuch as there were so many needs in Canto Grande.

Bill then informed us that since this plan had been approved already by the Eastern Province provincial superior Bud Colgan and his provincial council, and since the two bishops involved already had been contacted and informed of our immediate departure, there was nothing more to do except to obey. He ended by saying that for those reasons the reconsideration was being denied.

After receiving that letter only Diego continued to make several more personal attempts to see if he at least could remain in Chucuito with the Aymara Institute (IDEA) and live with the Benedictine community which had established a monastery in Chucuito in 1993. These special assignments were often allowed in the Holy Cross community. But that request also was denied.

I really thought Diego would leave the community, but he didn't. During the recent years, several members of Holy Cross, whose vision of the Church and Religious life and priesthood was similar to Diego's and mine, had opted to leave the district to minister elsewhere. Al Mahoney who had worked with us in Chucuito left in 2000 frustrated with many of the decisions that the Peru Holy Cross community was making at that time. Another, Gerry Barmasee, who had worked in Chile for many years before coming to the Peru district to be pastor in Chimbote in 1995, left the district to go back to Chile in 2001 after Bob Baker, then the new pastor in Chimbote, told Gerry that he could not return to reside in the Chimbote house after his sabbatical. Gerry had hoped to continue conducting his Bible workshops in Chimbote while living in the community house with Bob.

I think what hurt me most in this decision-making process was the way that it was done so secretly. No previous conversation on the part of the district authorities with Diego, Fidel or me. No dialogue with us. It was so unlike all my former experience of the use of authority in

Holy Cross during my time in the community. I felt great disappointment in our district leadership, and especially in Bill Persia who I had hoped as superior would follow the example of Fred Serraino who had held together this group of men with such different pastoral views and personalities. I think Bill was swayed by other people and by his own eagerness to begin the new mission in Tacna.

I also was very surprised with the provincial superior Bud Colgan allowing a district council to make a decision as important as closing a mission without consulting first with the people involved and without insisting that the plan be discussed with all the membership present in the upcoming district assembly scheduled for February 2004. When Bud was district superior we always discussed major decisions in assemblies.

I was hurt, also, that there was no outcry from anyone else in the district. I felt that this was an abuse of authority in our Congregation. I had seen and heard of such abuse in other areas of the Church since the election of Pope John Paul II in 1978, but I had hoped it would not reach Holy Cross. And here it was full force! With all of Bill Persia's enthusiasm to begin a new mission in Tacna, I felt that it was being built on the ashes of the Chucuito mission and especially on the personal sacrifice of Diego. It was a cruel decision, an unjust one the way it was made.

PREPARATIONS FOR THE MOVE

After all of our letters for recourse were denied, with deep regret and considerable ire Fidel, Diego and I started

222

to prepare for our departure from Chucuito scheduled for March 2004. Luckily, I had a vacation with Jorge Mallea planned for the week after Christmas, so I had a chance to get away and unwind a bit from all the tension.

One result of the district council decision was that our programs with the Holy Cross Family Institute were to be shut down in Chucuito. These projects had salaries attached to them for the Holy Cross men working on them, and since Fidel and I would be leaving, all three programs there, even the one headed by Sister Frances, were closed. It seems to me that in most of our moves during our years in Peru we in Holy Cross had little consideration for how those moves affected others.

To salvage in some way the work being done by the Family Institute team, I spoke with Simon Pedro, a Benedictine who had a similar program to ours called *Escucha* (Listen) which aided people who had suffered the trauma of terrorist violence. He offered to take into his structure the two men Wilber and Percy, who worked in the project with me, paying them a salary and thus keeping the Family Violence Workshops going in the schools. Thank you, Simon Pedro, for that offer and for being my spiritual director in Chucuito all those years since 1994 when I returned from my sabbatical year. I could not have survived in Chucuito or in the Prelature or in Holy Cross all those years without your wisdom and spiritual insights.

Diego finally was given permission to stay in Chucuito a bit longer than the rest of us after he insisted that in our contract with the Prelature, Holy Cross had to give Bishop Elio at least a six-month advance notice before leaving. During that time, he began making plans to turn the IDEA program over to Simon Pedro, who already was part of the IDEA team with him, Santiago Mendoza and Juan Mallea.

During the month of January 2004 while Diego and I continued to teach at the ESER summer school in Puno, I began to prepare the house for the move, packing up our things. We decided to take with us to Tacna all the furniture bought in 2001 for the new house in Chucuito.

At the annual gathering of Holy Cross men and women Religious in February 2004 in Lima, the Holy Cross Sisters expressed their frustration about the way the decision to leave Chucuito had been made without any consideration for the impact that it would have on them. They said that they had decided to come to the Prelature of Juli in 1986 to collaborate and to work with the Holy Cross men there. They felt that they had been overlooked and excluded from the whole conversation and decision-making process which also concerned them. Bill, who unlike some of the other Holy Cross men, enjoyed collaboration with the Holy Cross Sisters, answered them by describing his enthusiasm for beginning a new ministry in Tacna with the Sisters who already were working there, and that their loss in Chucuito was their gain in Tacna. Other Holy Cross men thought that the Sisters had no right to speak or interfere in a decision made by the men.

Besides not discussing with the Sisters beforehand, there had not been any conversation during the decision-making with anyone else affected by it, either. To me, the decision was totally contrary to the discernment process for leaving a mission expressed in our Rule, which calls for all kinds of consultations before taking any final resolution. These were sad days and sad times which I call "the dictatorship of the council."

Before I close this chapter and my life-giving but sometimes difficult years in the Prelature of Juli with the Aymara people, I want to thank the Lord for the wonderful years of life in a circular Church of brothers and sisters, and for the rich spiritual experience of those years. Chucuito was my home for almost twenty years, and I learned so much from the Aymara people during that time. It was a time when Peru was changing, and a time when for many of us the Church was moving farther and farther away from the hopes and dreams that we had held for the implementation of the documents of Vatican II. But even during these difficulties, I thank you, my Aymara friends especially, for accepting me among you for those many years and for sharing your friendship, your culture and your spirituality with me. I would not trade them for anything else! The joys of working and living with so many of you for so many years outweigh all the unpleasant experiences I have recounted in these last chapters.

9. TACNA 2004 - 2009

Closing and leaving the mission in the Prelature of Juli with a heavy heart, I departed from Chucuito on the morning of March 4, 2004. Diego was to remain there until the end of May, when he would go back to Chile where he continues to today, teaching at the Catholic University in Santiago, helping in Holy Cross parishes, and traveling often to the high Andes in Peru and Bolivia to give talks at Andean Theological Conferences. He decided to leave the District of Peru after his petitions to remain in the Prelature of Juli all were denied by the district superior Bill Persia and the district council. It certainly was a sad day for him and for all of us as our caravan proceeded out of Chucuito like a funeral procession.

A large truck led the way with our furniture, followed by Juan Mallea's small van carrying Jorge Mallea with his things that he used to leave at our house. Next was Wilber Mamani's van carrying me with my packed boxes, then the Holy Cross community car driven by Fidel carrying his things going with him to Canto Grande. We had loaded the truck the night before to get an early start. Thank you, everyone who helped with all that work.

It was a long, eight-hour drive to the city of Tacna. We arrived at about three o'clock in the afternoon at the house Bill Persia, Jorge Mallea and I had decided to rent there. The three of us had flown to Tacna in late February, after our district assembly in Lima ended, to greet the new diocese at their annual assembly and to choose the house we would live in. The building, owned by the Association of Peruvian Lay Missionaries (APM), was perfect for us. It was near the area of Vinani where we were to found a new parish, and it was convenient to transportation to the center of town. The house was unfinished and simple, as we all wanted. The second floor had no windows yet, and the roof was not finished. We put plastic on the windows and straw mats on the roof to keep the wind out.

Since we arrived earlier than expected, we had to wait for Bill Persia who had the keys and had gone into town. He soon returned, and we unloaded the truck and vans. Once we were somewhat settled, all of us who had come from Chucuito went into Tacna to have *pollo a la brasa* (Peruvian-style grilled chicken) to celebrate our safe arrival.

With Bill the next day we went to a Pacific Ocean beach about twenty miles away, where we enjoyed the afternoon with Juan Mallea, Wilber Mamani Cotillo and Percy Malaga with their wives and with Fidel's family. Thank you, all, for making a difficult move more enjoyable. The day afterwards we settled into our new life.

VINANI

Sunday we went to look at a piece of land the bishop told us was designated for a chapel in Vinani, a large area on the southern side of Tacna recently parceled out to people who had lost their homes in the 2002 earthquake. There was no electricity, water, or sewage installed yet. The people who had moved in had constructed straw-mat homes on small designated lots. To our consternation, we found that some had put their homes on the chapel land. I feared that it would be a big problem—perhaps even a legal fight for us—which would not be a good way to start out with the people we were supposed to serve. We spoke with them about our problem. The next day to our surprise they all had moved their homes across the street to land supposedly designated for a future market. It seemed to us evidence that they wanted us there.

That same day three men knocked on the front door of our house. They told us that they belonged to the Juan XXIII Movement, a new spiritual organization in Peru for lay Catholics. They had heard that we were going to start a new parish in Vinani where they lived, and they wanted to help us. So, we bought some wire, straw matting and wooden poles, and within a day they had our little chapel standing on the lot designated by the authorities. They also found enough small cement building blocks for us to use as seats in the chapel and to build a small altar. It was perfect! Thank you, Lucio Marin, Hernan Arma and the now deceased Humberto Cruz, for all your friendship and your help that day and throughout the years. We could not have done it all so quickly without you.

Lelia Ramos, from the same Juan XXIII Spiritual Movement, joined with the three men on the following Sunday to form our little, core Sunday Mass group. Each week afterwards we celebrated Sunday Mass at 7:00 am, since the people told us that in Vinani they gathered each Sunday at 8:00 am in their neighborhood housing association assemblies to discuss plans to have water, sewage and electricity installed in their neighborhoods and in their houses. The streets did not yet have public lighting. Each block had a public water pump from which people would carry their water home in pails.

Once established in Tacna the three of us joined the Tacna auto club. This allowed care for the car that Bill used for the parish, lessons for Jorge who wanted to learn how to drive, as well as use of the clubhouse which had a very nice outdoor swimming pool that I used during the warmer months from October to March. Tacna could be very cold in the winter months, and the pool was not heated. However, it kept me in shape to some degree. Swimming always has been something of a spiritual exercise for me since my youth when my cousin Jack Barnes, a La Salette priest, one of my vocation pillars, taught me how to swim and feel safe in the water.

MY NEW MINISTRY

Since I was interested more in education than in parish ministry, I went immediately to the Diocesan Office for Education of the Laity located with the bishop's offices underneath the Tacna Cathedral on the main square of the city. I learned that Santiago Estefaniak, the Maryknoll priest who had founded that office and had been working there for more than fifteen years, was just about to retire at eighty years of age. When I was in Chucuito, Santiago had invited me and the Family Institute team, as well as Diego and Al, to Tacna several times over the years to conduct workshops within his married-deacon program; so I knew him well. I would be able to replace him on this lay formation team coordinated at the time by Maryknoll Sister Martha Goetchel, and later by Maryknoll Sister Maria Lynch. The key lay members of the team were Javier Chacon, a teacher who also worked in the Diocesan Office for Religious Education (ODEC-TACNA), and Ana Maria Napa who was the secretary of the Diocesan Formation of Laity office.

I knew the work of the team from the times when I stayed at the Maryknoll Center House in Lima and had spoken with the other Maryknoll priests who had founded this program with Santiago in Tacna in the early 1990s. They had established the office to organize diocesan-wide programs on Bible and Faith Formation for adults, inviting the lay leadership and religion teachers from all the parishes and schools in Tacna to their Monday and Friday night programs. These were held in the three large classrooms in the diocesan offices under the cathedral. It was a perfect fit for the type of educational work I had hoped to do in Tacna, ever since the time in 2000 when I visited the bishop there with Jorge Mallea.

Just after our arrival in Tacna my good friends the Sisters of St. Joseph, whom I have mentioned several times in previous chapters, heard that I was now in town, and they invited me to give a retreat to their lay teachers at the Fe y Alegría school that they administered in Tacna. This furnished an opportunity for me to become known among the teachers. It seemed to me that God was preparing the way for me and for all of us to settle in Tacna after so many months of turmoil.

THE HOLY CROSS SCHOOL

In mid-April Bill, Jorge and I traveled back up to Chucuito to join Diego for the official closing ceremony of the mission there with Bishop Elio and other members of the Juli Prelature. It was a sad day for me, but also a joyful one with so many friends present to say goodbye to us and wish us well in our new mission in Tacna.

When we returned to Tacna, Bill, Jorge and I spoke with the St. Joseph Sisters administering their Fe y Alegría School, and with the Jesuits who conducted two schools in Tacna, one of which was for the poor. They both thought that we should start a school in conjunction with the new parish, since the Aymaran people in the poorer areas of Tacna really wanted good schools for their children. They also told us that it would be a helpful way to interest the people in Vinani who were mostly immigrants from the Puno area to participate in the parish. As I pointed out earlier, the people in Puno were not Sunday Catholics, since in Puno they usually live in small farming communities where there are no priests nearby for Sunday Masses. Bill, Jorge, and I all thought that this was a very good idea.

Jorge Mallea, who was a teacher like me and who had been transferred from his permanent teaching position at a Fe y Alegría school in Canto Grande to become part of the new team in Tacna, was especially interested. He had done a lot of studies in education while in Lima and wanted to continue in education more than in parish ministry.

Bill Persia, the new pastor in Vinani who also was the district superior who had promoted this move to Tacna, decided to present the idea of opening a new Holy Cross school as part of the new parish to his district council in Lima for their approval. In previous Holy Cross assemblies of all the Holy Cross Religious men in Peru, which we held twice a year in Lima, we had discussed starting a Holy Cross school somewhere in Peru. To his and to our surprise Dave Farrell, Bob Baker and Edison Chuquisengo (a recently ordained Peruvian priest who was then the Director of the Fe y Alegría school in Canto Grande), the three members of Bill's four-member district council who lived and worked in Canto Grande, were totally against the idea. Fidel Ticona, who was then studying in Lima, was the only council member who supported it. Bill told Jorge and me that during the first council meeting in which they discussed the Tacna school, Dave Farrell said to Bill that Holy Cross was only in Tacna provisionally.

This council had just closed the Chimbote mission and the mission in Chucuito to begin this new mission in Peru, and now at least one of the council, Dave, was saying that the Tacna mission was only temporary. We wondered what they were thinking to close the former missions only to start what they considered a temporary one.

During the following months, Bill tried to convince the three of his councilors, but to no avail. He needed the approval of at least two of them to begin a school sponsored by the Holy Cross Congregation, since the district council was the legitimate authority for such decisions in the district. He also would need the approval of the provincial superior Bud Colgan and his provincial council in the United States on which the Peru district depended. Bill invited his council members to visit the new mission in Tacna to see for themselves the need for a school, but for some unstated reason they would not come to visit. Bill continued to speak with them, hoping to change their minds, but they remained adamant in their vote against it. Their resistance to the idea of a school seemed to us beyond any reasoning.

In November 2004 Jim Lackenmier, the province treasurer, came to Peru for meetings in Lima with the district treasurer Dave Farrell. Bud Colgan, the provincial superior, asked Jim to visit Tacna while he was there. We had a very nice visit with him, and he seemed quite understanding of our point of view about the need for a school. We planned to show Jim the large piece of land that was being offered to Holy Cross by the Tacna educational authorities free of charge to build the school in Vinani. We hoped that Jim might be able to convince those in Lima who were opposed to the school. This gift of land was a great opportunity for the Congregation. We asked the little group of teachers who had become friends with Bill and Jorge and were working with us on the plans to start the school, to meet us when we visited the land with Jim after Sunday Mass. However, the Tacna educational authorities and the leaders of the neighborhood assemblies in Vinani learned about the visit, and there was a big crowd to welcome Jim. The crowd was a total surprise to us! What was obvious to all of us was that both the Tacna educational authorities and the people wanted us to start a school. Of that there was now no doubt.

There was no turning back the clock for the three of us, either, at least if we were going to have good relations in a parish in Vinani. We would have to start a school there one way or another if we wanted to retain the people's trust. We unfortunately had jumped the gun, presuming that the district council would give its approval, and had begun to include the Vinani people in the conversation. They were overjoyed with the idea, because the nearest school at the time was a long distance away. The parents had to personally transport the younger children and fetch them. The older ones had to walk or pay bus fare. That was very costly for poor families who worked long hours to survive. With the district council opposed to the school, it was going to be hard for us to say that we were not going to start one when that is what the people very much wanted.

Bud Colgan the Eastern Province provincial superior soon got involved in the community conflict. Bill Persia was scheduled to go on vacation in the United States at the end of November 2004, so Bud decided to invite him to a provincial council meeting while he was there to talk about these difficulties he was having with his district council.

In December another problem started up in Canto Grande. Dave Farrell and Bob Baker who were two of the councilors who voted to close Chucuito and send Bill to

Tacna to be the cornerstone of the new mission just a year earlier, were now asking the provincial superior to insist that Bill, as district superior, live in Canto Grande, near them, to handle the district business there. Bill was not only the district superior; he also was the pivotal person for the new Tacna mission as pastor of the new parish. So we wondered what was going to happen.

Bill, living in Tacna with us, had been traveling the twenty-hour bus trip to Lima to spend about ten days each month in Canto Grande taking care of the district business. At that time, Bob Baker, the assistant district superior, lived full-time in Canto Grande, so Bill presumed that Bob would handle any other business that cropped up there during the rest of the month. This is how it had been done when Dan Panchot, district superior in 1985, lived and worked in Chimbote when he replaced me in the parish there so I could go to Chucuito.

Another development was that the recently ordained Peruvian Edison Chuquisengo, who had been named the new director of the Fe y Alegría school in Canto Grande even before he was ordained a priest in 2003, had suddenly decided he wanted to leave the Congregation. Edison also had been named to the district council to replace Jorge Izaguirre when Jorge went to the United States to study pastoral theology in Boston in early 2004. Edison was one of the three district council members opposed to the school in Tacna from the beginning.

After Bill's meeting with the provincial council in the United States, the provincial superior Bud Colgan decided to visit Peru himself in January 2005 to speak personally with all the members of the district about some of these problems. When he spoke with me his main concern seemed to be where the district superior should live rather than about the school.

After speaking with all the members of the district individually during the month of January 2005, Bud the provincial superior decided that Bill had the option either to go to Lima to live and continue as district superior, or renounce being superior and stay in Tacna. Even though there was a community assembly coming up in a month's time in February, Bud made the decision beforehand with the district council.

Bill chose to stay in Tacna, giving up the office of district superior to which he had been elected unanimously in the chapter of 2003.

THE PARISH DIOCESAN SCHOOL

Shortly after that decision was announced, Bill, Jorge and I discussed again what to do about the school, since that is what the people wanted and what they expected of us. We decided finally that if the Holy Cross community did not want to start a new Holy Cross school in Tacna, we would speak with the bishop to see if he might be interested in a diocesan parish school there in Vinani among the poor. The bishop was very interested. Since we already had permission from the community to establish the parish, we figured that we could start a parish school as part of the parish project with only the bishop's approval. To our way of thinking we did not need the district council's approval to do that. The provincial superior finally accepted this, but he told Bill that if there were a parish school in the parish under the sponsorship of the bishop, it would not receive any financial aid from Holy Cross. He insisted that Bill ensure that the bishop in Tacna understood and accepted those terms. Thank you, Bishop Hugo Garaycoa, for agreeing.

So off we went with the plans to open the diocesan parish school in April 2005 with Jorge Mallea as founder and principal. A lot of the ground work for the school had already been done with the help of Vinani neighborhood assemblies and now with another new small group of teachers. The first group of teachers had been convinced after Jim Lackenmier's visit in November that Holy Cross would not start a school in Vinani. Discouraged they backed out—except for Professor Luciano Quispe Cutipa, a faithful friend to Jorge, Bill and me since the beginning of the school project. We could not have started the school without his help that first year. Heartfelt thanks to you, Luciano.

The educational authorities informed us that we could not open the school if it did not have water and sewage installed. So Bill Persia got a financial grant from Europe to put in bathrooms connected to a water and sewage system that the mayor had recently installed in Vinani five blocks away from the school. Bill had to buy a lot of pipes to make the connection, and then build the bathrooms. Thank you, Bill, for doing all of that.

The small teacher group put their money together and put up their straw mat classrooms on part of the land designated for the parish. The Jesuits and the women from the Lions Club gave us some discarded school desks and blackboards, so we were ready to begin classes in time for the start of the school year in March. Nevertheless, we had to wait until mid-April to receive official recognition from the Peruvian educational authorities. That first year about two hundred students enrolled in a kindergarten, all six years of grade school, and the first year of high school. The number shows how great the need was for a school in Vinani.

The parents trusted us enough to enroll their children in March even though the school was still waiting for official recognition. Due to the late approval date, the newness of the school and their limited yearly budget, the educational authorities could not give the school all the salaries we needed for each of the six grade-school classrooms. So, the six teachers got together among themselves and decided to split the three government salaries among the six of them so that all of them could work that year. Thank you for your generosity and solidarity, faithful lay teachers.

In all this I was so happy for Jorge Mallea. Now he had his ministry. Bill was pastor of the parish, and I had my educational ministry with the diocese while helping in both parish and school as needed. God had been good!

CHANGES IN THE AIR

In late 2005 a new auxiliary bishop was appointed to aid Bishop Hugo Garaycoa who had accepted Holy Cross in Tacna. Marco Antonio Lara Cortez was a young Peruvian diocesan priest from the Chiclayo diocese in northern Peru near Cartavio. He had been formed there by Opus Dei, a conservative organization in the Catholic Church founded in Spain at the beginning of the twentieth century and supported by Pope John Paul II and later by Pope Benedict XVI as a bastion of Catholic doctrine. During the past years, some twelve new bishops had been named in Peru from Opus Dei. It was rumored that Peru was to be an experiment to see how well the more conservative elements in the Catholic Church could take control of an entire Latin American country.

Marco Antonio was not a full member of Opus Dei, but an associate. In September 2006, he became the new bishop of Tacna when Bishop Hugo retired. He did not come into the diocese claiming he had all the truth like some newly appointed Opus Dei bishops tried to do in other dioceses, and as was happening in the Prelature of Juli, where the new Opus Dei bishop was refusing to renew the contracts of the Maryknoll priests whose congregation had founded the prelature back in 1957. Bishop Marco Antonio was a friendlier type of the Opus group. Jorge, Bill, and I had little difficulty with him. In fact, he was very supportive of us in many ways with regard to the parish and the new parish school in Vinani.

In the same year 2006 the Holy Cross Sisters, who had been working in another parish in the southern area of Tacna since their arrival in 2000, decided to build a residence and work with us in Vinani. Bill Persia was helping Sister Raquel to get land there, but the project really progressed when Sister Frances Savoie, who had worked with me in Chucuito, was transferred to Tacna. She found a nice piece of land in Vinani and got the official papers for it in record time. In fact, Bill was still working on getting papers for another piece of land for the parish church from the Tacna city authorities when she got her piece of land. The parish school was built on most of the land that originally had been set aside for the parish church and other parish buildings, so now additional land was needed.

THE CHRISTIAN WORKER MOVEMENT

During the early years in Tacna, I decided to organize a group of the Christian Worker Movement (MTC) that I had known about for years and which had been part of the Chimbote parish pastoral plan, as I described in that chapter. Hernan Arma, Lelia Ramos, Lucio Marin with his wife Patricia, and Humberto Cruz, who had helped us establish the parish at the beginning, and a few of the teachers at the school came to the first meeting held in the straw mat parish church. After a year of meetings, we got in touch with the national MTC movement in Lima, and they accepted us as a group in formation for the movement.

Our MTC group organized many fundraising activities for the parish. Once they sold *pollo a la brasa* (Peruvian grilled chicken) to buy the wood for new benches for the church and a new wooden altar. One of the MTC members, a carpenter, did the manual work. They also helped with school fundraising activities organized by the teachers, like the yearly bingo. MTC was one of my favorite ministries, ever since I had worked with the Young Christian Workers (JOC) and the Young Christian Students (JEC) movements in Chimbote and in Cartavio. MTC followed the same social action methodology at each meeting, reflecting on the socio-political reality in the light of Scripture, and then looking for ways to act to better the lived situation. I still believe that these kinds of movements are the salt of the Church, because they are "small Christian communities" which are not dependent on a priest or Religious like me. They can function by themselves no matter who the pastor is. Many parish groups are often overly dependent on the pastor, and for that reason soon disappear when the priest is transferred elsewhere.

FAMILY COUNSELING PROGRAMS

During those first years in Tacna I was invited to help in a state-run program for addicts at the regional hospital. Most of the participants were men addicted to alcohol or drugs. A few were women, mainly with gambling addictions, and adolescents with computer addictions. They were a rewarding group to work with, eager to share their stories and to learn. They were honest about their lives and wanted to change them. Later that year another group of doctors and specialists began a similar privately-run program for addictions in which I also collaborated. I helped in the morning once a week.

Almost as soon as we arrived in Tacna I decided to initiate the Family Counseling School as I had within the Family Institute project in Puno. I still had some funds left over from the Puno project, so I invited Wilber, Percy and Marlene to come from Puno to lead family workshops on self-parenting, first with the forty-plus teachers at the Fe y Alegría school administered by the St. Joseph Sisters, then with the staff of the Jesuit-run social center in Ilo, as we previously had done in 2002-2003.

The self-parenting program was geared to help persons reflect on the parenting they had received as children and how they might alter any negative effects so as to establish a healthier self-esteem. These workshops with the team from Chucuito helped me to find new people in Tacna who could constitute a new family-counseling team there. Wilber, however, continued to come occasionally during all my years in Tacna, both to visit me and to help me with workshops. Thank you, Wilber for your help and your friendship all these years.

So many people were interested in the family counseling school in Tacna that I had to divide them into two study groups which, as I explained in the last chapter, were essential to socialize the material studied at home during the week. One study group met in the morning in the diocesan offices, and the other met at night at the home of one of the participants. Another group of students formed in the city of Ilo, located on the Peruvian coast about two hours north of Tacna by bus. I usually met each week with each of the study groups, excepting the one in Ilo where I went once a month. Sisters Kay Conroy and Zelma Leblanc, whom I had known in Cartavio, were now living in Ilo, and they helped me with the study groups there through the years. I found new students for the family counseling school through my teaching in the Tacna program for lay leadership. As I explained earlier, it was a diocesan program established by the bishop and the Maryknoll priests in the early nineties to train lay people to assume leadership positions in the Peruvian Church where there were few priests. It had resulted from the Second Vatican Council's call for all baptized members of the Church to assume a more active role in Church life as followers of Jesus. I had been involved in this type of ministry since my arrival in Peru. I was convinced that the future of the Church in Latin America depended on lay people becoming more actively involved in ministry and decision making. It was the backbone of all my ministry in Peru through the years. Sadly, some Church people were still insisting on emphasizing vocations to the ministerial priesthood and vocations to the Religious life. I have no problem with that if it is kept in perspective, with the lay Baptismal vocation recognized as the primary vocation. That vision of mine had already caused me problems in the past, if you recall, when I defended Rudi on the ODEC team in the Prelature of Juli.

I was very busy in Tacna, and I helped both in the parish and in the parish school, as well, when asked to do so by Bill or Jorge. However, just as with Diego in Puno, my auxiliary service to the people of Tacna and to the diocese rather than full-time in the Vinani parish, the Holy

Cross institutional ministry there, fostered my reputation of "doing my own thing" among those in Peru who were working full-time in the Holy Cross institutions. It was only one more step to calling me lazy for not contributing to the growth of Holy Cross in Peru.

The founder of Holy Cross, Basil Moreau, wanted the priests and Brothers and Sisters of Holy Cross to offer their services to help the local Church as auxiliaries. If that meant establishing Holy Cross institutions, fine. However, I believe that it also meant sometimes doing what others were not yet doing. I felt that in Tacna as in Puno, while I was helping as needed in the Vinani parish, a Holy Cross institution, and in the parish school, I also was accomplishing other ministries that no one else or few others were undertaking. I am proud of my work, whatever the opinion of a few in Holy Cross.

THE MONEY PROBLEM

In mid-July 2006, Jim Lackenmier, as the provincial treasurer, sent Bill a letter regarding Bill's seeking financial grants for the parish school without getting Holy Cross approval. Bill responded, explaining that the school was a parish school, so he got the necessary approval for the grants through the bishop who was the person responsible for the school. That was the way that Diego and I also had gotten financial help in the Juli prelature for the Chucuito parish and for the religion teacher training team (ODEC) and for the Aymara Institute (IDEA), all of which were not Holy Cross institutions, but were Holy Cross auxiliary work in diocesan institutions in collaboration with the Prelature of Juli and the local bishop. There apparently was a growing concern in Canto Grande that the school in Tacna was obtaining funding from the same donors who gave to Holy Cross grants for the Holy Cross ministries in Canto Grande, and that that might affect somehow the amounts Canto Grande received. Apparently there also was a fear that donations to the district might be designated more for Vinani than for Canto Grande because at that time Vinani looked poorer and more in need.

Canto Grande was a huge parish with over 250,000 people within its boundaries. It was the size of a diocese here in the United States. It had nineteen chapels which here in the United States would be big enough to each be considered a parish. That was the reason why the shortage of priests in Canto Grande was always a problem for the Peru district. The Canto Grande parish had a great need for sacramental priests just for Sunday Masses. Holy Cross also was administering a large Fe y Alegría grade and high school there with over 2,000 students. Additionally, it had a school for disabled children and youth named Yancana Huasi. And the Holy Cross Family Institute, about which I wrote earlier, had its national headquarters there. Canto Grande was a booming, growing enterprise.

As I recounted, Dave Farrell had asked the chapter of 2003 at the request of the bishop of Chosica to accept the Canto Grande parish in perpetuity, which meant that another bishop could not easily throw Holy Cross out. The chapter of 2003 had debated the pros and cons of doing that, but in the end the decree presented by Dave received the necessary majority vote for approval. So, Canto Grande was ours, and it was to be the centerpiece of the Holy Cross presence in Peru.

Bill was quite upset with Jim Lackenmier's letter. He spoke with me one evening shortly afterwards about his plan to leave Peru in March 2007. He told me that he was out of patience with what he considered the continual negativeness towards the Tacna mission.

Bill knew that in February 2005 after the district assembly I had spoken with Bud Colgan, the provincial superior, about possibly leaving the district to return to the United States, if that was what he thought would be best under the circumstances. I did not want to continue living and working in the district with a lot of anger in me. I was very upset that Bud had named Bob Baker to replace Bill as district superior, especially since Bob was one of the councilors who had made life so difficult for Bill when he was superior. I felt that Bob, who had been living in Canto Grande and had been Bill's assistant at that time, could easily have helped Bill manage the district while Bill continued living as the district superior in Tacna. But he would not do that. Even though he was the assistant district superior, he felt that it was Bill's job, not his. He also was very opposed to the school in Tacna from the very beginning, although at the time he had never visited Tacna. However, when the provincial offered him Bill's position as district superior, he was quick to accept it.

I also had worried at the time that possibly quite a few of the Peruvian members disagreed with my opinions. I did not want to be an obstacle to what the Peruvians in the community wanted, especially if the young Peruvian members of Holy Cross were finding my views or ways difficult. During the debates at the community assemblies many of them remained silent and seldom participated.

On the other hand, during all those years, the young Peruvians often spent time with us in Tacna. They came during their summer breaks from studies. The Latin American novices from Mexico, Brazil, Chile and Peru also spent time with us during their pastoral month in July. They all seemed always to enjoy the time with us both for the work they did at the school or in the parish and for our style of community living. The young Peruvians also seemed to like spending time with Bill, Jorge, and me at table or during the social periods of our community assemblies or gatherings in Lima twice a year.

Then a year later during the chapter of 2006 I was nominated by some of the Peruvians to be a candidate for the position of elected councilor for the new district council that was being elected to serve under Bob Baker. He had been reappointed as district superior by the provincial for a three-year term. I lost that election by one vote.

After the affirmation that the 2006 election gave me, I spoke to the provincial again telling him that I had changed my mind about leaving the district. I had decided to stay on, because I felt that a good number of the Peruvians seemed to want my voice heard on the district council. I was always a very vocal person, and I had spoken my mind both when I had been on district councils in the past with Bud and during community assemblies. That openness and honesty about my thoughts and feelings bothered some people in the district.

I often was critical of council decisions, too. My experience of Church and Holy Cross in the past had been one of discerning in community and making decisions together as a community. Since the chapter of 2003 I felt that Holy Cross had become more of "a dictatorship of the council," with the superior and his council making important decisions outside of community assemblies and without much community consultation, especially with the people who would be affected by the decisions. I also thought that the provincial superior in the United States was overly involved in the district decision-making and was listening mainly to a few, thus excluding the voices of others in the district with different opinions and points of view. I felt that Holy Cross was taking on the authoritarian, militaristic style of Church which was so very present in the manner both Popes John Paul II and Benedict XVI operated, and was apparent now among many of the newly appointed Peruvian diocesan bishops named by them. Holy Cross in Peru seemed to me to have turned to a more clerical top-down pre-Vatican II style of Church, and I was vocal in my criticism about that both in my words and in my actions. It put me in a very singular place in the Holy Cross district. I certainly put wood on the fire in community meetings!

So, in July 2006, I felt sorry that Bill felt now that he needed to leave the district for his own mental and emotional health. I think he was very hurt by all that had happened in his regard while he was district superior. I think that he was angry that both Bob and Dave who had opposed him when he was superior, had been named as the new superior and assistant superior in his place. He was also tired of seeing all his plans for bettering the new mission in Tacna and his efforts looking for funds for that purpose being constantly criticized and opposed. He just wanted out of it all. Bill rarely spoke openly about what was going on inside himself, but I felt that was his state of mind at that time, even though I knew he loved working in Vinani in the parish and helping Jorge with the new school. He had put a lot of energy into this new parish mission which he had been responsible for starting up. Bill also was a voice like me in the district, and a companion on the journey. I would miss him deeply! Both Jorge and I would miss him in the parish, too, because we would have to assume Bill's share of the ministry there. Thank you, Bill, for our years together in Tacna.

Bill left in early December 2006. He went directly from the Tacna airport, where Jorge and the Holy Cross Sisters and I saw him off, to the airport in Lima and then immediately on to the United States. He did not want to stop in Canto Grande.

After Bill left, Jorge and I had to take on much more of the parish ministry. Since arriving in Tacna I had helped Bill with celebrating the Sunday liturgies which I enjoyed doing in the parish. Bill led the music at Sunday Mass with a small choir he had formed with some of the teachers at the school. He also celebrated daily Mass in the chapel even though practically no one attended. Sometimes the teachers felt sorry for him and would attend Mass with him if they had late meetings. Bill would then drive them to the center of town in the community car that he had for his use. When he left Tacna, the daily Mass was canceled. Both Jorge and I still felt that we needed to build the Sunday Mass community up first, and then when they wanted a daily Mass we would begin with a weekday Mass. That was a thorn of contention for many years from the beginning, with those who believed that if you were an ordained priest you had to celebrate daily Mass in the parish no matter what. Once again there were community tensions from different visions of priesthood and Church community development.

Many of the teachers at the school and the four founding lay people of the parish had helped Bill out with faith formation classes and with the preparation for the reception of the Sacraments on Sunday afternoons. All this collaboration continued after he left.

Remembering what had happened to the Chucuito mission in 2003 I wondered what would happen to Jorge and me, since we were now a community of only two!

THE PARISH AND THE SCHOOL IN VINANI

Shortly after Bill left, Bob Baker became very supportive of the Tacna mission. He asked each of his four councilors to visit Tacna. We had good visits with three of them, and we were happy that they finally were getting to see the mission, and especially the new school, first hand. They all were delighted with the parish and the parish school. Only Dave Farrell was too busy to visit, because he was very involved in the Holy Cross institutions in Canto Grande.

Bob visited us often, and we had very enjoyable days with him. He named Jorge pastor of the Vinani parish in August 2007. He also seemed to have changed his mind about the parish school, because he became very supportive of Jorge's work there. From my many years in Peru with Bob, I was accustomed to his going through highs and lows in his relationship with me and with others. I hoped he would stay on a high with us in Tacna.

Occasionally Jorge and I would go for a day off to the Chilean city of Arica, located just across the border from Peruvian Tacna. It was only a forty-mile trip by bus or *colectivo*, but usually took about two hours because we had to pass through both border customs on the way.

The school continued to grow in numbers of students and teachers each year under Jorge's leadership. I helped him by offering days of reflection for the teachers—using Basil Moreau's booklet on Christian education—and participating with Jorge in the process of evaluating the teachers each year during January for the renewal of their contracts with the school. Most of the teachers were friends, and Jorge and I enjoyed spending time with them. Many of them became members of the Christian Workers Movement (MTC), and some of them studied family counseling in the Family Counseling School and took Bible classes in the programs for the Diocesan Formation of lay leaders where I taught. Thank you, teachers of Vinani, for your friendship and for all that you did for the school and parish during those years.

MINISTRY IN TACNA DURING 2007

In early January Jorge's father died in the farming community of Cutina Capilla where Jorge had grown up, near the city of Juli in the Prelature of Juli. He had been sick for some time. That year Jorge's nephew and my godson Daniel Mallea lived with us for a time while studying at the university in Tacna. We had room, because Bob still had not yet assigned a third person to live with us. Juan Tuesta, one of the young professed in the Congregation who had been asked to leave the community recently, also lived with us briefly while at the same university.

During that year, I continued to bring my History of Holy Cross in Peru up to date. I already had written several papers since the founding of the mission in 1963 and presented them at the Holy Cross Family History Conference in the United States.

In August 2007 I was invited to travel to Santiago, Chile by Chilean Holy Cross priest Pepe Ahumada, the rector of St. George College, our high school there, to give talks on our founder Basil Moreau to the parents and teachers. On that occasion I visited several of the ex-Holy Cross Peruvians who had left the community while studying theology and had stayed in Chile.

In September Jorge and I celebrated the beatification of our founder Basil Moreau with a lovely, simple celebration with the Holy Cross Sisters in Vinani. It coincided with the anniversary of the parish and school. We celebrated a Mass at which several Religious congregations in Tacna participated and then enjoyed a dinner party at a nearby restaurant. It was a joyful day for us.

Later that same year I was invited to Chimbote to celebrate the Mass for the twenty-fifth anniversary of the presence there of the Sisters of the Holy Cross (American branch). In November I went, as well, to Chucuito to preside at a Mass honoring the twenty years of the Sisters of Holy Cross (Canadian branch) in the Prelature of Juli.

Also in November I went to Chile to meet up with my friend Bob Comiskey who was traveling from the United States with his wife Nancy. He had been ordained with me in Rome, and later left the community to marry. Together we visited our two Chilean friends from Rome Mario Irarrázaval and Sergio Concha.

In Lima I conducted the Maryknoll Fathers' annual retreat at their Center House. It was during a difficult period for them, because the new Opus Dei bishop in the Prelature of Juli had decided not to renew the contracts of the three remaining Maryknoll priests who were still working in that prelature founded by their congregation. I shared with them the Spiritual Exercises of St. Ignatius which can be helpful in trying times. I had been introduced to the Exercises during my thirty-day retreat back in 2000.

That year, 2007, I conducted many workshops on the topic of forgiveness in the Tacna schools. My godson Wilber Mamani Cotillo came down from Chucuito several times to help me with the large groups. Our diocesan lay formation team also began to offer these workshops in our Friday evening programs, and some of the students who had graduated from the family counseling school helped me out, too. The entire Marriage Preparation

Team from the parish of St. Martin in Tacna studied the family counseling course together that year. Along with assisting Jorge in the parish, it was a very busy time for me.

HOLY CROSS

In December 2007 Bob and his council made the decision to move the Holy Cross men's summer annual meeting to the days right after Christmas rather than have it at the usual date in February when we could meet together with the Holy Cross Sisters. Jorge and I complained about the change for that reason. We also pointed out that not only was it very difficult to get inexpensive air tickets around Christmas, but especially that it also was a time when there was a lot of work to do to close the school year. Even the Holy Cross men who worked in the Fe y Alegría school in Canto Grande often were absent during the meeting that year. However, decisions in the district council continued to be made more and more around the desires and for the convenience of the Religious in Canto Grande. Since neither Jorge nor I were members of the council, we had neither voice nor vote in these decisions and were not consulted beforehand.

Since the mid-1980's all the Holy cross men and women in Peru had gathered together for a week of Holy Cross family assembly during the month of February when it was easier for all, especially for the Holy Cross Sisters to meet. This year Bob announced that the February 2008 assembly with the Sisters would be optional for the men. Then he assigned the Peruvians in formation, who usually enjoyed these gatherings, to summer studies and pastoral work during those February dates. Despite these decisions by Bob and his council, I was happy that Peruvian Holy Cross Sister, Marcelina Quispe, became a teacher in the Vinani school that year, so Holy Cross collaboration in Tacna, at least, was still alive and well.

In 2008 Bob and his council made plans for a third Holy Cross priest to join Jorge and me in Tacna. Jorge and I hoped that it would be young, recently-ordained Alfredo Hernandez, who was from the Chimbote parish and who had been working in Canto Grande. We both knew Alfredo from our time in Chimbote. He had been my student while I was a teacher there, and he joined Holy Cross in 1994 when Jorge was doing vocation ministry in the parish. Alfredo had spoken to us often about his interest in working with us in Tacna.

Bob and his council opted, instead, for an interchange of personnel with the Holy Cross district in Chile. It was felt that this interchange would strengthen the ties between the two districts, which already were collaborating in formation programs with a novitiate in Huaycan outside of Lima and a theology program in Santiago. So the Peru district assigned Alfredo Hernandez to work in Chile, while the Chilean district assigned to Tacna elderly North American Gerry Papen, who had been in Chile for years and who was suffering at the time from early-stage memory problems.

Gerry arrived in Tacna in February 2008 accompanied by Sergio Concha, a Chilean friend of his and mine who recently had left the community. I knew Sergio from when I studied in Rome. I was very happy to be able to spend some time with him again after so many years. Way back in the early 1970's he had visited me in Cartavio. Since then I had seen him a few times when I went to Chile for community meetings or on vacation with Jorge Mallea. Thank you, Sergio, for that week-long visit.

Gerry had a lot of difficulty adapting to life in Tacna. He often got lost when he went out alone. He could not find sufficient pastoral work he could do in the Vinani parish, so he wound up spending most of his day moving stones from one area of the parish school patio to another. It was neither a just nor kind decision to assign him to Tacna where he was way out of his comfort zone. It was obvious in our conversations with him that he had been very happy and well-adjusted to his life and ministry in a parish in Santiago.

In July 2008 Don Fetters, the novice master at the time, who had come to the Lima novitiate after several years as district superior in Chile, told Jorge and me that several novices would be coming to Tacna for their August pastoral experience. It was quite normal. We had hosted Holy Cross novices during their pastoral month several times in the past, as well as young Peruvians in formation, both professed and postulants, during their summer and mid-term pastoral experiences. When Bill Persia was still with us, they helped him organize a summer school in the parish and aided with a parish census. This year they were going to assist Jorge at the school.

In our community meeting in Tacna Gerry offered to direct the novices' program, since he had more time to spend with them, and it would give him something to do. He made plans to spend a few weeks during July at the novitiate with his friend Don and then travel back to Tacna with the two novices. The three of us drew up a plan for the time that they would be with us that Gerry could present to Don at the novitiate. According to our plan, the novices would go with Gerry to daily Mass at the nearby parish or to where Gerry might be celebrating Mass, just as the novices did in Canto Grande parish if they were not in the formation house where a daily Mass was celebrated.

I believed that the novices' formative pastoral experience should show them how community life is lived in an active house, organized around the members' ministry schedules, unlike a house of formation, organized around the study schedule. Our community in Tacna was an active house, and I did not feel that we should be dishonest with the young by changing our schedule or life style just because they were visiting us. They should see life in an active house, because one day that would be the schedule they would be living.

In our house in Tacna each member took turns organizing daily morning prayer around a theme or a reality that we were living at that time. Each leader of prayer selected hymns, psalms and readings that were appropriate to the theme of the day. Then we shared prayer around our needs, concerns and hopes. We did not merely pick up the official Church prayer book and recite the psalms. We also did not celebrate daily Mass in the house, since we were usually only two, nor did we have daily Mass in the parish after Bill left. These were different points of view between our house in Tacna (and before that in Puno when Diego and I lived there) and the houses in Canto Grande where most of the Holy Cross men had a more formal, official morning prayer, even though they did not have daily Mass in their houses, either, except in the formation house itself. In Canto Grande usually one of the priests celebrated daily Mass each day in one of the chapels in the parish, and the others might or might not attend.

Suddenly, however, in early August just before the community meeting in Lima, Don the novice master told us that the novices would not be coming to Tacna. They were all going to live at the formation house in Canto Grande. Once again, we had no part in the decision. The news came with no explanation as to why the change had been made, even though I personally asked Don why. He did not seem to know, or simply would not say. Only afterwards, Jorge Izaguirre who was on the district council again at the time, hinted that the reason might have been because we did not have daily Mass in our house in Tacna. We never got a clear answer to our inquiries from the district superior or anyone else.

In September Bob suddenly decided to send Gerry back to Chile before his planned year in Tacna was finished. So, after six months Jorge and I were alone again.

That same month, I was invited by the Holy Cross Brothers in Brazil to give another workshop on Holy Cross history to their five novices in Santarem in the northeast jungle. I first had been invited there in 2003. I enjoyed these opportunities to spend time with the young

Brazilian men considering life as Holy Cross Brothers and with my good friend Brother Ronald Hein who had a ministry with street children in Santarem.

During the whole year of 2008 we tried to buy our house in Tacna, which had been put up for sale at the end of 2007. Bob Baker told us that his council at first did not approve buying the house, but afterwards he had spoken with them one by one and convinced them to approve it. The sale was problematic because the owners did not have their papers in order, but Bob put down half the purchase price, so we were hopeful to finally conclude it. Jorge and I were very happy about the decision because we felt it would give some permanence to the mission in Tacna. Unfortunately it dragged on all year without being finalized, because the owners' papers continued to be delayed.

In November I went on an eight-day retreat at the Maryknoll Center House in Miraflores in Lima. I usually did my retreats in those years at the Maryknoll house in La Paz, Bolivia, but this year I had decided on Lima. It was to be my last visit to the Center House, because it was being sold. The Maryknoll congregation was down in numbers in Peru, and the house was much too big for them. They were going to buy an apartment only for themselves in Lima, so they no longer would have accommodations for people like me. I had been staying with them since 1972. From then on I would have to stay with the community in Canto Grande, very far from the Lima city center.

On my return to Tacna the Maryknoll Sisters invited me to guide them, too, in their discernment process to make some major decisions in their Peru mission.

In mid-December 2008, Bob Baker came to visit us as he usually did a couple of times a year. The visit seemed to go well, as always.

At the end of the month, Jorge finally got his permanent teaching position transferred from the Fe y Alegría school in Canto Grande to our new parish school in Vinani. It had taken him five years to obtain the transfer; it was not easy. We celebrated it on December 28.

THE 2009 DISTRICT CHAPTER

Just before the Christmas holidays, the provincial superior Bud Colgan phoned me to ask if I would keep my name in as one of the three candidates with the highest number of votes on the straw ballot for the position of new district superior. I was happy that Bud was going to allow an election during the 2009 district chapter in January. For this reason, even though I did not desire the position, I told him that I would leave my name in. I believed that in the district we should have elections, and I felt that Bob Baker should have the opportunity to be elected by the membership and not just be named by the provincial superior as he had been previously.

In mid-January 2009 Jorge and I went to the district chapter held at a retreat house outside Lima. It began as usual with the district superior Bob Baker's presentation of the state of things in each house of the district. There was no mention at all about our mission in Tacna. I was about to say something to Bob when Jorge Mallea spoke up and asked him why he had not mentioned Tacna in his report to the chapter. Personally, I figured Bob probably had skipped a page in his notes accidentally, because he seemed very nervous during his presentation that day with the provincial superior Bud Colgan sitting there presiding. But even after Jorge's question to him, Bob did not try to offer an explanation. He just sat down, and there was silence in the room. No one else said anything.

Jorge had prepared a wonderful little video on the parish and school in Tacna that we wanted to show during the days of the chapter, so that the membership in Canto Grande could see the advances made there. But the coordinator of the chapter, Jorge Izaguirre, kept telling us that there was no free time in the chapter schedule to show it.

Bud continued the chapter session by asking the delegates to approve legislation that would allow him to name the district superior in the next chapter of 2012. The provincial superior had that right even without chapter permission if he thought that there were not three suitable candidates for the position on the nominating ballot. He had used that right back in the chapter of 2006, and had just used it again in this chapter with his appointment of Bob Baker as district superior. I and several others, especially the Peruvians, spoke strongly against this. I thought that we had the right to elect, and that we had suitable candidates. After debate, the legislation was not approved by the chapter.

Then Phil Devlin who had founded the Fe y Alegría school in Canto Grande presented legislation that obligated the district superior and his council to send donations earmarked by the donor for a certain ministry directly to the people in charge of the ministry for their use, instead of holding the donations in a common fund until the ministry presented plans for the use of the monies and they were approved by the district superior and his council. In recent years the latter had become the district practice. Jorge and I in Tacna also had had similar difficulties receiving donations sent for Tacna. Sometimes the funds never reached us. Following a lengthy discussion, the chapter approved this legislation after modifying some of the strong, harsh language in the original proposal.

At all previous chapters, there always had been added to the chapter legislation a statement about the places considered the official Holy Cross works of the district. I remember it so well, because down through the years at former chapters Diego and I often had to struggle to get the Chucuito mission included in it, because some did not feel that our work in the Prelature of Juli was an official Holy Cross ministry. But during this chapter of 2009 no one even mentioned the statement. I thought that was strange, but then, since I often had found it a thorn in my side, both when Diego and I were in Chucuito and then even later in the chapter of 2006 when a few others did not want to recognize the parish school in Vinani as a community work, I decided to let it pass and not to say anything about it.

The chapter ended a day earlier than planned. Many remarked what a calm chapter it had been, because there had been so few heated discussions during it.

THE DAY AFTER

Before we left, the provincial superior Bud Colgan told me that he was making his official provincial visit to all of us and that he would like to speak with Jorge and me the next morning in Canto Grande, while we both were still in Lima. He also said that he wanted to speak with Alfredo Hernandez, the young Holy Cross priest who had been sent to Chile the year before in the district interchange. I thought that maybe Alfredo was going to be assigned now to Tacna, since Gerry had returned to Chile.

That evening after we arrived back at the formation house in Canto Grande, most of the Peruvians (except for Jorge Izaguirre) with the novice master Don Fetters and I went out to Larcomar, a commercial recreational spot in Lima in Miraflores to have dinner out and to attend a play at the theater together. It was a happy, relaxed evening in that large commercial, recreational complex overlooking the ocean. We had a very nice time.

The following morning at the formation house in Canto Grande after Mass and breakfast Jorge Mallea finally got a chance to show the video he had prepared about Tacna to the young Peruvians. They all seemed impressed.

After that it was time for me to go for my provincial interview. So I walked into the room where Bud Colgan, provincial superior, was meeting with me. I was surprised to see that the district superior Bob Baker was sitting off in a corner of the room. I sat down across from Bud. Immediately, he announced to me that Bob and the district council (composed of Anibal Nino, elected councilor, the assistant district superior and head of formation;

Jorge Izaguirre, elected councilor and pastor of the large Canto Grande parish; Dave Farrell, district treasurer and head of the Holy Cross Family Ministries and Yancana Huasi School for the Disabled; Brother Tom Giumenta, director of the Fe y Alegría School in Canto Grande) unanimously had voted me out of Peru and that he and his provincial council unanimously had approved it. What a bomb!

I looked over at Bob in the corner of the room and asked him why he had not said anything to me about this while visiting us in Tacna a month earlier in December. Once again, as in the chapter when Jorge had asked him about not mentioning Tacna in his report, the only response was silence. Again I asked him why he and his council had made such a drastic decision without ever first sitting down and talking with me. I wanted an answer from him. He responded only that he had suggested to his council that I might be assigned to Canto Grande to work with the lay leadership school there, but they had vetoed that possibility.

Bud spoke then, and said that he personally thought that this change might be good for me. He suspected that I might be having a priestly vocation problem because of my attitude toward celebrating daily Mass both in the house and in the parish. I answered that I knew that others in the Congregation and in the Peru district had similar views as mine about daily Mass. I knew that not everyone in Holy Cross in Canto Grande went to daily Mass, either, unless they were the celebrants, and I named a few of them.

Bud got very defensive and cited the Constitution in our Holy Cross Rule that mentions the obligation of daily Mass for all the Religious when possible. I responded that I had heard that that Constitution was one that Rome inserted into all the rules of Religious congregations even though many did not practice it. I said that for me the Mass is a community celebration at which a priest presides to serve a community of people, and not just a daily pious practice for the priest when no one is present. I added that for me Jesus' ministry was a lot broader and deeper that that, and that He told us to do what He did and to live as He lived. I could see that Bud was getting upset with me, as he always did when I said things that went against his personal beliefs about the Mass, the priesthood and Religious life.

Then Bob spoke up and told me that besides the problem with daily Mass, there was another practice of mine that was causing scandal with the young Religious. I always stayed at the Maryknoll Center House in Miraflores when I came to Lima, even though he had recommended that I stay at the formation house in Canto Grande. I reminded him that he himself, before becoming district superior, also had stayed at the Maryknoll House when he came down from Chimbote, and that we both had stayed there for the same reasons. We both liked to go to a movie and visit the city and relax. Canto Grande was too far out and too difficult to get to and from, especially late at night. Besides that, the community in Canto Grande was not the most hospitable or sociable, because they usually were too busy or too tired to spend time with visitors, and so it was not, for me anyway, a relaxing place to stay. Then, back to the previous topic, I told Bob that I knew that he himself was one of the community members who was not a big fan of daily Mass. So, I asked him, why was he signaling me out for things that he himself did or had done!

Bob ignored my question and continued. He said that on his visits to Tacna, he noticed a lot of DVD movies and English-language novels in our living room there. He accused me of reading novels and watching movies all day long. I was amazed that he could jump to that conclusion. His accusation was based on the existence of books and DVDs as can be found in most recreation rooms of the Congregation! That was no basis to know how much time we spent with them. Jorge and I watched a DVD occasionally at night to unwind after our work was finished, and I always read a bit of a novel just before going to bed to relax myself. I challenged Bob that he never had seen me reading novels or watching DVDs during the day on his visits to Tacna, because I didn't do it. But I told him that I had seen him during the day on his visits to Tacna reading novels up on the roof of the house. Why was he accusing me of doing exactly what he did when he came to visit us in Tacna?

I told them that if those were their only reasons for expelling me from Peru, then it was clear they really were very desperate to be rid of my voice and my way of being a Religious priest in their midst, because the concerns they were citing certainly did not warrant such action. I said to them I would leave Peru with a clear conscience. I knew in my heart that they must have other reasons than these if they were expelling me from the district.

Bud Colgan told me that Bob Baker and his council wanted me out of Tacna and Peru by March 1st, a little more than six weeks from that moment. I told him that I could not possibly leave that soon. I had pastoral commitments for the coming year already planned in Tacna with the pastoral teams that would need to be attended to before I could leave. Most of the people on the teams were on summer vacation during January and February, so I could not meet with them until March. Once again there was silence from Bob. The provincial said that he would consult Bob about the date later.

I asked them then what was going to happen to the parish and school mission in Vinani. By then I expected only the worst, but at the same time I was hoping that Bob would send Alfredo Hernandez who was still working in Chile to replace me in Tacna, since the interchange with Gerry had not worked out. Bud said that they would have to see about that later.

I was so angry with the secrecy and half-truths and outright lies that I was on the verge of crying in front of them, but I would not give them that satisfaction. So I stood up and told them that since I had been accused by the district superior and his council of not being worthy to continue ministry in the district, judged by them without any face to face dialogue beforehand about the accusations, and sentenced to exile by the provincial superior and his council also without any previous communication, I had nothing more to say, except that this was not at all the way I thought the Constitution on obedience and authority was supposed to be exercised in Holy Cross. I walked out. I was so angry that I could not bring myself to shake their hands.

I went directly to the chapel where I sat for two hours with Jesus, crying and wondering if this might be one of those strong signs He often gave me during my lifetime, like my original call to Peru when I was in Rome.

As I sat there with Him, I reflected that I probably should have seen this coming during the last years. I had continued to put wood on the fire by speaking out in assemblies about my way of seeing things in the district. I often had advised myself during those years to keep my mouth shut during the community assemblies and chapters. If I had been quiet and sung the company song, all this might not be happening to me. If I had celebrated daily Mass and not continued to stay at the Maryknoll House and had not insisted on my way and my belief system, maybe things would have been different. But then I realized that doing so I would not have been true to who I am. I would have been false and hypocritical. All those thoughts and many others went through my mind.

It was clear that secrecy, a complete lack of transparency, had become the norm for making serious community decisions in the Holy Cross district of Peru. It had been used to close the Chucuito mission in 2003. The manner of dismissal had become typical, too. I remembered what I had heard often in recent years from some of the young Peruvians who had been thrown out of the formation program. They each told me that suddenly one day, they were invited into a room at the formation house where the district superior Bob Baker and the head of formation Anibal Nino were sitting. Then they were told by Bob and Anibal that they were being dismissed immediately from their temporary vows in the Congregation, right in the middle of the school year, rather than in January when their annual vows came up for renewal. There were no warnings or notices beforehand; the decision usually came as a complete surprise to the young Peruvians. They said they were given a bus ticket and some money and told to leave by the following morning. Many of them, especially those Aymara from the Puno area who had been suddenly dismissed, came to visit Jorge and me in Tacna afterwards. At first I thought that they were angry and exaggerating. But then it happened to me the same way.

Jorge and I, and several other Peruvians like Alfredo, Jose Luis and Fidel, often wondered, too, what was going on in the formation program, but when we asked what the reasons were for these sudden, immediate dismissals, no explanation ever was given by Bob Baker the district superior. We were always told that these decisions were private matters that should not be discussed with others outside the district council. Dave Farrell would tell us that we should not be questioning decisions made by the district superior and the head of formation. We should just accept and obey.

I was so angry that I even considered leaving Holy Cross. I thought about staying in Peru as a diocesan priest in Tacna. I have never been so angry in my life. As I write about it now and recall how the decision about me was made, my suppressed anger rises again in me.

I knew that I and others in the district had different visions of Holy Cross' mission in Peru and on Religious life and on priesthood, but I never thought the authorities in the Congregation would take action so extreme, so secretive and so lacking in brotherliness. It was how I imagined people might be treated in the business world. But in a Religious community I expected more mutual support, more respect for diversity, more compassionate treatment and caring dialogue between those with different views.

Leaving the chapel with my head still spinning, I went looking for Jorge to find out what had happened to him during his visit with the provincial. He told me that his interview was similar. They told him that the Tacna mission was being closed immediately. The bishop had already been informed. Jorge was to be back in Canto Grande on April 1st. Jorge told them that that date would be impossible for him. After all, he was the principal of a parish school and could not possibly leave when the school year was just beginning. So, they gave him until July 1st. That news made me all the angrier, because Bud had told me just two hours earlier that they did not know what they were going to do with the Tacna mission! It was obvious that everything had been carefully planned beforehand and cleverly kept secret from the district chapter which had just ended. The closing of a mission is usually the decision of a full district chapter and not the decision of just the district council. But then there was the precedent of the closing of the Chucuito mission in 2003!

I believe that the provincial superior and the district superior and his council wanted to keep my expulsion and the closing of the parish and school in Tacna a secret from the chapter because they were worried that the chapter would not agree with them. To this day, I do not think the district chapter would have approved the closing of the Tacna mission whatever the needs in Canto Grande. The mission in Tacna was going too well, and most of the Peruvian members of Holy Cross really liked it, and a few hoped to work there someday.

Looking back on all this now I know that the reasons for expelling me were not the ones they stated. Those in provincial and district authority at the time were concerned that my voice was becoming too influential among some of the Holy Cross Peruvians. That is why they did not entrust the closing of Puno and then the closing of the Tacna mission to the entire district membership in those respective chapters. They calculated that they might not have enough votes with my voice opposing their plans. My name had been voted onto the nominating ballot for district superior in 2009, and but for one vote I would have been elected district councilor in 2006. I had become too much of an obstacle to making Canto Grande the center pin in Peru and to focusing all human and financial resources on the Holy Cross institutions in Canto Grande. With me expelled they would be free of me, and have an excuse, as well, for closing down the Tacna mission. With only the Canto Grande mission left standing, all the Holy Cross men and all financial donations would be devoted to the Canto Grande ministries. These are the real reasons, not those given to me. And they had to act quickly because Bud Colgan was approaching his term limit as provincial superior, and the new provincial elected might be less sympathetic to their vision.

Jorge and I had lunch as planned at the formation house where we were staying. Bud and Bob and other district council members involved in these decisions went out for lunch that day, so they did not have to sit at table with us. We shared our heartbreaking news only with the Peruvian Jose Luis Tineo, who also was often vocally critical of the ways of the district council. I remember that Jose Luis embraced Jorge and me and cried. Thank you, Jose Luis, for your tears and for your loving care and brotherly concern for Jorge and me that day. We both needed to feel that. Jorge and I left for the airport to return to Tacna right after lunch as we originally had planned to do.

MY LAST DAYS IN PERU

As you can imagine it was a very sad time for me. I had hoped to live out my life in Peru and die there. Peru was, and still is, home for me. When I shared my frustration and anger about how I had been treated by my community with Holy Cross Sister Frances Savoie, who had worked with me on the religion teacher training team (ODEC) in Chucuito and was now working in Vinani, she helped me to get over some of the resentment I was feeling toward Holy Cross. She reminded me not to blame the whole Congregation for the actions of a few. Thank you, Frances, for those wise words that I later would discover were so true.

Shortly after returning to Tacna I wrote to the provincial Bud Colgan asking him to delay my return date until April 1st. After consulting with Bob, he finally said yes to that. So, I began the work of organizing my ministries so that they would continue without me. I was fortunate to know people who were willing to take on the family counseling school ministry. In fact, the graduates from the various groups that had completed their studies in the family counseling school program wanted to form an official organization of family counselors. I was enthused with their suggestion. We immediately called a few meetings to begin the legal process of setting up that association. My other ministries already had their own leadership, since I worked as an auxiliary priest with them. I helped them prepare for the coming year without me.

Jorge and I decided to file appeals to Hugh Cleary, the Superior General of Holy Cross, who was the maximum authority in the Congregation. Hugh had been provincial superior of our Eastern Province from 1994 to 1998 before being elected superior general of the Congregation in 1998. I knew Hugh as a good friend. We often had interacted socially when I was visiting from Peru on vacation in the United States. My most important appeal at the time was to keep the Tacna mission open.

While we were waiting for a response from Hugh, many people and groups in Tacna wrote letters to him, with copies to Bud and Bob, asking for a reconsideration of their decisions. They asked especially that the Congregation remain in Tacna. I thank the Sisters of Holy Cross who worked with us in Tacna and the Sisters of the Holy Cross who knew me well from Chimbote, who both sent letters from both their general administrations and their Latin American councils. The Maryknoll Sisters in Tacna with whom I worked and, of course, the Vinani parish and parish school communities and the members of the Adult Workers Movement (MTC) also sent letters asking for a reconsideration particularly with regard to the closing of the Tacna mission.

Bud Colgan, the provincial superior, was completely silent about the letters. Bob Baker's response from Canto Grande was a phone call to Jorge telling us to stop causing more problems by forcing people to write those letters. Bob did not like any criticism, especially from the Sisters.

As I expected, Hugh Cleary, the superior general, did reply to our appeals with a long letter to both Jorge and me. Unfortunately he came down on the side of the district and provincial authorities. I understood his position. Two levels of Congregational authority, both the district and the provincial superiors, had approved both my expulsion and the closing of the Tacna mission. It would have been very unlikely that a superior general would intervene taking a position against them. It would not have been good company politics.

In his long letter of reply to me and to Jorge, Hugh did tell us that he had taken the time to speak several times with the provincial Bud Colgan before deciding to uphold the decisions taken by the district and provincial administrations. I did think, though, that it was a sad commentary about community authority that Hugh had not thought that it was important to speak directly with Jorge and me. Finally Hugh put on paper the reasons for my expulsion, which were the same ones that Bud and Bob had given me verbally. Hugh also stated that the reason given by Bud for not bringing up the closing of the Tacna mission in the chapter was that the members of the district council would have to mention the personal problem of my expulsion, and that this was considered a personal, delicate matter never discussed by chapters. I find it hard now to accept that Hugh did not recognize that the reasons given for my expulsion were so obviously inadequate. He went on to comment how much the Holy Cross Sisters and others in Tacna appreciated Jorge and me. He ended his letter to me by saying that he thought that this might be the best move for me personally.

District superior Bob Baker and the district treasurer Dave Farrell shut down our community bank account in Tacna immediately. Jorge had to travel to Lima, twenty-two hours each way on the bus, to pick up cash for our monthly house needs. While there he was told that he would have to move out of the house on March 31st when I left. No one told him where he was to go. The Holy Cross Sisters in Vinani invited Jorge to stay with them, but Bob Baker would not allow it. Finally, I spoke with the owners of our house who told me that Jorge could stay in the house until July since the official documents needed for the sale of the house still were not in order, so they could not sell it to someone else before that date.

During all those days, no one from the community in Canto Grande phoned us to support us or to ask how we were doing. I often wondered if the others even knew what was going on. When Bill left the district in 2006, some of the young Peruvians later told me that they had not known he was leaving until after he had gone. Or maybe the young Peruvians were afraid to identify with us. Or maybe they were in favor of the decisions. I really do not know. The silence saddened me, however. If they did know, this was a poor commentary on community life. I had felt the same in 2004 when Diego announced to the Holy Cross men during the annual community assembly that he was leaving the district to go back to his home district of Chile. Diego had thanked the men for his years among us. When he finished speaking the men simply stood up and walked out for the next session without any word of thanks or applause or fraternal embrace. Only the Holy Cross Sisters spoke up during the following session, sometimes with tears in their eyes, thanking Diego and me for the years working together with them in Puno.

In February Jorge and I both traveled to Lima for the annual gathering of the Holy Cross men and women. The Sisters were all there, but only Brother John Benesh came from the men's community in Canto Grande. The other men had decided not to attend. In 1985 John had come to Peru thanks to my invitation. Thank you, John, for your presence at that assembly. It meant a lot to me. During the gathering in which I gave a last-minute talk on Holy Cross history, since Bob had not shown up for his scheduled talk, the Sisters helped both Jorge and me to heal somewhat from the blows we had received. Thank you, dear Holy Cross Sisters.

Afterwards Jorge returned to Tacna for his work at the school while I went to Cartavio, Trujillo and Chimbote to say my goodbyes to my dear friends there. In early March I went to Chucuito/Puno to do the same. And of course, in Tacna during those weeks we had lots of goodbye parties.

Fortunately, during the month of March Jorge and I did not have too much time to lick our wounds. A serious problem between the parish school and the educational authorities arose. According to the agreement between the Holy See and Peru, the Church authorities presented candidates for the teaching jobs in parish schools, and the Peruvian government accepted or rejected them. The right to nominate or present the teachers was the right of the Church authorities. In early March the educational authorities told the parish school in Vinani that it had to choose six teachers from among the educational authority's list of teachers with permanent teaching positions who needed to be transferred to a new job. This was blatantly against the agreement. So, with the consent of the Bishop of Tacna, Jorge as principal and I as representative of the bishop in the parish diocesan school started conversations with the educational authorities in Tacna, together with three other parish schools in Tacna that were suffering a similar situation. We had endless meetings with the educational authorities that seemed to go nowhere, but at least for Jorge and me this effort, to help the school have the teachers we felt would best serve the students, took our minds off what was happening to us. By the end of March the situation still had not been resolved, and Jorge with the consent of the bishop had begun a civil process against the educational authorities for abuse of authority.

Meeting with the bishop during that month to keep him informed about what was happening at the school in this difficult situation led him to learn what was happening to us in our Holy Cross community. He expressed his regret to us and expressed surprise that Holy Cross was pulling out so abruptly from his diocese without prior conversation with him and without giving him more time to find replacements. Thank you, Bishop Marco Antonio, for your support during that month of March.

After one of those meetings with the bishop I felt sorry for his situation, so I decided to swallow my pride and write a letter to Bob and his council offering to comply with whatever they asked me to do if they allowed me to stay at least until the end of the year. This would solve the problem that the bishop had finding replacements for us so quickly. I thought it might be a way for me to stay in Peru long enough to keep the Tacna mission open. The immediate reply the next day from Bob was NO.

The day before I was to leave, Dave Farrell broke the long community silence by phoning to thank me for my years in Peru. He acted surprised that I was leaving! I always thought he was quite brave phoning me that way. I realized he was taking a victory lap.

On March 31st, the Holy Cross Sisters came to the Tacna airport at 5:00 in the morning to say goodbye to me. Jorge accompanied me to Lima. Arriving there we went to the Sisters of the Holy Cross house in Jesus Maria neighborhood and spent the day together. In the evening, Jorge and my compadre Felipe Calderon, father of my godson Isaac, and his family came to the Lima airport to say farewell. And so, off I flew from my beloved Peru where I had hoped to live out my final days. But that plan of mine was not to be. God had other plans for me.

10. UNITED STATES 2009 - 2018

If I were to give this chapter a subtitle, it would be
MY TIME OF EXILE. I landed at JFK airport in New
York City on the morning of April 1, 2009, on the LAN
direct flight from Lima. My only lifeline was the hope
that I would be able to return to Peru at least occasionally
for visits to friends and extended family. I was downcast
and heartbroken. My dream had come to an end. I had
thought I would live out my last days in my beloved Peru
and die there among those with whom I had lived and
worked all my ordained priesthood. But it was not to be.
"Why?" I asked myself.

George Lucas, assistant provincial to Bud Colgan,
met me at the airport in New York and drove me to the
provincial house in Bridgeport, Connecticut. He told me
that he had been visiting in Uganda, Africa, where he had
been district superior, while all these decisions about me
and the mission in Tacna were decided. He gave me the
impression that he had known nothing about it. I found
that hard to believe, but I said nothing. However, I recently learned from another person on Bud's provincial
team at that time that he, too, had known nothing about
my being expelled. George had always seemed open to
what I was saying when he visited Peru, but I think he
usually backed Bud's decisions. He seemed to me to be
the faithful, loyal assistant who really would have pre-

ferred to be back in Africa where he had spent most of his priestly life.

On arrival in Bridgeport, the provincial Bud Colgan and the treasurer Jim Lackenmier received me warmly, as if I were just arriving on vacation as in earlier years when I stopped at the provincial house coming from Peru. Bud said we would speak about my new ministry in the United States after lunch.

When Bud, George and I had our meeting, I told Bud that I was planning to write him a letter later, sometime when I felt less emotional about all that had happened to me recently in Peru. Bud talked about possibilities for a new ministry for me in the United States. He had communicated with the Fall River diocese in Massachusetts regarding Hispanic ministry work for me there near our community at Stonehill College where I could live. He had set up a meeting for me with a contact person in that diocese, whom he suggested I phone as soon as possible. Afterwards, George took me out to buy me a new clerical black shirt which Bud insisted I wear for my interview. I had not worn one in years.

I already had written from Peru to the St. Petersburg diocese in Florida where Holy Cross had opened a new Hispanic parish in Dade City the year before. My friend Dan Kayajan, a younger Holy Cross priest who had spent a year in Peru in 1992, was engaged in Hispanic ministry there with Bill Persia who had been with me in Tacna.

The next day Jim Lackenmier drove me up to our community residence at Stonehill College near Boston to pick up a car for my use. I stayed the night with the

Stonehill Holy Cross community. Once again it was just like when I came on vacation from Peru. No one said anything about my return. I don't think they knew why I was back. Then, the following day, I drove to Holy Cross' house in Dartmouth, Massachusetts where twelve of our elderly, retired priests lived. I had asked to spend some time at this house, because Fred Serraino, my friend from Peru who was superior there, had invited me to do so. Dartmouth was a great community for me during the next four months. Many of these men are deceased now. Thank you, all, for receiving me so well and helping me to heal. May you rest in peace.

NEW MINISTRY

Almost at once I set up an interview with Bud's contact, the director of Hispanic ministry in the Diocese of Fall River, who spoke with me about several possibilities in that diocese. He told me that there might be an opening in one of the larger Hispanic parishes near Stonehill College. The other possibility was to perform educational ministry across the diocese in seven different parishes with Hispanic communities. I found that last offer enticing, since I enjoyed the teaching part of parish ministry. I was afraid, however, of driving long distances between the parishes during winter months, because I had not driven in wintertime in years. I also was not sure if the pastors in these parishes would welcome my help. Dan Kayajan, who had worked in this diocese a few years before, had helped to create its diocesan pastoral Hispanic plan. In more recent years, however, there had been many changes of the priests who were now pastors in these parishes with Hispanic ministry. I said I would think about it.

In the meantime I waited to hear from Joan Morgan, chancellor of the St. Petersburg, Florida, diocese, to whom I had written from Peru about the possibility for Hispanic ministry there. I knew our Holy Cross parish in Dade City where Dan and Bill worked did not need any more priests, but I thought that I might be able to live with Bill and Dan while working in another nearby parish. When I had spoken with Joan previously, she had said to me that it was not a question of *if* but *where*.

So, three weeks after arriving back from Peru, while I was on a bus going from Kings College in Wilkes-Barre, Pennsylvania, where I had been visiting the Holy Cross community, to Baltimore, Maryland, on my way to visit a friend, I received a call on my cell phone from Art Proulx, the pastor at Nativity parish in Brandon, Florida. He informed me that I had been assigned by the St. Petersburg Diocese to serve the large Hispanic community in his six-thousand-family parish. None of the other priests in the parish spoke Spanish, so I was very much needed. I was thrilled at this news; I said I would like to visit the parish.

I traveled down to Florida the next week. First, I spent some time with Holy Cross priest Bob Wiseman, a community friend of mine who worked in another parish in that diocese. With Bob I then visited with Dan and Bill at our Holy Cross parish in Dade City. And then we all went to a diocesan assembly where I met many priests of the diocese. Afterwards I spent two nights and a day at

Nativity Parish. I told the pastor Art Proulx that my provincial wanted me to live either with Dan and Bill or with Bob, but Art told me that Nativity parish was too distant from either one of them, so I would need to reside right there at Nativity. Then I spoke with the provincial about my visit to Florida and my desire to work there. After consulting with Jim Lackenmier, the treasurer, who was more favorable to me working in the St. Petersburg diocese because the financial benefits there were better than those in the Fall River diocese, I was given the green light to accept the new ministry at Nativity parish. So, after four weeks back in the United States I had a new job, which would begin on August 1, 2009.

RENEWAL TIME

I asked the provincial for some renewal time before beginning this new ministry, and I was given permission. However, before that renewal I participated in June in the Holy Cross Eastern Province provincial chapter in which all the members of the province were delegates, and during which we elected a new provincial superior. Bud Colgan had finished the maximum nine-year term as provincial. Jim Lackenmier, the actual provincial treasurer in Bud's administration was one of the candidates for the position, but he was not elected. A majority of the province wanted a change of leadership style. Tom Looney, a theology professor at Kings College, was chosen by the membership.

After our provincial chapter ended, I attended the Holy Cross spirituality program in Le Mans, France, where Holy Cross was founded in 1835. It was a profound spiritual experience for me to walk where our founders had walked and to reflect on their lives. Our founder Blessed Basil Moreau also had suffered at the hands of his priests and Brothers, dying at the end of his life outside the community. Thank you Marianite Sisters of Holy Cross, who were the only ones loyal and faithful to the founder all his life, for making available to me that great spiritual renewal program.

Afterwards, I went to visit my friends Hermann and Bridgette Beer in Karlsruhe, Germany. They had come to Chucuito parish when I worked there back in the 1990s. I also stopped in England to visit with my friends Roger and Josie Masters and with Chris Mann and his wife Moira, both couples whom I knew from my diaconate in 1967 in their parish in Aldershot, England. Spending time with these friends who knew me over so many years gave me the opportunity to share with people who could help me to work through it all. All these visits to friends in Europe made this a healing time for me.

In July I made an eight-day Ignatian retreat at the Jesuit retreat house in Faulkner, Maryland. It helped me to walk through the pain I was experiencing and to find new life here in the United States. Marilyn, a lay woman, who was appointed to be my spiritual directress during the retreat, understood intuitively where I was in my life journey when I shared with her during our first meeting what had just happened to me in Peru.

I remember I went into the retreat thinking that when it was over I would write the letter to the provincial which on the day of my return from Peru I had told him I would do. However, during the course of the eight days I came to realize that Jesus, who had been treated unjustly too, had written no letters to Herod or Pilate or Judas. So I decided at that time not to do it. Marilyn walked me through the passion narratives in the gospels, helping me to come out at the end into a sort of new, resurrected life.

When the retreat was over, I felt like a heavy burden had been lifted off my shoulders. I was re-energized to move on with my life. So, after four healing months, also spent visiting family and friends and resting at the Dartmouth house, I headed by car and auto train to my new ministry as associate pastor for the Hispanic community at Nativity Parish in Brandon, Florida, in the Diocese of St. Petersburg.

NATIVITY PARISH IN BRANDON, FLORIDA

I arrived in Brandon a few days before August and quickly settled into my new room with the two suitcases of my life's belongings that I had brought back with me from Peru. Art Proulx welcomed me to the parish team graciously and quickly put me to work. The parish had been understaffed the whole month of July. Art, a dedicated pastor, was tremendously kind, understanding and patient with my inexperience in U.S. parish work. I had so much to learn about duty days, preparation for the Sacrament of Marriage in this country, and visits to the nearby hospital and nursing homes. It all was very new to me. Parish ministry in Peru had been very different.

Nativity is the largest parish in the St. Petersburg diocese, so the days were full of sacramental activity. So much so, I had little time or energy for any real teaching, which I was more interested in doing. I did accompany the Hispanic Bible group and teach them occasionally. I also organized a few workshops on forgiveness and on family communication in an organization called Families in Search of Jesus. This was a group of Hispanic families (couples with children) that gathered twice a month on Saturday night. During their meeting the parents had time alone to reflect on their family life and their actual difficulties and to pray together. The children had their own space for games and some faith formation with a young adult. I enjoyed working with this group because they were full of energy and joy.

I especially remember Eneida and William, a young couple not yet married who took me under wing during my first months there. We often went out after the Saturday night meetings to the nearby city of Tampa. Thank you, Eneida, and may you, William, rest in peace.

I also was interested in the Hispanic Basic Christian Community Movement that was active in the parish. These were like the "small Christian communities" with whom I had worked in Peru. Fifteen or twenty people, often couples, gathered weekly in homes to pray and reflect on their lives in the light of the Scriptures. Most of the groups were composed of elderly people. They were interested in attracting new, younger members and forming new groups. So, the "small Christian community" did some house to house visits in neighborhoods near the parish hoping to find people interested in forming new small communities. Those visits were a big success. During the first year, we formed several new "basic Christian communities" in new neighborhoods in the parish. Thank you, Hispanic laymen and women, for this great effort to reach out to new people.

Rafael Ramirez with a few others was already engaged in new ministry in the outlying Mexican migrant worker trailer camps, so I threw some of my energy into helping them to form new Christian communities there. We expanded that ministry to include other migrant camps within the parish. All this reminded me of my ministry years in Macate.

I also tried to interest the parish's English-speaking "small Christian communities" in strengthening themselves by doing something similar. However, they were more hesitant, inasmuch as they were less numerous than the Hispanics and shyer and perhaps fearful of visiting neighborhoods and knocking on doors.

During my time at Nativity I made many friends in the Hispanic community. Miguel Leiva, a Chilean who knew Holy Cross in Santiago, Chile, had lived in one of our Holy Cross parishes there. He and I became and still are good friends. We visit when I pass through Brandon occasionally. Thank you, Miguel, for your friendship.

I also met up with several Peruvian families. David and Alejandra Dioses and their two daughters became my Peruvian family in Brandon with whom I visited often during those years. Since then they have returned to live in Peru. Thank you, Dioses family.

I spent two years at Nativity parish in Brandon. I enjoyed the work with the Hispanic people there very much, but I missed living with members of Holy Cross. So, each Sunday after the Spanish Mass I drove to our Holy Cross community residence in Cocoa Beach, or up to Dade City to spend time with Bill and Dan, or over to Largo where Bob Wiseman worked, to spend my free day with them. In west Florida, Bob, Dan, Bill and I formed a little regional community in the St. Petersburg diocese. The four of us met monthly for dinner and/or a movie or concert. Thank you, guys. I could not have re-entered life in the United States without your friendship, care and support.

I thank all of you, members of Holy Cross in Florida, for making me feel so welcome. You brought to mind Sister Frances' words to me before I left Peru when I was so angry with Holy Cross there. She reminded me that I should not blame all the Holy Cross community for what a few Holy Cross people did to me in Peru.

FROM MISSION TO MISSION PROGRAM

In February 2010 I participated in the From Mission To Mission Program held in San Antonio, Texas with seven other returning missionaries. One Sister who had ministered forty years in Sweden had departed there much like I had left Peru. I shared my story with her and the others, and listened with interest and respect during these life-giving days. We all noted how the members of our Religious communities had little interest in listening to our stories. When they did, they usually had trouble understanding, because they had no experience in another culture. It often has occurred to me that if I had not lived in Peru I would have become a different person. My life as a priest would not have been the same. I continually thank the Lord for the opportunity He gave me to work in Peru. Involvement with people different from myself was mind-opening, and it lifted me out of my preconceptions and my prejudices.

The program was excellent for giving us returning missionaries the chance to re-examine our lives and re-enter the world of the United States that is so different from the worlds where we had lived and loved so much for so many years. At the beginning of the program we each put a little flag on a world map on the wall to indicate the country where we had ministered. Most of us had been more than twenty years in Asia, Africa or Latin America. At the closing ceremony, we were asked to move our little flag to the area in the United States where we would be or already were ministering. What an emotional moment that was for all of us!

I moved my flag from Peru to Florida with tears in my eyes, but also with the realization that I was the same Tom Shea whether here in the United States or in Peru, with the same gifts and weaknesses that were mine to put at God's service for his people, the poor and the marginal-ized—no matter where I was. What an insight that was for me! I could still do the same work here that I had done in Peru! Thank you, Lord, for bringing me again out of the darkness of depression and despair into new life with new energy to serve you among your Hispanic people here in the United States. Thank you, Julie Lupien, the wonderful coordinator of the From Mission to Mission program, for creating this program and guiding us through it with your gentle kindness. And thank you my brothers and sisters, fellow-travelers on this journey of returning from our beloved adopted countries, for sharing your stories with me as together we re-entered this new foreign world of the United States.

THE NEW PROVINCIAL

Shortly after his election in June 2009, Tom Looney, the new provincial superior of the Eastern Province, told Bill Persia and me that he wanted to speak with us about the district of Peru before he traveled there. He said that he wanted to hear what had happened recently to me in Peru. He already knew part of the story because before his election he lived at Kings College, where since 2006 Holy Cross Peruvian priest Fidel Ticona was studying and living while working with the Hispanic community in a nearby parish.

Fidel had been in Chucuito with Diego and me. He had to leave Chucuito when he was assigned to go to Canto Grande to prepare himself to be the new director of the Holy Cross formation program there. This reduction of our community number to two had been a reason given by the district superior Bill Persia and his council for closing the Chucuito mission in late 2003. After Fidel finished his preparatory program of studies in 2006, the new district superior Bob Baker and his council decided that he was not the person they wanted for the formation program, so he was sent to study family counseling at Seton Hall University in New Jersey in a study-from-home program. Tom had heard a lot about the Peru district and Canto Grande from Fidel. Thank you, Tom, for phoning us, and for listening attentively to each of us in a two-hour conversation. (Fidel received his degree in 2010, and Fred Serraino, Tom Looney and I went to his graduation.)

At that same time Jorge Mallea, who was still in Tacna, was experiencing more difficulties with Bob Baker and the district council. Jorge and I spoke almost weekly on the phone, and he told me how he continued to be mistreated. I shared this and my story with Tom. After Tom visited the Peru district personally, it seemed to me that there were some slight improvements in the use of authority there. I especially thank you, Tom, for helping my good friend and fellow Religious Jorge Mallea at that time.

During his two years as provincial before our province merged with the Indiana Province of the Congregation to form the new United States Province of Priests and Brothers in June 2011, Tom visited the communities in our Eastern Province, during which he spoke with each of us personally. He visited me twice while I was working at Nativity Parish. After each of these visits, he wrote a three-page letter to me affirming the person I am and suggesting areas in my life that I might consider to work on. He did that for all the Religious in the Eastern Province. He was considered a great listener. He was very affirming of each person, and never overly critical.

After two years at Nativity Parish I asked Tom if I could move to the Cocoa Beach house in the Orlando diocese in Florida so that I could live with the community there. I found diocesan parish living quite lonely. Tom at first thought I was doing such a great job at Nativity that I should stay there another year. When I related that to Brother Denis Fleming, a friend of mine from formation days who was then the local superior at Cocoa Beach, he and the local Cocoa Beach community, many of whom also were contemporaries of mine from formation days, encouraged me to ask Tom to reconsider my assignment to Nativity because there were now two available rooms at Cocoa Beach. After some time of prayer, I did ask Tom to reconsider, since the bishop in St. Petersburg just recently had named a young, newly-ordained, Hispanic priest to Nativity. I felt that I easily could leave the work with the Hispanic community in his hands.

Tom did so, assigning me to live at Cocoa Beach just a few days before the merger of our Eastern Province with the Indiana Province, forming the new United States Province of Priests and Brothers. Thank you, Tom. I will never forget that act of kindness to me.

Thank you also to all the Holy Cross members in Florida who encouraged me to make this move to Cocoa Beach. I especially thank Bob Wiseman who himself had just received a change of assignment to leave Florida to go to Stonehill College.

NEW HISPANIC MINISTRY

I moved into Cocoa Beach on October 1, 2011, and I have been here ever since. I love this house by the ocean, and I love the wonderful community of ten priests and a Brother, with many of whom I shared life when I was beginning formation back in the early 1960's. I often say that if I cannot be in Peru, this is the second-best place for me. I came full circle in Holy Cross, living now with the men I started out with in our formation house at Stonehill College some fifty years ago.

Another event in my life that I consider a miracle was my finding a new Hispanic ministry so quickly near Cocoa Beach. I knew that I wanted to continue working with Hispanic people when I moved here. On arriving, I phoned a priest with whom Bob Wiseman had put me in contact a year earlier who was doing Hispanic ministry at Our Lady of Grace parish in Palm Bay, which is located about thirty-five miles and an hour's ride from our Holy Cross residence. To my surprise this priest had just left Our Lady of Grace, so there was an opening and an urgent need there for a Spanish-speaking priest, since the pastor Leo Hodges did not speak the language. After an interview with the pastor and his associate Martha Lushman, I knew that God had chosen Our Lady of Grace for me. From our first meeting it was clear that Leo, Martha and I were going to work well together, because we shared a common vision of the Vatican II Church. Thank you, Leo and Martha.

Leo asked me to do the Spanish Mass and an English Mass each Sunday and then to be available eight hours on

Tuesdays and Wednesdays to counsel Spanish speakers, as well as to help with two Spanish Bible workshops. I also would help with the portion of the faith formation program for the Spanish-speaking parents who brought their children on those days. This could not have been more providential for me. I did not have to do the many parish tasks that I had done at Nativity, which included daily Masses, duty days, and visits to the sick in their homes and at the hospital. I could just dedicate my energies to Sunday liturgy and to teaching and counseling the Hispanic community as I had done in Tacna. God is good. I had come full circle in ministry, too.

I have been at Our lady of Grace five years now, and I continue to enjoy ministry there, even though due to distance I have not gotten to know as many of the Hispanic people as well as I did in Brandon where I lived closer by.

These past years I also have expanded my Hispanic ministry in our area. Father Karl Bergin, the pastor at Our Lady of Lourdes parish in Melbourne, asked me in April 2014 to help with his large Hispanic community which was experiencing some internal conflicts. I met with them on several occasions to hear what they had to say about the problems in their community. Then I helped them to reorganize their pastoral committee which the conflicts had broken apart. This committee coordinated the activities of all the Hispanic groups in the parish, and it was this committee's voice that the two Hispanic delegates took to the pastor's parish council. After an effort by everyone, I think that they now are doing quite well. I still occasionally go there on Wednesday nights to celebrate a Spanish

Mass and offer a Bible workshop to the Hispanic parents who bring their children for faith formation.

I continue to enjoy this educational ministry at both parishes. Thank you, Karl Bergin and the Hispanic community for inviting me to minister at Our Lady of Lourdes in Melbourne. Thank you, Leo and Martha, for inviting me to Our Lady of Grace. Thank you, Emmanuel, the new pastor at Our Lady of Grace for retaining me.

OTHER ACTIVITIES

This Hispanic ministry keeps me busy enough, but it also allows me time for a partial retirement, which includes the pleasure of reading, swimming at the Y, writing these memoirs, attending conferences, walking on the beach in front of our residence, and some traveling which I always have loved to do. I enjoy my Thursday nights at Nolan's Irish Pub with my friends Jeff Njus, a diocesan priest, and Bob Birmingham, who is the Faith Formation director at our Holy Cross parish, St. John the Evangelist, in nearby Viera, Florida.

In 2011 Dan Kayajan encouraged me to participate in the first gathering of The United States Association of Catholic Priests (USACP). It was founded by thirteen diocesan priests who felt that the priest's voice was not being heard by the bishops. Since its inception, this association has grown to over a thousand members. I try to attend all its annual conferences, because it has been very helpful. I also have been able to attend several conferences on immigration, both in San Antonio, Texas, and at Holy

Cross' University of Notre Dame. I try, as well, to go to the New Ways Ministry conferences every five years. I personally feel that we as Church need a lot of education in those areas.

I also have been able to visit Peru several times since leaving in 2009. These trips in some way dull the pain of not living there year-round. Each time I have stayed about a month, bypassing the Holy Cross men in Canto Grande, but always visiting the Holy Cross Sisters. Holy Cross Peruvian priests Jose Luis Tineo, Alfredo Hernandez and Jorge Mallea come into Lima to have a meal with me. I spend most of my time in Peru visiting my friends in Cartavio/Trujillo, Chimbote, Chucuito/Puno and Tacna.

In 2013 I traveled with Fred Serraino and Bill Persia during the fifty-year anniversary of Holy Cross' presence in Peru to celebrate our friendship with the people in Cartavio, Chimbote and Tacna where Holy Cross had ministered and we each had worked. In Cartavio my friends there arranged for me to receive the medal of the municipality from the mayor who was a former student of mine in the Cartavio high school. What a great joy it was for me to receive that honor!

In 2014, I was invited back for the fifty-year anniversary celebration of the high school in Cartavio where I had taught. I was received royally as an ex-teacher by the principal of the school during that visit, and I enjoyed seeing again so many of my former students and renewing friendship with them on Facebook.

In 2015 Jorge Izaguirre, the Peruvian Holy Cross priest whom I knew as a high school student in Chimbote back in the 1980s, invited me back to Peru for his Episcopal Ordination. Jorge had been named Bishop of the rural mountainous Prelature of Chuquibamba located in the southern Andes of Peru near the city of Arequipa. Thank you, Jorge, for that invitation. It meant a lot to me.

In 2016 I was invited to travel with a tour group organized by Our Lady of Grace parish. The twelve of us on the tour, including my cousin Bob Barnes, had a great two weeks traveling in southern Peru and meeting with my friends there.

During that same year, John Phalen the new master of novices in the Latin American Holy Cross novitiate outside Lima where I used to teach the novices, invited me to conduct my Holy Cross history workshop for the five novices. Thank you, John, for that invitation and for the warm welcome back I received from both the men and women of Holy Cross in Peru.

PERUVIAN VISITS TO THE UNITED STATES

My good friend Holy Cross priest Jorge Mallea has visited me here in the United States twice. The first time was in June 2011 when I still was working at the Nativity parish. Jorge came to the United States for the Eastern Province's closing ceremony. He came again in January 2014, this time to Cocoa Beach, and we toured southern Florida. These visits of his recalled the many vacations we took together in Peru. Thank you, Jorge.

My compadre Felipe Calderon, father of my first Peruvian godson Isaac, also has visited me here twice. In

June 2013, he came for my birthday celebration at Cocoa Beach, after which I drove him up the east coast to Stonehill College to visit Jim Chichetto, whom he knew from living with the Holy Cross community in our house in Cartavio. Larry Olszewski and Fred Serraino, whom Felipe also knew from those days in Cartavio, both reside in Cocoa Beach as well, so we had some enjoyable times together with Felipe. I enjoy time with Larry and Fred, and with Bill Persia who also lives here now. We are the Peruvians in the house.

In June 2014 Felipe returned, and I drove him across the United States. I had mentioned during his first visit that I always wanted to travel across the United States by car to see this nation of my birth, but because I was out of country for so many years, first in Rome for theological studies and then forty-one years in Peru, I never had had the opportunity for it. So happily, Felipe said that he would come back to do it with me, and we did. It was a wonderful, memorable month-long trip together. Thank you, Felipe, for your visits and friendship which reaches way back to my first year in Cartavio.

THE END OF MY STORY...SO FAR

I have come to the end of my Peru story, it seems. Undoubtedly I have forgotten to include the names of some persons and events. There are so many wonderful people among whom I lived and worked in Peru. I visited many when I lived in the country and afterwards during my trips back there. I have stayed in touch with coworkers and friends over the years by email and more recently with Facebook. I thank each one of you and all of you for being important in my life. Even if I have not mentioned you by name, know that I carry all of you always in my heart.

In my story I have written, as well, about people with whom I had conflicts during my years in Peru. Hopefully both they and I have learned some positive things from those events. Conflicts are part of every life journey. So, I thank God for them, too.

My journey with God has not ended. I continue to walk with Him, ready for whatever unexpected designs He may have for me. Since I first responded to His call to Peru those many years ago, I have tried to listen attentively to His voice in the decrees of Vatican II, as well as in the Medellin documents that apply those decrees in Latin America. I embraced that orientation faithfully during the early years of Church enthusiasm, creativity and hope, and later during the more difficult years when the Church seemed to me to be looking backward rather than forward, stifling creativity, fearing anything new, and imposing once again clerical control on all aspects of Church life. Here in the United States I still try today to minister for Jesus in that light, inspired as well by Pope Francis who I believe is showing us once again the way to new life for our Church and our global world. I trust the Lord to continue to guide me and protect me on my journey with Him as He has done always in the past.

EPILOGUE

What do I say at the end of my journey with the Lord in Peru? The sentiment that rises repeatedly within me is THANKSGIVING.

THANK YOU to God who created me as I am and walks with me through my life's journey, giving me the experiences and people I needed just when I needed them. THANK YOU, my family, my childhood neighborhood friends, my grade and high school friends, my community friends in Holy Cross, and everyone with whom I have shared. THANK YOU, all the people in my life who have been God's messengers, His angels.

When I recently celebrated fifty years of priesthood with family and friends in Albany, I had the opportunity to thank more than one-hundred-forty people present for their influence and help on my life's journey. I thank you all again, and everyone who has walked with me during all these years, both living and deceased; your names are written in my memory and in my heart. God resides in each of you, and I thank Him for the gift of having you in my life. I thank Him, too, that I have been able to stay in touch with so many of you.

I thank God for the gift of *my life as it is*. When I was asked at the Attleboro renewal program during my sabbatical in 1993 if I would change anything in my life journey, I said no. Even though there have been very difficult and lonely moments on that journey, I mostly have been happy. I have tried to learn from all my experiences, supported by my friends in Peru and elsewhere, and I am grateful to you all.

I remember that at Attleboro, the seven other persons in the group told me that the word that best described me for them was *strength*. I never pictured myself as a strong person, but several pointed out that I seemed to have such strong views. I heard that said of me in Peru, as well, both within my community and by others among whom I lived and ministered. In that respect, my strength may also be a weakness. It often has served me well, but at other times has brought difficulty and conflict into my life. No doubt I can be quite assertive. But I thank you, Lord, for giving me that strength, because it enabled me to grow out of childhood weakness to become your minister those forty-one years in Peru. Without your strength, Lord, I never would have gotten there nor stayed.

During all my life I have tried to follow Jesus' path as best I can, and to use my gifts for teaching and preaching with which He particularly has endowed me to build His kingdom of justice and love. Jesus is my guiding light. Whatever I have accomplished I owe to Him. My prayer is a continual THANK YOU.

As I complete this memoir, my life journey continues on, in Jesus' service. You have called me, Lord, and I am still answering. I listen attentively for Your voice in our times.

It is my hope that you, my reader, may be able to discover in your own life God's guiding hand and God's love that is there for all of us in Jesus. My life is not special. It is just the one given to me. I have tried to pick it up as best I can. That has always been the challenge—to try to be and to do my best with this greatest gift, life itself. May that be true for each one of you, too.

I would be happy to hear from you. You can reach me at <u>tomashea@hotmail.com</u>.

Made in the USA
Middletown, DE
21 May 2018